CRISIS IN NORTH KOREA

Hawai'i Studies on Korea

HAWAI ' I   STUDIES   ON   KOREA

Crisis in North Korea

The Failure of De-Stalinization, 1956

Andrei Lankov

University of Hawai'i Press, Honolulu
and
Center for Korean Studies, University of Hawai'i

Library of Congress Cataloging-in-Publication Data

Lankov, Andrei.
Crisis in North Korea : the failure of De-Stalinization, 1956
/ Andrei Lankov.
    p.   cm.—(Hawai'i studies on Korea)
Includes bibliographical references and index
ISBN: 0-8248-2809-7 (hardcover : alk. paper)
1. Communism—History. 2. Korea (North)—History. 3. Korea
(North)—Politics and government. I. Title. II. Series.

DS935.L36 2004
951.9304/3—dc22

2004018509

 The Center for Korean Studies was established in 1972 to coordinate and develop resources for the study of Korea at the University of Hawai'i. Reflecting the diversity of the academic disciplines represented by affiliated members of the university faculty, the Center seeks especially to promote interdisciplinary and intercultural studies. Hawai'i Studies on Korea, published jointly by the Center and the University of Hawai'i Press, offers a forum for research in the social sciences and humanities pertaining to Korea and its people.

University of Hawai'i Press books are printed on acid-free
paper and meet the guidelines for permanence and durability
of the Council on Library Resources.

Designed by inari
Printed by The Maple-Vail Book Manufacturing Group

Contents

Preface

THE 1956 CRISIS IN North Korea and the subsequent changes in North Korean society—the subjects of the present book—have not been adequately accounted for in academic literature. That an unsuccessful attempt at replacing Kim Il Song in 1956 and the subsequent Sino-Soviet actions occurred is known. Rumors about these important events were quite widespread at the time, and foreign observers eventually became more and more aware of the general outline of the incident. Thus the "August incident" of 1956 is briefly mentioned in all general surveys of North Korean history. Some other events and trends mentioned in the present book have also been long known to students of North Korea. For example, the increasing influence of Mao's China and the gradual shift to nationalism from 1957 have been noted by virtually all experts on North Korean history. However, until recently it was impossible to give a detailed account of these important events and their political background, because virtually all materials relating to the key incidents of these critical years had remained secret and inaccessible to scholars.

In the early 1990s the situation changed considerably. In the periods 1992–1995 and 1998–2000, I managed to locate a considerable amount of relevant material in the Russian archives. During the heyday of perestroika and glasnost in the early 1990s, some materials from the Soviet Embassy in Pyongyang and other documents from the former Soviet Foreign Ministry archives were partly declassified and temporarily opened to scholars. Unfortunately, what was made available was but a fraction of the total, and even this material does not necessarily comprise the most important or revealing documents. To this day some of the more important documents remain classified and thus inaccessible. Among the documents still classified are, for example, virtually all telegraphic exchanges between the Soviet Embassy in Pyongyang and the Foreign Ministry in Moscow (containing discussions of all urgent matters and the direct instructions of Moscow), all contemporary materials of the Soviet Communist Party Central Committee, all materials of the intelligence services, and most of the regular embassy reports. The chance of gaining access to these documents does not look promising at the time of this writing, especially because the period of relaxation in the former Soviet archives did not last very long; since the mid-1990s, admittance to the archives has once again become especially restricted and selective.

The most common type of material found in the Foreign Ministry archives are the so-called records of conversation *(Zapis' besedy)*. These documents had to be compiled by every Soviet diplomat after he had an official or semiofficial encounter with a North Korean. Normally, these typewritten records were produced within a few days after the actual conversation had taken place, but they were based on handwritten notes made during the conversation or immediately following it. The title always indicated basic information (name and position) about the Soviet diplomat and his Korean interlocutor, as well as the conversation date. Handwritten notes were usually destroyed soon after a final typewritten text was compiled, although, as we shall see, there were some exceptions to this rule. Initially the records of conversation were all classified as either "secret" or "top secret" (i.e., the second or third level of the four levels of Soviet classification). To the best of my knowledge, none of these documents has been published or previously used by historians. Meanwhile, the party archives are much more diverse, including various documents sent to Moscow by authorities in Korea.

Between 1987 and 1995, I conducted interviews with some former Soviet diplomats and North Korean officials now residing in the Commonwealth of Independent States (CIS). Information from these interviews is also used in this work. The North Korean émigré community in the Soviet Union numbered a few hundred people in its heyday in the early 1970s. These people were Soviet citizens of Korean extraction who had once worked in the Democratic People's Republic of Korea (DPRK) but had to escape to the Soviet Union in the late 1950s. Some of them provided me with interesting data that would hardly have been obtainable in any other way.

Another source of information for this book is the official North Korean press, especially articles published in the *Nodong sinmun,* the leading North Korean daily. The press in the DPRK, as in any Stalinist country, was subjected to the strictest censorship and control, and therefore the widely used expression "official press" in these circumstances is a tautology, given that no other press but the official one could possibly exist under a Stalinist regime. With the benefit of hindsight, though, it is surprising how much information one is able to extract from the press in conjunction with other sources. The availability of such information is a by-product of the dual role of the press in a Communist-ruled country. According to a famous dictum of Lenin's, the newspapers were not only "collective propagandists" but also "collective organizers." As a "collective propagandist," a newspaper of a (ruling) Communist Party might and often had to distort and deceive, but being a "collective organizer" as well, it also had to hint at the path that the party and its leader were going to take at any given moment, even though the language used to formulate such hints could be quite nebulous or deliberately obscure. The language employed was basically a code that was well understood (and meant to be understood) by the more sophisticated contemporaries, who knew all the party jargon and were trained to grasp the real meaning behind official idiom. Indeed, training in these somewhat esoteric language interpretation skills has always constituted an important part of the "political education" in the countries of Leninist socialism. Subtle changes in wording might often be far more important than an article's content, and the positioning of an article on a page might be a significant message purposely addressed to an experienced reader—usually a party cadre.

Still, the information available remains far from complete, despite the greatest of efforts to obtain it. Apart from the above-mentioned deficiencies with respect to Soviet material, access to Chinese data, which in this case are of equal or even greater importance, still remains a dream. In the course of time many more documents will surface in the Moscow archives (not to mention the Pyongyang and Beijing archives), and some of these documents may force us to reconsider our current assumptions about North Korea in the 1950s. Yet the materials currently available already provide us with a considerable amount of new information about the "August incident" and the activities of the opposition within the North Korean leadership during the summer of 1956, as well as subsequent changes in the North Korean society.

The distribution of available materials is quite uneven—much more is known about some incidents and developments than about others. For example, Soviet diplomats carefully traced the preparations for the August Plenum by recording all of their conversations with Korean officials. As a result, sufficient information is available on the developments in June and July 1956. However, when the embassy discussed the situation with Moscow, such exchanges, because of the obvious urgency and importance of the situation, were possibly conducted via telegraph and have therefore remained classified and unavailable to scholars to this day. Moscow's instructions that were wired to Pyongyang by telegraph fall into the same category. Therefore little is known about the Soviet reaction to the crisis when it began to unfold in late July 1956. Nor is an official report available of the fateful confrontation that occurred in the late morning of August 30, 1956.

Undoubtedly, a quite detailed Soviet account of this incident exists, but it remains beyond my reach. Nevertheless, additional accounts can substitute for the inaccessible report. The subsequent plenum of the Korean Workers' Party (KWP) Central Committee in September 1956 was attended by a Soviet delegation led by Anastas I. Mikoyan, and it is certain that a detailed report of this event exists somewhere in Moscow. However, because the Mikoyan group was officially considered a party delegation (as opposed to a government delegation), its reports were kept in the party archives and therefore were not made available even in the early 1990s. As a result, information about the August events and especially the September events is incomplete in comparison with information about earlier and later developments. At the same time, a wealth of information is available regarding the purges that followed the failure of the "August opposition" and culminated in a secret trial of the opposition leaders in 1960. Special attention was given in the sources to the plight of the Soviet Koreans in 1956–1960, and other aspects of the North Korean "Great Purge" were recorded as well. The significant changes in the regime's ideology were also widely reflected in the contemporary North Korean press. More examples are available, but the main problem is clear: because of the nature of the sources, information is unevenly distributed.

I am still working on these topics, and, with a certain amount of luck and effort, more material might become available in the future. Recent developments make me particularly skeptical of such a possibility, though; quite probably we will have to wait many years, if not decades, for new data to emerge. However, the available material provides us with fresh and fascinating insights into one of the most important turning points in North Korean political and social history. I believe that the data are both of interest and of practical value to students of DPRK history. I decided to publish the present book in the hope that it will soon be augmented by new publications and new research in the area. In the meantime the conclusions that can be drawn from the materials at our disposal are necessarily of a preliminary nature, and I hope that readers will bear this in mind. Very often we are forced to ask questions that cannot be answered with any certainty.

Another shortcoming of this book, of which I am fully aware, is its inevitable "Soviet angle." Indeed, the inner developments of North Korea are here often described from a specifically Soviet-Russian point of view, with perhaps too much attention given to the ensuing problems of Soviet-Korean relations or to problems that simply found some resonance among people who came from a Soviet background. This aspect of the book is largely due to the nature of the sources available and also to my own experience. I believe that further work by colleagues from other countries and with different backgrounds will eventually provide students of North Korean history with a more balanced picture.

Although the events in North Korea in 1956 have remained obscure for decades, some works offer a context to this current study. Among works that describe the 1956 crisis and the subsequent changes in North Korean society, I must mention that particularly relevant material can be found in *Communism in Korea,* by Robert Scalapino and Lee Chong-sik, and in *Kim Il Sung: The North Korean Leader,* by Suh Dae-sook, as well as in other general works of North Korean history. Among South Korean works, I recommend Kim Hak-jun's *Pukhan 50 nyŏn sa* (Fifty years of North Korean history) and Ch'oe Sŏng's *Pukhan chŏngch'i sa* (Political history of North Korea). The latter two books are based on the recent research of South Korean, Japanese, and Western scholars who have uncovered new material on North Korea's early history.

In the South Korea of the late 1990s one can discern a considerable increase in academic interest toward the history of North Korea. In this, the Far East Research Institute of Kyŏngnam University in Seoul has played a special role. The institute publishes a somewhat misnamed quarterly, *Hyŏndae Pukhan yŏngu* (Studies of modern North Korea), which contains articles of remarkable quality that are mostly about North Korean history rather than current politics.

Among publications dealing with the campaign against the Soviet Koreans in 1955, sections of Brian Myers' *Han Sŏl-ya and North Korean Literature* are noteworthy, as is Masao Okonogi's article "North Korean Communism: In Search of Its Prototype." Both publications contain interesting material, each with a slightly different focus. Myers' book is primarily concerned with literary politics, whereas Okonogi concentrates on industrial policy discussions after the Korean War.

Acknowledgments

THERE ARE MANY PEOPLE without whose constant support and encouragement this book would never have been written. I would like to express my gratitude to my Korean colleagues Dr. Yu Kil-jae (Kyŏngnam University), Dr. Kim Sŏk-hyang (Korean Institute for National Unification), and Dr. Sŏ Tong-man (Korean Institute for National Security), whose support and advice have been vital to me. I am also very grateful to my wonderful coworkers at the Australian National University and above all to Professor William Jenner, Dr. Kenneth Wells, and Dr. Shin Gi-hyun. My Russian friends and colleagues were instrumental in my gaining access to the necessary material. They also provided me with both a research infrastructure and valuable suggestions, not to mention moral support and intellectual stimulation. I therefore would like to thank Dr. Vitali Naishul, Oleg Plaksin, Dr. Alexander Soloviev, Dr. Andrei Illarionov, Mihail Kisilev, Boris Lvin, and Dr. Nikolai Dobronravin. I thank the Russian State Archive of Photographic and Cinematic Material for allowing me to reproduce the photographs presented in this book.

I would also like to express my gratitude to the witnesses of the North Korean events of the 1950s and their families. Not all interviews were used in this work, but these talks gave me a better understanding of the atmosphere of 1950s Pyongyang and of the personalities and inner motivations of people whose activity is discussed in the book. Hence, I extend my gratitude to Gen. Kang Sang-ho, Dr. V. P. Tkachenko, Lira

Hegai, Maia Hegai, V. V. Kovyzhenko, G. K. Plotnikov, Kim Ch'an, Sim Su-ch'ŏl, and many others.

I reserve very special thanks to Balazs Szalontai, a Hungarian scholar who is currently researching the Communist world of the 1950s. He not only provided me with valuable information about his recent findings in the Eastern European archives but also was a constant source of interesting and valuable observations and remarks. In addition, he found time to read the entire manuscript carefully and to provide me with thoughtful and extremely useful comments.

Note on Romanization

THE ROMANIZATION OF Korean names used in this work follows the McCune-Reischauer system except where other spellings have become commonly accepted, as in the case of Kim Il Song. For consistency's sake, the spelling follows the modern South Korean pattern in cases when it differs from the current North Korean spelling (e.g., *Nodong sinmun,* not *Rodong sinmun;* Yi, not Ri or Li). Consonants are shown vocalized when between vowels, but not at the beginning of words (a surname and a given name are treated as two different words). Chinese names are romanized according to the pinyin system, and Russian names according to the Library of Congress system, with similar exceptions for commonly accepted spellings (e.g., Khrushchev, Mikoyan). Whenever possible, the translation of the names of official North Korean institutions and government agencies follows Suh Dae-sook's book *Korean Communism, 1945–1980: A Reference Guide to the Political System,* currently the most comprehensive Western publication on the DPRK bureaucracy.

Introduction

FOR THE COMMUNIST CAMP, the mid-1950s were years of great importance. These few years altered forever the political, social, and cultural
landscape of most Communist countries and changed the meaning of
the term "World Communism." For us—recent witnesses to the far
more spectacular collapse of the Communist system in the early
1990s—the changes of this earlier period might appear less impressive
than they would have at the time. Nevertheless, in the 1950s these
transformations were indeed substantial, and they determined the direction of the "Communist bloc" for the next few decades. Indeed, the
mid-1950s created a framework within which the Communist camp
continued to function until its demise in 1989–1991.

To a large extent these changes were driven by the de-Stalinization
campaign in the Soviet Union. Nikita Khrushchev launched this campaign in a somewhat hectic attempt to create a new, more humane
model of Leninist socialism, and by the mid-1950s it was gaining mo-
mentum. Khrushchev and his supporters wanted reform, but their reform plan had one important caveat: the party must remain in
permanent control—both domestically, in the Soviet Union, and internationally, in the other Communist states of Europe and Asia. These
controversial developments in Moscow were rapidly changing the entire face of the Communist world, which comprised at that time some
dozen countries in Eastern Europe and East Asia. The reactions to the
challenge of de-Stalinization in the hitherto solidly uniform and strictly

1

controlled Communist camp were varied and mixed. In some countries the local elite chose to follow Moscow's footsteps and eventually created —or rather, imported—a more liberal post-Stalinist version of state socialism, albeit still very restrictive and occasionally repressive. In other countries the local leaders did not follow suit; either they embarked on more radical experiments and distanced themselves even further from the original Stalinist model, or they struggled even harder to preserve the old patterns and, in the process of doing so, occasionally proved themselves more Stalinist than Stalin. These two latter approaches appeared and indeed were quite different. Nonetheless, liberal reformers and "national Stalinist" conservatives were, in a sense, performing the same function: they were dissolving the prescribed uniformity of early Communism and undermining the once unbreakable domination of the movement by Moscow. The Communist world changed irrevocably during the mid-1950s; in fact one could argue that after this period there was no longer a coherent "Communist world."

The uncertainty and doubt among the rulers filtered down to the ruled and triggered riots and revolts on a scale hitherto unknown in the Communist world. In 1956 in Hungary and Poland the people, under nationalist and/or democratic slogans, openly challenged their Communist governments, and in the case of Hungary only the large-scale Soviet intervention prevented the popular insurrection from overthrowing the local Communist government. Elsewhere substantially different ideas inspired the rebels: during the less known but bloody events in Soviet Georgia, Stalin's own homeland, local youth rioted to protest the new policy of de-Stalinization and to protect the "honor" of the deceased leader, whom they perceived to be their great compatriot and benefactor. Still, until 1956 open revolt had been simply unthinkable in most circumstances, and if it did occur, as it did in Germany in 1953, it was promptly and decisively suppressed.

Of these few pivotal years, 1956 can be singled out as an "annus mirabilis" (or "annus miserabilis," depending on the individual's political taste). It was the year of the Soviet Twentieth Congress; the year of Khrushchev's "Secret Speech" and official denunciation of Stalin; the year of the Hungarian uprising; the year of the Polish riots and strikes; a year of increasing tensions in China; and the year of the first Soviet-

Yugoslav reconciliation. For many Communist states the politics, problems, and achievements of the ensuing decades had their genesis in events of the mid-1950s. After 1956 the earlier uniformity of the Communist camp disappeared forever, and the original "Communist monolith" no longer existed.

North Korea was no exception. The mid-1950s were an important turning point. In 1953 the Democratic People's Republic of Korea (DPRK) emerged from the Korean War as an especially poor but otherwise unremarkable "people's democracy," still supervised and sponsored by Moscow. It had some peculiar characteristics, but by and large it remained firmly within the Moscow-approved framework of a "people's democracy." This situation was to change quickly, however. It is a well-known fact that North Korea—together with Albania, Romania, and China—was one of the few Communist regimes to reject the new Moscow line (with varying degrees of radicalism) and to remain more or less loyal to the old Stalinist pattern, a pattern that was increasingly reinforced with fierce nationalistic rhetoric. This new political course of "independent Stalinism" became more obvious after 1960, but its foundations were laid in the period 1955–1960.

Of the many important events that took place in North Korea in the mid-1950s, the abortive attempt to replace Kim Il Song in August 1956 and the subsequent impact on North Korean society is of particular interest. This attempt was a major milestone in the country's political history. It marked the end of the early North Korean power structure and the birth of Pyongyang's version of "national Stalinism." The "August events" were to become the only known open challenge to Kim's supremacy from within the North Korean political system in the almost half-century reign of the "Great Leader." The open rebellion of high-level cadres was made possible by an excited and more confident atmosphere common in the Communist capitals of the mid-50s, a time known as "the thaw." A general feeling of impending change, a vague but powerful hope for a better society, and the eventual development of a more dignified and less repressive kind of socialism mixed with a lingering uncertainty among the populace and eruptions of adventurous opportunism from top party dignitaries. The motives of those who joined the expanding ranks of the reformers differed quite markedly—

from nationalist fervor to leftist idealism and political careerism. Nevertheless, the reformers were united in their rejection of the old Stalinist ways, which were seen as immoral, inefficient, or both. This atmosphere threatened recently established regimes and their leaders from Warsaw to Pyongyang. Some fell, while others remained in power. Kim Il Song and his group survived the challenge. Not only was he able to continue his former policies, but he also began to steer the country in a new direction, one that differed significantly from the political course followed by a majority of the Communist regimes of Eastern Europe.

In terms of international relations, the failure of the August opposition and the eventual fiasco of an abortive Sino-Soviet political intervention demonstrated that Kim Il Song had consolidated his position and was no longer the puppet of foreign powers. It also indicated that under the new dispensation, Moscow had neither the wish nor the power to impose its will on the easternmost (and, at that time, one of the most remote) of its clients. After 1956, Kim Il Song began to cautiously, yet persistently, cast off the shackles of Soviet-Chinese tutelage. He also started to get rid of some Soviet-style policies that had been imposed on his country. The "imported Stalinism" of the late 1940s began its gradual transformation into "independent Stalinism." This process was visible before the 1956 crisis, but it was greatly facilitated by those dramatic events. The coeval gradual rupturing of relations between Moscow and Peking also meant more diplomatic opportunities and more space in which to maneuver. Once Kim Il Song had ensured domestic support, he could use these opportunities to his own advantage. Internationally, the North Korean policy of maintaining an equal distance from the two Communist giants began in the mid-1950s, although it took a few years for this policy to mature. This policy had manifold consequences, the most important of which was North Korea's ability to avoid direct involvement on either side in the Sino-Soviet schism.

The outcome of the 1956 crisis in North Korea was even more important domestically. It was a personal victory for Kim Il Song, and his reign eventually became the longest in the history of the entire Communist world, concluding with an unprecedented dynastic succession. However, the crisis was not only about personal power. Its outcome also determined the peculiar direction of North Korean development over the following decades and laid the political foundations for the creation of a distinctive Pyongyang brand of Stalinist state socialism, later known as *chuch'e* socialism. The term *"chuch'e"* (in the later North Korean sense) was coined by the North Korean leader on December 28, 1955, in the midst of his offensive against the Soviet Koreans, on the eve of the pivotal year. Prior to 1956–1957, North Korea had been quite a typical "people's democracy," in many respects not unlike similar regimes in Soviet-dominated Eastern Europe.

However, in the aftermath of the events of 1956–1957, North Korea gradually transformed itself into a much more idiosyncratic Communist state. It became a tightly controlled and extremely militarized state devoted to a fanatical personality cult and a particular type of ideology far removed from "orthodox" Marxism-Leninism, even in its Stalinist form. Eventually these changes resulted in *chuch'e*'s replacing Marxism-Leninism as the official ideology of the state. These changes also led to a significant degree of independence from Soviet (and Chinese) control and interference, but this independence was not transformed into any meaningful material or social gain for the country's long-suffering population. With the wisdom of hindsight, we know that the entire project of state socialism was economically inefficient, even ruinous, but the degree of inefficiency varied greatly within its various incarnations. Unfortunately, North Korea opted for a particularly hopeless variety of this generally inept concept. As a result of the changes in North Korean society in the late 1950s and early 1960s, the Pyongyang elite established themselves as masters of their country's destiny, while the common populace gained virtually nothing at all.

The main task of this present work is to track the developments that led to an open clash within the North Korean leadership in August 1956, to provide a detailed picture of what came to be called the "August group," and to investigate the history of subsequent developments, as well as to study the impact these events had on North Korean politics and society. In doing so, I investigate how North Korean "national Stalinism" was brought into the world. Given the nature of the currently available sources, the focus is necessarily and unavoidably on old-fashioned political history. This is a common problem in studies of

North Korean history; the field still suffers heavily from a severe short-age of source material. It will be many years, if not many decades, before an in-depth study of North Korean social, cultural, or intellectual his-tory will become possible. Such an endeavor requires access to a large amount of primary sources, currently completely unavailable, as well as careful preliminary work that would lay the foundation for further studies. Nevertheless, whenever material was available and relevant to the thrust of the arguments, I have discussed some of the important changes in North Korean society and culture.

1 North Korea and Its Leadership in the Mid-1950s

THE DEMOCRATIC PEOPLE'S REPUBLIC of Korea (as North Korea is officially named) formally came into being on September 9, 1948, shortly after the Republic of Korea had been proclaimed in Seoul. The creation of two rival Korean states, neither of which recognized the legitimacy of the other—each claiming to be the sole legitimate authority on the entire Korean Peninsula—was a by-product of the intensifying rivalry between the USSR and the USA, former allies that by then were busy waging a cold war. On the whole, the Korean scenario was similar to that of Germany; in both countries two zones of occupation were originally conceived primarily for the sake of military convenience. However, in both cases the two zones had been quickly transformed into two rival states, each supported by either the Soviet Union or the United States (in Korea's case, China's involvement on the North Korean side must also be noted). However, there were some important differences between the Korean and German situations. The internal political competition between the Left and the Right in Korea was much more intense, and the country itself was perceived by its Great Power patrons as peripheral and marginal enough to risk a military confrontation—something neither side would dare undertake in Central Europe. This combination of fierce internal rivalry and Great Power scheming resulted in a violent clash. The Korean War erupted in 1950 when the North invaded the South. The war developed into a major international conflict when first the Americans and later the Communist Chinese were forced to rush

into the peninsula to save their respective Korean allies from total collapse. The war was bloody and dramatic. All of the participants (except
the South Koreans) scored spectacular military victories at different
times during the conflict, and all (except the Chinese) faced total disaster
at other times. Millions were killed and wounded, and entire cities were
wiped out. The scale of devastation was probably without parallel
throughout the entire history of Korea, but the general outcome of the
war was inconclusive. Korea remained divided.

Internally the DPRK was, to a significant extent, the creation of the
Soviet generals and political advisers, although some of their actions
met with a positive response and received the support of a majority of
North Koreans. In general, however, as the only Asian country occupied
by the Soviet Army after World War II, North Korea was receiving the
usual mixture of Soviet guidance and pressure and thereby following
the path of other Moscow-controlled territories. The institutions of the
Stalinist state were implanted into North Korea with only minor
modifications. In the DPRK of the early 1950s, one could encounter all
the salient features of such a regime: a one-party political system (de
facto, if not strictly by the book), a state-controlled and state-run
planned economy, intense propagation of the Stalinist interpretation of
Marxism-Leninism, an obligatory adulation of the USSR and the Soviet
experience, as well as numerous Soviet-style institutions in virtually
every field of life.

The framework for all these changes was provided by the concept of
the "people's democracy." Stalin and his ideologists developed this concept from the earlier United Front theory. In the mid-1940s the concept
was authorized chiefly for the Soviet-occupied territories of Eastern
Europe, but later it was applied elsewhere as well. In practice, all Soviet-
controlled Communist countries had to follow the prescriptions of this
theory, but in more independent Communist states like Vietnam or
China its impact was less obvious, though still perceptible. According to
this concept, all newly emerged Communist societies were considered
to be immature and not yet fully socialist. In order to successfully construct a "complete socialism," they were supposed to pass through a
prolonged period of transformation. During that period, industry had
to be nationalized and collective agriculture was to be eventually imple-

mented. Those changes could, however, be gradual and slow, so for a relatively long period of time a "people's democracy" (as such emerging socialist societies came to be called) retained some private businesses (normally small), private agriculture, and even some political parties other than the ruling Communist Party. The effects of this theory were twofold. On the one hand, it provided a theoretical justification for some flexibility to accommodate the concessions to local realities that were sometimes deemed unavoidable. These regrettable but necessary deviations from orthodoxy were easily justified because they occurred in an immature socialist society (indeed, not yet really socialist). On the other hand, it was this concept that drew a distinct line between the fully socialist society of the USSR and the immature "semisocialist" societies of the new Communist states. In doing so, it reinforced the doctrinal foundations of Soviet supremacy and Moscow's stance as the supreme arbiter of international Communism.

Nevertheless, despite its uniqueness as the only "people's democracy" in Asia (China and Vietnam, not being under direct Soviet influence, were less frequently given this description), the DPRK was fairly similar to its East European counterparts. Of course, some local specifics were present. Remarkable features of the DPRK included the very rapid establishment of a mass party; the decisive replacement of "old," supposedly pro-Japanese bureaucrats by new cadres who were recruited from the "masses" in a great hurry; an unusually harsh and successful assault on the Christian churches, their priests, and their active followers; and the peculiar nature of the land reform, which combined a drastic reduction of private landownership with a relatively soft approach to the "class enemy." Some of these phenomena might have been products of Chinese influence, but in general the North Korean political and social structure followed the prescriptions of the "people's democracy" theory quite closely. In the social sphere, North Korea boasted a structure that was fairly typical of a "people's democracy." The nationalization of its large and medium industries was completed at a very early stage in 1946, although some small private retail trades and handicrafts were tolerated, albeit restricted, until the late 1950s. Just after the end of the Korean War in December 1953, private businesses still conducted 32.5 percent of the entire retail trade in the country, but their share soon began to decline.[1]

The Stalinist collectivization of agriculture began in 1954, and by December 1955, 49.0 percent of peasant families had been pressed to join the agricultural cooperatives.[2]

Politically, the DPRK was run by the local Communist Party—known as the Korean Workers' Party (KWP)—or, rather, by its self-appointed bureaucracy. On paper, the country had numerous democratic institutions, which included an elected parliament and elected local councils, but the elections were uncontested (one candidate, one seat) and heavily controlled by the authorities, and the candidates were handpicked by the party functionaries. Formally, the party itself also had many democratic features—vestiges of a much earlier pre-Stalinist, or even pre-Leninist, tradition of revolutionary Marxism—but these bore next to no relevance to the realities of political life. Virtually all decisions were made with the hierarchies of KWP committees, from factory or school committees right up to the Central Committee, and party conventions merely rubber-stamped the committees' decisions. The committees, although technically elected, were for all practical purposes handpicked. The recruitment of a new member was decided by the committee itself and confirmed by a committee at a higher level. Occasionally, the higher committees could also appoint members to the subordinated bodies.

The creation of any formal factions had been anathema to all Leninist parties from the early 1920s, and the accusation of "factionalism" was a very serious one. Nevertheless, this did not mean that Communist parties were united, even if for a while they were able to successfully project a public image of unbreakable internal unity and discipline.

This disunity was especially true in the case of the Korean Workers' Party. The Korean Communists had never constituted a monolithic body. On the contrary, the entire early history of the Korean Communist movement was a history of fierce feuding between competing groups. In December 1928, when even the direct intervention of Comintern cadres was not enough to reconcile the antagonists and calm the situation, a desperate Comintern headquarters took the unusually drastic measure of formally disbanding the Korean Communist Party.[3] All subsequent attempts to reestablish the party in the 1930s and early 1940s were also plagued by the same problem. Endless internal feuds were fueled partly by minor political or ideological disagreements but mostly by naked power struggles and personality clashes. By the time the Japanese colonial rule collapsed in 1945, Korea had no functioning Communist Party but only small groups of underground leftists, scattered across the country, who were more numerous in the South and especially in Seoul, the traditional political and cultural center of Korea.

Thus, factions and the factional spirit—which later came to be known as *chongp'a* and *chongp'juŭi,* respectively—were a constant and bitter feature of the Korean Communist movement by 1945. The conditions of the Communist takeover in North Korea strengthened these earlier tendencies. By 1945 the northern part of Korea had neither any considerable Communist organization nor any Communist leaders of nationwide importance, since the prominent Communists were all active in the U.S.-occupied South. Hence, when the Soviet authorities tried to establish a friendly government (that is, a preferably Communist one, under the circumstances) in this strategically important region, they had few choices but to look for ethnically Korean Communist cadres elsewhere. This meant that the entire North Korean elite during the first years of DPRK history was to consist of people who had spent their previous lives in diverse places and whose pre-1945 political and personal experiences had been quite dissimilar. When the North Korean Workers' Party was officially established in August 1946 (by merging the North Korean Communist Party with the North Korean New People's Party), it consisted of four rival factions with very different social, cultural, and educational backgrounds, as well as varied political orientations.

Of these four groups, it was the Domestic (or Underground) faction that appeared strongest in the early days of Liberation (i.e., liberation from Japanese rule). This faction comprised former underground Communists active in Korea prior to 1945. Of all Korean Communists, they were perhaps the closest approximation to the Soviet Bolshevik "Old Guard" or the East European "Underground Workers." They combined a lifelong commitment to Communism with a high intellectual and educational level. After the Communist Party had been officially disbanded by the Comintern in 1928 and ceased to exist as an organized body, various Communist groups continued their activities throughout Korea. In August 1945, when the rapid Japanese withdrawal created a power vacuum in the country, some left-wing leaders grasped the opportunity, gathered in Seoul, and promptly reestablished the Communist Party of Korea. The most remarkable of these South Korean Communists was Pak Hŏn-yŏng, who by then had acquired almost legendary status among Korean leftists. In 1945, Pak became a leader of the reborn party. For a time even the Communist organizations of the Soviet-occupied North technically recognized the supreme authority of Pak Hŏn-yŏng's Seoul-based Central Committee. But by late spring 1946, under Soviet tutelage the North Korean Communists created an independent Communist Party of North Korea. A few months later, after a merger with the New People's Party, the Communist Party changed its name to the North Korean Workers' Party. This party, however, initially included surprisingly few members of the Domestic factions, because so few underground Communists had been active in the North prior to 1945. Meanwhile, the Communist Party of South Korea (renamed the South Korean Workers' Party after merging with several minor leftist groups) kept growing and, in spite of constant persecution by the American military authorities and Washington-backed rightists, transformed itself into a formidable political force that engaged in, among other things, substantial guerrilla activity. Thus the small number of pre-1945 underground Communists were joined by another generation, who had underground and/or guerrilla experience in the South and had been recruited to the party after 1945. This younger group was closely connected to the older Domestic faction members and was generally perceived as belonging to the Domestic faction. However, perpetual police harassment eventually made most of the Communist leaders leave their homelands for the North. In 1949 the Workers' parties of the North and the South officially merged, and the Domestic Communists were incorporated into the Korean Workers' Party, by then dominated by other factions.

The Guerrilla faction consisted of former guerrillas who had fought the Japanese forces in Manchuria in the 1930s and/or had run intelligence-gathering and logistics networks for the guerrilla movement there. Most of them had escaped to the USSR circa 1940 and remained there until Liberation. They were ethnic Koreans, but by the early 1930s most of them were living not in Korea proper but in Manchuria, where there was a substantial Korean minority. In the USSR they received some additional military training and for a few years served in the Eighty-eighth Independent Brigade. This special Soviet Army unit was composed mostly of former Chinese and Korean guerrillas and was led by Zhou Bao-zhong, a Chinese officer who was himself a prominent former guerrilla. Contrary to later pronouncements of the North Korean propaganda machine, prior to 1945 these people had weak if any connections to the Communist movement in Korea proper, and though they were fighting in units of the Chinese Communist guerrillas, they remained largely unaware of the exiled Korean intellectuals in Yan'an, the rustic capital of Red China, let alone the underground activists in Seoul. The guerrillas themselves were of humble origins (mostly peasants) and lacked a good—indeed any—education. Most of them were virtually unknown outside their native villages.[4] Very soon, a young but prominent guerrilla commander whose nom de guerre was Kim Il Song (born Kim Sŏng-chu in 1912) came to be perceived as the supreme leader of this faction, though initially some other former guerrillas were able to rival his authority. The final victory of the Guerrilla faction—initially the weakest of the four factions—was assured in early 1946 when Kim Il Song, with Soviet support, secured his position as supreme leader of North Korea. In spite of the obvious lack of administrative experience and proper education among former guerrillas, Kim Il Song gradually appointed them to the most senior posts within the state and party bureaucracy, though it was not until the early 1960s that a former guerrilla affiliation became the necessary precondition for any aspiring member of the North Korean supreme elite.[5]

The Yan'an faction was made up of Korean leftist intellectuals who had emigrated to China in the 1920s and 1930s and had spent many years at the Chinese Communist headquarters in the town of Yan'an. There, while working mostly within the Chinese Communist Party, they also created some specifically Korean organizations, of which the Korean Independence League was the most remarkable. These Koreans from Yan'an were mostly cultured and well educated, and their leader Kim Tu-bong was one of the most outstanding Korean linguists of his generation. In their ideological outlook they were quite similar to the members of the Domestic faction, although a long period of exile had partly undermined their understanding of Korean realities and made them more susceptible to the ideas and trends that spread from Mao's China. A less sophisticated but tougher and practically minded part of the Yan'an faction consisted of ethnic Koreans who had fought with the Chinese Communist Forces (CCF), as the Chinese Red Army was often called in the West. Noteworthy among the latter was an ethnic Korean general known widely by his nom de guerre, Mu Chŏng (his real name was Kim Mu-chŏng). A Korean émigré, he achieved prominence in the Chinese Eighth Route Army and later played a significant role in the initial stages of the Korean War. Mu Chŏng and other generals with Chinese experience formed the backbone of the North Korean army on the eve of the Korean War. In the late 1940s entire units of ethnic Korean soldiers were transferred from China to become integral parts of the Korean People's Army (KPA), the North Korean armed forces. The Yan'an faction members returned to Korea in 1945–1949, but their political activity met with some obstacles because excessive Chinese influence over Korea was not exactly welcomed by the Soviets even at this early stage. Still, many former "Yan'an" exiles with military backgrounds were appointed to the DPRK armed forces, while the leader of the "civilian wing," Kim Tu-bong, even became a titular head of the North Korean Communist Workers' Party and later the state.

The fourth faction, the Soviet faction, comprised Soviet Koreans—mostly former schoolteachers and low-to-medium-level party cadres who were sent to Korea by Soviet government agencies during 1945–1948. They had been recruited from a large ethnic Korean diaspora in the USSR. Their main task was to act as both supervisors and advisers in the administrative bodies of the new North Korean state. On the whole, the Soviet Koreans possessed both an education and a considerable amount of technical competency, not to mention formidable administrative experience. They were the primary conduit of Soviet traditions and expertise into the North Korean society. For this reason their imprint on North Korean institutions was to be extremely enduring. Greatly outliving their personal political importance, this imprint can still be observed to this day. Most of the Soviet faction, however, were born or at least educated in Russia, where they had spent most of their lives. Being second- or third-generation overseas Koreans, they were thoroughly Russified in their habits and worldview. Until the late 1950s the Soviet Koreans preserved close ties with Moscow and often technically retained Soviet citizenship (although the citizenship question was not clear-cut, given that the majority failed to renew their expired Soviet passports). They spoke mainly Russian with their families and educated their children at the Yuk ko jung (the Sixth High School in Pyongyang), where Russian was the main language of instruction and all students had a Soviet background. Generally, they felt ill at ease in Korean culture. On the other hand, their previous experience generally made them very efficient and reliable officials. This group boasted few leaders, with Hŏ Ka-i, an able and determined midlevel party cadre from Soviet Central Asia, being initially the most prominent.[6]

The backgrounds of the factions and the life experiences of their members were quite different, and tensions among the factions were unavoidable. The intellectuals from the Domestic and Yan'an factions had little in common with the uneducated but resilient former guerrillas or with the purge-hardened former Soviet bureaucrats. They occasionally even spoke different languages: Russian was a natural medium used among the Soviet Koreans, who were also openly proud of their Russian upbringing and education, while the Yan'an sojourners were fluent in Chinese and strongly influenced by the spirit of Mao's emerging China. All but the Domestic Communists were strangers to North Korea as well, for they had spent decades overseas or had been born on foreign soil. Even the local Communists, who were mostly from the South, did not always feel comfortable in the North. Furthermore, most of them were strangers to one another. It is probable that before 1945 the Yan'an faction members had a vague idea of the ongoing guerrilla activity in Manchuria, but they seldom knew its leaders personally. The connections that both the Yan'an intellectuals and the Manchurian guerrillas had with the Communist underground in Korea prior to 1945 had been tenuous at best. Neither of these groups had known much about the Soviet Koreans—who in turn had been cut off from any information about their country of origin until 1945—and they almost certainly had known nothing of any other Korean Communist groups (those Soviet Koreans who had been imprudent enough to maintain overseas connections were much more likely to have fallen victims to

Stalin's Great Purge in 1936–1938). It can be said that pre-Liberation Korea was an ideal breeding ground for factionalism.

The important political decisions in post-1945 North Korea were made by the Soviets, and they offered their unequivocal support to Kim Il Song, whose relative youth (he was 33 in 1945) and lack of contacts would otherwise have scarcely afforded him much of a chance of achieving supremacy in North Korean politics. Kim was chosen for the role of the future North Korean leader primarily because of his Soviet Army background and the good rapport he had managed to achieve with the Soviet military. His rise also signaled the eventual but slow advance of the Guerrilla faction. During the first decade of his rule, however, Kim Il Song was scarcely more than a first among equals: he did not have majority support within the ruling elite, which comprised members of all four opposing factions (in the 1948 Central Committee their representation was numerically almost equal). Unless Kim rid himself of these potential rivals, his power could be neither full nor safe.

During the Korean War (1950–1953) and soon afterward, Kim Il Song succeeded in eliminating the entire Domestic faction, which was by far the most vulnerable faction because of its lack of foreign support. He also managed to weaken significantly the Yan'an and Soviet factions. The associates of Pak Hŏn-yŏng, and later the man himself (the founder of the Korean Communist Party in its post-1945 reincarnation, whose formal supremacy was briefly recognized by Kim Il Song in late 1945), were accused of "informing the Japanese secret police," "spying for the USA and South Korea," "planning terrorist actions," and other absurdly improbable crimes. As was customary at the time, Kim Il Song staged a show trial of the former underground Communists in August 1953 that was reminiscent of contemporary trials in other "people's democracies." The defendants delivered the customary self-abasing confessions, were "found guilty," and mostly were sentenced to death. The show trials of 1953 and 1955 (the latter a low-profile, almost closed trial of Pak himself) were accompanied and followed by a large-scale witch hunt. As a result, by 1955–1956 all but a handful of former underground Communists had been purged. A good pretext for these purges was provided by their close connections with the leaders of the Domestic faction (undoubtedly true, especially considering the traditionally personal nature of Korean politics).

The purge of the former local Communists had another goal as well. The Korean War almost ended in complete disaster, but Kim Il Song never took responsibility for the military debacle of 1950. To save his own reputation, he had to find convenient scapegoats who could be blamed for things that went wrong. The South Koreans and some Yan'an generals became his scapegoats. The former group were faulted for their alleged inability to start a large uprising in the South that, as they had promised before 1950, would be an instant reaction to the North Korean invasion of the South.[7] The Yan'an generals (notably Kim Mu-chŏng) were made responsible for the military disasters of October and November 1950, when the North Korean army was annihilated by the U.S. forces.

Another important event that marked the end of the Korean War and signaled the increasing independence of Kim Il Song from his one-time sponsors was the purge of Pak Il-u and Hŏ Ka-i. At that time those two men were probably the most prominent members of the Yan'an and Soviet factions, respectively. The leader of the Soviet Koreans, Hŏ Ka-i, fell from grace in late 1951 and committed suicide in 1953 under suspicious circumstances (indeed, many people believed he was secretly assassinated by Kim Il Song's agents).[8]

The prominence of Pak Il-u among the Chinese Koreans was rather less significant than Hŏ's influence on the Soviet Koreans, but as a Korean representative in the Chinese-Korean Joint Command, Pak played a major role as a contact between the Chinese and North Korean generals during the war. He was often perceived as "Mao's man in Korea," because of his reputed close relations to the chairman. This made him an obvious source of political danger, so Kim Il Song did his best to limit Pak Il-u's influence after the war and finally purged him in early 1955. Around the same time, another prominent and vocal leader of the Yan'an faction, Ch'oe Ch'ang-ik, was criticized by the Great Leader, although in his case the criticism did not lead to complete demotion.

The purge of both Hŏ Ka-i and Pak Il-u, the accusations against whom were patently absurd, indicated a more independent position of Kim Il Song after the Korean War. Both Hŏ Ka-i and Pak Il-u had grown too influential and, given the foreign support they could rely on, were potentially dangerous rivals of Kim. Before 1950, however, Kim Il Song could hardly do much about these figures, who were widely viewed as the embodiment of Moscow and Beijing's predominance. The purges of Pak and Hŏ were an omen of things to come. In 1953 or 1954, Kim Il Song dared not do much about any other members of the Soviet or Yan'an factions. The support of Moscow and Peking was of vital importance to him, even after the end of hostilities, and he had good reason to believe that in the event of an attack on either faction the reaction from the "elder brothers" would be swift, decisive, and harsh.

From the early 1950s onward, the role of leader in the Yan'an faction was increasingly played by Ch'oe Ch'ang-ik. A first-generation Korean Communist, Ch'oe was prominent in the Seoul Communist underground as early as the mid-1920s, being one of the "founding fathers" of the native Korean left-wing movement. Eventually Ch'oe moved to China, where he became one of the principal leaders of the Korean Independence League—the embryo of the New People's Party and later of the Yan'an faction. During and after the Korean War, Kim Tu-bong remained the most respected and technically the most senior of all Yan'an leaders, but he had never been particularly interested in politics (or, rather, in political intrigues) and was, to all appearances, content with his role as a respected figurehead. As for the Soviet faction, it lacked common experiences and a tight network of longtime personal contacts like those so strong among the former Yan'an exiles. The failure of Hŏ Ka-i, the focus of the Soviet Koreans, was a significant and irrecoverable loss. After Hŏ Ka-i's death in 1953, Pak Ch'ang-ok was sometimes perceived as the most important of all Soviet Koreans. Pak, a former low-level Soviet official and intelligence operative, eventually became a chairman of the State Planning Commission and a Politburo member in North Korea. However, despite his considerable ego and ambitions, Pak lacked the moral authority and charisma of Hŏ Ka-i and was unable to replace him fully.

The Korean War changed the entire domestic situation in North Korea. Economically the war greatly weakened the devastated country, while politically the North Korean authorities emerged from the conflict stronger than when they entered it, to some extent because it was Chinese, not Soviet, troops that fought in the war. Beijing, not Moscow, had rushed to the rescue when the North Korean regime was facing imminent collapse. Consequently, throughout the Korean War, China's influence grew and Soviet political influence waned; it thus became possible for Pyongyang to play one Great Power against the other. Moscow and Beijing were still at that time close partners, but the first cracks in their doomed alliance were already beginning to appear.

During the war, the North Korean government also amassed substantial practical experience. In the course of the fighting, a new state and party bureaucracy, including quite formidable security forces, emerged—or, to be more precise, grew considerably. The newly recruited personnel in the army headquarters and government offices consisted of predominantly young people in their twenties and thirties whose entire education and worldview had been shaped by the new official ideology; their core political and social experience was war and its accompanying spirit of iron discipline, sacrifice, and obedience. Significantly, Kim Il Song was the only leader this younger generation of cadres had ever known. In addition, the fortunes of war had been especially capricious, and most regions of the country had been occupied at least once by troops of both sides. This meant that the majority of potential troublemakers had ample opportunity to leave the North with the crowds of refugees, thus relieving the North Korean authorities of the bothersome necessity of dealing with them at a later stage. Therefore, in 1954, Kim Il Song—and for that matter the entire North Korean regime—had reason to feel more secure than in 1948.

Kim Il Song's logic in seeking to eliminate other factions was simple. In light of the intense and endemic factional rivalry and the Korean tradition of political factionalism, it was inevitable that Kim Il Song should see all other factions as sources of potential danger. This suspicion was fueled by the fact that two of the four initial factions had enjoyed quite intimate relationships with powerful neighbors. By 1955, Kim Il Song had already destroyed the core of the Domestic faction and was considering what to do next. Backed by the two Great Powers on which Kim Il Song and his regime greatly depended, both the Soviet and the Yan'an factions were far less vulnerable than the Domestic faction. By the end of 1955, however, the international and domestic situations had changed to such an extent that a (still cautious) challenge to the influence of these two factions was possible.

Although Soviet influence in Korea had waned by 1955 in comparison with that of 1946 or 1950, it remained considerable. The time had passed when Soviet Embassy officials would check the texts of speeches that North Korean leaders intended to deliver at public meetings or would confirm all major army appointments and promotions.[9] No longer did all principal political decisions of the Pyongyang government have to receive the formal prior approval of the Soviet Politburo.[10] Still, all things Soviet were officially considered admirable and superior, and many an institution was shaped according to the Soviet pattern, a fact that nobody bothered to conceal at the time. Russian was also by far the most widely taught foreign language. The wholesale emulation of Russian and Soviet culture remained an essential feature of the North Korean cultural landscape. Soviet books, Soviet movies, Soviet plays, and Soviet songs were everywhere, and a considerable number of elite young Koreans studied at Soviet universities. Coverage of the Soviet Union in the North Korean press was ubiquitous, and minor incidents of official Soviet life were reported in great detail. Even some essentially local Soviet events, such as anniversaries of rather obscure Russian writers, were often seen as deserving extensive coverage in the North Korean press.

Some—but not all—former Soviet Koreans frequented the Soviet Embassy and engaged in long conversations with diplomats. Information from the official records of such conversations is widely used in the present book. However, the general assumption that the Soviet Embassy regularly and persistently used the Soviet Koreans to manipulate North Korean politics appears to be an overstatement. Few if any traces of such attempts are to be found in the available declassified papers—at least those written after 1953 (most earlier documents were either destroyed during the war or remain classified). Occasionally a Soviet diplomat was willing to use this channel of influence, but it was far from a routine practice. In most cases, as the documents clearly demonstrate, the Soviet officials chose to be passive listeners to their Korean interlocutors and tried to avoid making recommendations, giving orders, or even expressing a clear-cut position on the vast majority of politically sensitive questions. Thus the image that was extremely popular in the 1950s in both Western and especially South Korean propaganda—that is, the image of a Soviet Embassy acting as a kind of shadow government to

North Korea and of Soviet officials acting as vigilant supervisors of the North Korean regime or omnipotent puppet masters behind the scene—is an exaggeration. Such an image may have been close to the truth in the late 1940s, but by the mid-50s the situation had changed considerably. The new Moscow line of "noninterference with the domestic affairs of fraternal countries," initiated by Khrushchev, was not just a slogan. The "noninterference" of course had its limits, and those limits were quite narrow (as most East European countries were to learn in due course), but the epoch of petty patronage had effectively ended soon after Stalin's death in 1953.

The cautious attitude of the Soviet diplomats and their reluctance to make risky decisions probably reflected not only the new government policy but also something less altruistic: their own personal backgrounds and their own personal agendas. Few of the Soviet diplomats were Korean specialists; Korean specialists began to appear in the embassy only in the late 1950s and, even then, initially at a junior level. Not many of the Soviet diplomats of the period had experience of World War II or the post-Liberation Soviet occupation of Korea. In the late 1950s the majority of the embassy staff had neither sufficient background knowledge nor particular personal interest in North Korea.[11] For them the country was just another overseas posting, and in fact one of the least desirable. Therefore the Soviet diplomats did not want to do anything that would jeopardize their chances of eventually getting a promotion or posting to an enjoyably decadent Western capital. The general approach to North Korea is well reflected by two jokes, quite popular among Soviet diplomats of the 1950s and often retold even today. In one of these jokes, the DPRK (or KNDR, in Russian) was mockingly called *kndyra,* a combination of the country's official name and the Russian *"dyra,"* "a hole, a destitute and boring place." Another joke was "Kuritsa ne ptitsa, Phenyan ne zagranitsa" (Chicken is not a bird, Pyongyang is not abroad)—with implications not of closeness but of a lack of "overseas" refinement and career prospects.

Indeed, in comparison with the majority of Soviet diplomatic missions, a typical diplomat's existence in the Soviet Embassy in North Korea was boring and unrewarding. Social life in Pyongyang, a city ruined by the intense American bombing, was a wasteland. The economic conditions also left much to be desired: even if the diplomats had money, they could not spend it on high-quality goods, because such goods were not to be found in the Pyongyang shops, not even in the special shops exclusive to members of the foreign community. Given that easy access to foreign currency and Western consumer goods was becoming an increasingly important incentive for aspiring diplomats in the Soviet Union, this lack was a serious shortcoming in North Korea. It is therefore understandable that many diplomats hoped to escape eventually from such a dreary place. It would be a mistake to generalize, given that some investigative and resourceful diplomats did their best to understand the situation (e.g., Ye. L. Titorenko, to some extent V. I. Pelishenko, and, later, V. P. Tkachenko), but for the most part, Soviet officials had good personal reasons to be cautious and therefore passive. After all, as every bureaucrat knows only too well, the chance of being punished for a lack of action is usually less than the chance of getting into trouble for a wrong action. The rapid and unpredictable changes in Moscow's politics and ideology also contributed to the situation. The political uncertainty in the Kremlin meant that the definitions of right and wrong were perilously nebulous, and the Soviet diplomats had ample reason to fear that certain actions, quite permissible and even laudable at one stage, would be considered inadequate, contemptible, or even criminal sometime later. Such worries were understandable and justified, but there is no doubt that they greatly restricted the Soviets' ability to react to the challenges of the new situation.

From the Soviet point of view, the general situation in North Korea did not appear to warrant serious concern, at least when compared with a potentially restive Eastern Europe. In many countries of Eastern Europe, anti-Soviet trends were all too obvious. In Poland, Hungary, and to a certain extent East Germany, the USSR was seen as a new incarnation of the traditional enemy, Russia, and nationalist ferment was ever present. In other Communist countries the forces of internal resistance were also influential, and the Soviet supervisors of the local governments would never overestimate their popularity or stability. Korea, where nationalism was traditionally directed largely against the Japanese and where the base for the internal anti-Communist opposition was obviously weak, did not look like a potential trouble spot.

Of course, apart from the popular discontent, Soviet domination posed another danger: "national Communism" of the Yugoslavian, Titoist type. With the wisdom of hindsight, we now know that this danger was quite real. However, in 1953–1955, Kim Il Song probably appeared to be a very unlikely candidate for becoming another Tito. North Korea, especially after the war, appeared to be too dependent on various forms of Soviet aid, and Kim's own background as a relatively unknown leader who had been chosen and promoted by the Soviet military authorities presumably precluded any kind of "anti-Soviet" action by him. But these calculations eventually proved wrong.

After 1953, the year of Stalin's death, the political landscape in the Communist world changed rapidly, profoundly influenced by the newly emerging situation in the Soviet Union. The entire Communist camp (with the probable exceptions of China, North Vietnam, and Yugoslavia), since the time of its inception, had been geared to react instantly to any major changes in Moscow. De-Stalinization began in 1953, almost immediately after Stalin's death. The pace was initially quite slow, since Khrushchev had to take into account the likely opposition of the Stalinist Old Guard and was probably not entirely sure himself of the direction he would take. Thus, in 1953–1954 the importance of the entire process could be easily underestimated from abroad. However, in a couple of years it became clear that Khrushchev and his supporters meant business and that they were going to undertake a major renovation of the state socialist project. The concentration camps of the infamous Gulag were emptied, censorship relaxed, contacts with overseas improved greatly, and the space for independent social activity, though still severely restricted, expanded considerably. Some of the more dubious components of Stalin's ideological legacy were discarded, including the notorious concept of "permanent sharpening of class struggle in a socialist society," which gave theoretical justification for the endless escalation of purges and terror for decades after the Communist takeover. However, the part of the new Soviet program that leaders of the fraternal Communist countries had to worry about in particular was the new conception of leadership. The personality cult (this rather inadequate and euphemistic term was coined at this time)—an excessive glorification, even deification, of one almighty leader—was officially condemned, and "collective leadership" was proclaimed the new ideal. The political structure of the new Communist state remained essentially authoritarian, but the single godlike figure on top was to be (in theory at least) replaced by the collective rule of the politburo or some similar body.

Another important and potentially menacing part of the new ideological package was the theory of "peaceful coexistence." This new concept emphasized that major wars between Communist and capitalist camps, hitherto considered unavoidable and indeed beneficial to the final triumph of Communism, might and must be avoided. According to the new doctrine, the eventual victory of socialism would essentially be won through peaceful competition, although it did not completely rule out small-scale military confrontation in less important parts of the globe. In the late 1950s, Khrushchev sincerely hoped to outproduce capitalism, and the seemingly robust Soviet economy of his era made these hopes look at least plausible. Most other Communist regimes did not mind this peaceful approach to global competition, but for North Korea, locked in a fierce confrontation with the U.S.-backed South, this theory looked dangerously like an attempt to appease the "American imperialists," to find a compromise with the enemy. In the mid-1950s the North Koreans were hardly planning a new attack against the South, but as their substantial military spending indicated, they did not rule out the possibility that an opportunity for such an assault would arise in the more distant future. They also had to be ready for a possible attack from the South, even if in 1955–1960 such a possibility looked rather remote. In such a situation, Pyongyang feared that "peaceful coexistence" would also mean that the Soviet Union would be less willing to provide direct support of North Korea in the event of a new military confrontation with the South and its American backers. Thus the "peaceful coexistence" theory—however reasonable—was interpreted as a probable "theoretical justification" for the perceived Soviet willingness to sacrifice the interests of its junior partners for the sake of world peace.

Although these new ideals were sometimes rather vague, they still appeared quite menacing to the old-fashioned Stalinist leaders of the Communist bloc. Hence, these leaders faced a new and dangerous dilemma: should they try to accommodate the new trends, or should they distance themselves from Moscow? Both paths were fraught with danger. Official recognition of the new line was tantamount to an invitation to attack the current leaders for their former Stalinist ways, and in many Communist countries local party opposition, supported by dissatisfied or ambitious cadres (and occasionally relying on widespread public discontent), did not fail to use this opportunity. Distancing themselves from the USSR was an equally perilous task, given that Soviet economic, political, and military support was an important precondition for the survival of many Communist governments. In addition, at that stage nobody could be sure about the limits of Moscow's tolerance and its possible reaction to such deviant behavior.

2 The Soviet Faction under Attack

IN NORTH KOREA the first attempt to react to the new, uncertain, and potentially menacing international situation occurred in 1955. Before then the North Korean leadership had generally ignored the unfolding de-Stalinization campaign in the Soviet Union. However, by the end of 1955 attempts at a response began, and the initial actions from Pyongyang did not bode well for those who either hoped for an eventual liberalization of the regime or simply wanted to follow the Soviet line. The events of late 1955 indicated that North Korea would distance itself from its main benefactor and aid donor. The first manifestation of this tendency was a campaign directed against some of the more prominent members of the Soviet faction, although that faction was probably not seen as the sole source of danger. In the North Korean political world, ridden with factional antagonism, any "other" was a source of danger, and Kim Il Song was aware of this. As the purge of Pak Il-u and the attacks on Ch'oe Ch'ang-ik testify, Kim did not exactly love the "Chinese Koreans" either, but the situation in late 1955 obviously made the Soviets more dangerous, because they could become a fulcrum for local reformism.

I suggest that Kim Il Song's decision to do something about the Soviet faction and its political role in North Korea was almost certainly influenced by the unfolding de-Stalinization in the USSR. This process not unexpectedly troubled the young North Korean leader, who was only forty-four years old in 1956. Like other Communist countries,

North Korea had a political and social system closely modeled on the Stalinist system, and the personality cult of Kim Il Song—the cult of "the little leader"—had been patterned after the cult of "the big leader," Stalin. The Stalinist influence was also evident elsewhere, from an industrial policy with an emphasis on heavy industry to the fine arts and the show trials of fellow Communists. Hence any diminution of Stalin's prestige spelled grave danger for Kim Il Song's own authority. Kim had good reason to fear that his rivals would employ the "little leader, big leader" analogy to accuse him of establishing his own personality cult, as subsequent developments in Korea (the August Plenum) and some other Communist countries would reveal. In many places, local "little Stalins" were ousted by political rivals (Bulgaria), popular protest (Hungary), or both (Poland).

By 1955, Kim Il Song and his entourage, the former Manchurian guerrillas, had many reasons to feel uneasy about the new situation, and it is likely that they perceived the Soviet faction as a major threat to their authority. After the Korean War, approximately 150 Soviet Koreans held important positions in the North Korean Workers' Party and government. Once they had been key political players, had enjoyed the backing of the omnipresent Soviet military, and up to the early 1950s had exceeded any other group in influence and power. By 1955, however, the influence of the Soviet faction had weakened somewhat; the gradual promotion of former guerrillas and other people who were perceived as personal supporters of Kim Il Song had been implemented at the expense of other groups. It is likely that Kim Il Song and his inner circle had never really felt much sympathy toward Soviet Koreans, but it was the continuing de-Stalinization in the USSR that made the Soviet faction look especially dangerous. Maintaining close connections with the Soviet Union, the Soviet Koreans were easily influenced by the "Soviet spirit"—a more liberal influence than the influence of Mao's regime over the Yan'an faction. From Kim Il Song's point of view, the Soviet Koreans were more likely to raise ideas of reform, to criticize his personality cult, or otherwise to cause trouble. By late 1955, Kim Il Song was working out a strategy for the next phase of his struggle for absolute supremacy, beginning by targeting the Soviet faction. It is not clear whether his real aim was to eliminate the Soviet faction or merely to check its influence and teach potential troublemakers a lesson, but the latter possibility seems more likely.

The new policy that slowly began to be implemented in 1955 seems to have been not only a reaction to the challenge of de-Stalinization but also a logical development of Kim Il Song's earlier line. For him, de-Stalinization brought both challenge and opportunity. Kim was not only a ruthless manipulator but also a nationalist who had spent a good deal of his life fighting for Korean independence. For many if not most East Asian Communists, Marxism was first and foremost an efficient anti-imperialist doctrine, a theory of fighting for national rather than social liberation, for national rather than social equality, and Kim Il Song undoubtedly shared this viewpoint. Toward the end of his long life, when Communism was obviously going out of favor worldwide, he openly referred to himself as a "nationalist." This was hardly a surprising revelation, and in this regard Kim resembled other "peasant-Communist" revolutionaries of East Asia. Evidence suggests that Kim Il Song considered any foreign influence to be evil by definition. Indeed, it is quite possible that he was actually averse to the Soviets and their dictates from the very beginning, even though he used them (or more precisely allowed them to use him) to achieve power. Kim had had no choice but to endure an omnipresent Soviet influence from 1945 onward, but by the mid-1950s, when he had established a firm grip on the country, he decided to draw the line. Now the disturbing developments in the USSR not only made this plan even more urgent but also created the conditions for its realization.

Throughout his entire political career, Kim Il Song proved himself to be a remarkable master of political manipulation who often used the same, invariably successful trick: he would single out a particular enemy who appeared the most threatening at any given time, and then he would create around himself a broad coalition that included virtually everyone but the targeted victim. In this manner he skillfully let his temporarily less dangerous enemies destroy the more threatening ones. The fall of the Domestic faction in 1953–1955 was a good example of this tactic. Kim Il Song's accusations against the former underground Communists, however improbable and even absurd, were enthusiastically supported and promoted by members of all other factions, who saw the former underground Communists as potential rivals or simply wanted to gain some extra power or privilege at the Domestic faction's expense.

While contemplating an attack on the Soviet Koreans, Kim Il Song was able to draw on the support of much of the Yan'an faction, not to mention that of the loyal former guerrillas. Mutual rivalry and suspicion had always poisoned the relationship between the Soviet and Chinese Koreans. The leaders of the Yan'an faction, the most important of whom at that time was Ch'oe Ch'ang-ik, used every opportunity to set Kim Il Song against the Soviet Koreans. In turn, the Soviet Koreans attempted to prove to Kim Il Song that the Yan'an members were incompetent or untrustworthy in order to obstruct their promotion. For example, during a lengthy conversation with Kim Il Song in late 1955, Pak Ch'ang-ok, the de facto leader of the Soviet faction, spoke out against the Yan'an faction, actively criticizing the actions of the "Chinese Koreans."[1]

The assault on the Soviet faction in late 1955 was not an unheralded event. In one of the few academic publications that deal with the campaign against the Soviet Koreans in 1955, Masao Okonogi considers that the quest for greater political autonomy, to which Kim Il Song and his entourage attached their own greater personal power and security, began in 1954 and was thereafter associated with the search for a new economic strategy.[2] In 1954 and 1955, Kim supported a policy that prioritized the development of heavy industry over the production of consumer goods. The latter, consumer-oriented policy was in part associated with the Soviet Korean leader Pak Ch'ang-ok, the then chairman of the State Planning Commission and hence the DPRK's chief economic strategist. Furthermore, as Okonogi notes, in the period after Stalin's death attention was increasingly drawn to the special qualities of "Koreanness" and the unique achievements of Kim Il Song.[3] Okonogi's observations are true, but the known Soviet materials do not pay much attention to the industrial policy dispute, and it seems that this controversy was not taken very seriously at the Soviet Embassy and went unnoticed by the diplomats. At any rate, neither the dispute over heavy industry in 1954 nor the gradual spreading of Kim's personality cult after the Korean War resulted in an immediate open attack on the Soviet faction.

Hence, the main reason the Soviet Koreans found themselves under attack in late 1955 was almost certainly a contemporary development in the USSR. By then it had become clear that the Khrushchev reforms were going to be radical, and his break with the Stalinist tradition was visible. We can surmise that under these new circumstances Kim decided he could no longer afford to pretend that nothing serious was happening over the border.

It seems likely that Kim Il Song's decision to eliminate the Soviet faction was also prompted by a less significant event—the open opposition of some high-ranking Soviet Koreans toward the promotion of Ch'oe Yong-gŏn, a former guerrilla and one of Kim Il Song's most loyal lieutenants. At least this was the view of some contemporary observers. As Pak Yŏng-bin later recounted to a Soviet diplomat, Kim Il Song had recommended Ch'oe Yong-gŏn's promotion to the Political Council (the official name of the North Korean Politburo until April 1956) "before the April Plenum (1955)"—that is, sometime in the late winter or early spring of 1955—but had been met with strong opposition from prominent members of the Soviet faction. During the April Plenum of 1955, Kim Il Song managed to include Ch'oe in the Political Council anyway. In September 1955, Kim Il Song again raised the issue of Ch'oe Yong-gŏn's promotion and hinted at his possible appointment as premier (instead of himself), but once again Kim encountered resistance from such Soviet Koreans as Pak Ch'ang-ok, Pak Chŏng-ae,[4] and Pak Yŏng-bin.[5]

It is now apparent that the promotion of Ch'oe Yong-gŏn was just another step in Kim Il Song's general strategy, aimed at further strengthening the influence of the former guerrillas at the highest level of the North Korean bureaucracy. There was, however, a serious, albeit purely technical obstacle to such a promotion. As incredible as it might seem, Ch'oe Yong-gŏn was officially considered as never having been a member of the Korean Workers' Party, let alone its Central Committee. Since 1946 he had been the leader of the Democratic Party, which the official propaganda labeled "a petty bourgeois party." The Democratic Party was established by the famous right-wing nationalist Cho Man-sik in November 1945. For a while it was a genuine political party; it even dared to challenge the Soviet authorities and the Communists. Its short-lived independence came to an abrupt end in January 1946 when Cho Man-sik was arrested after an open confrontation with the Soviet authorities over the political future of Korea. However, the Democratic

Party was preserved by the North Korean leaders (after a thorough purge, of course) to maintain the fiction of a United Front, as well as to initially control this significant number of potentially troublesome non-Communist elements within North Korean society. Ch'oe Yong-gŏn, a former Manchurian guerrilla commander who also happened to be a onetime disciple of Cho Man-sik, was made Cho Man-sik's deputy in November 1945. After Cho's arrest, Ch'oe was appointed chairman of the Democratic Party in February 1946. In this capacity as a leader of the Democratic Party, he played an important role in North Korean politics and technically even acted as a commander of the North Korean armed forces at the beginning of the Korean War. His real influence as an ex-guerrilla and Kim's old comrade-in-arms was also substantial. By the mid-1950s the Democratic Party had fulfilled its role as a front organization and, for all practical purposes, had ceased to be a political party. It had essentially been transformed into a propaganda institution, so there was no need to retain a politician of such prominence in such an expendable organization.

In fact, Ch'oe Yong-gŏn was secretly a member of the Workers' Party; he was an "agent of influence" within the Democratic Party whose main task was to prevent that party from becoming an independent political force. In May 1956, for example, a Soviet diplomat noted in an embassy paper that Ch'oe, despite being the Democratic Party's chairman, was a member of the Workers' Party.[6] It is not clear whether in 1955 Ch'oe was a card-bearing member of the KWP, but the possibility appears quite likely. Even if he was not a secret KWP member in the strict sense, his official party affiliation was a purely technical issue. Given that Soviet diplomats were aware of Ch'oe Yong-gŏn's real affiliation with the Workers' Party, it is unlikely that high-level Soviet Koreans were ignorant of his role. However, Ch'oe's formal membership in the Democratic Party offered an excellent pretext for resistance to his promotion and was frequently cited in many of the relevant debates. The Soviet Koreans also insisted that Ch'oe Yong-gŏn was unsuitable for promotion because of his alleged lack of competence—they labeled him an "incompetent official."[7] In reality, the strong opposition to Ch'oe Yong-gŏn's promotion appears to have been a result of factional rivalry; Ch'oe was considered an opponent of the Soviet faction. As early as

1954 he and the leader of the Yan'an faction, Ch'oe Ch'ang-ik, had attempted to have some Soviet Koreans dismissed from their posts (at least this was suspected at the time by the Soviet Koreans).[8] The Soviet Koreans were certainly not keen to see a high position occupied by someone they perceived as a political foe. From Kim Il Song's point of view, however, attempts to block Ch'oe Yong-gŏn's promotion were aimed at weakening the position of the former guerrillas and were thus akin to an open challenge to his own authority.

Although problems associated with Ch'oe Yong-gŏn's eventually successful promotion to the KWP Political Council were an early broadside in the anti-Soviet campaign, the promotion was still a relatively minor issue. As has been mentioned, the threat posed by de-Stalinization was arguably a much more important consideration with future implications, and all of these uncertainties could have been reinforced by the behavior of many Soviet Koreans in the mid-1950s. As might be expected, it was the Soviet Koreans who began to discuss openly the problems of the personality cult. This occurred in 1955, and the attempts at discussion and the subsequent clashes are mentioned in Soviet Embassy papers from early 1956. Some Soviet Koreans even insisted that it would be desirable to launch a Khrushchev-style campaign against the personality cult in North Korea. In most cases this would have been a naive view, divorced from the harsh realities of North Korean politics; many Soviet Koreans, wanting to improve the North Korean situation, would have taken the slogans about "mutual criticism" at face value, while in some cases the motives would have been somewhat less altruistic—some people may have hoped to profit personally from the new political situation. It would appear that in general the Soviet Koreans were influenced by the new winds blowing from Moscow, by the new atmosphere of hope and expectation, and were quite genuine (albeit somewhat naive) in their attempts. When Pak Yŏng-bin was appointed head of the Agitation and Propaganda Department of the KWP Central Committee in February 1955, thus becoming one of the party's chief ideologues, he dared to suggest to Kim Il Song that it might be necessary to cease the "excessive use" of Kim's name in the North Korean media.[9] In this endeavor Pak Yŏng-bin was supported by Pak Ch'ang-ok, and obviously this was not the sort of suggestion Kim Il Song would welcome.

Soviet Koreans in more lowly positions also showed signs that they had been "contaminated" by the dangerous ideas of de-Stalinization. In December 1955, Song Chin-p'a, the former chief editor of *New Korea* magazine (a North Korean foreign-language propaganda monthly), was dismissed after initiating discussions concerning the personality cult with his coworkers. Curiously, he was also accused of referring to the secretary of the party organization on the monthly editorial board (who had earlier criticized him) as "an anti-Soviet element." In addition, Song Chin-p'a was said to be hostile toward Han Sŏl-ya, an official North Korean writer and leading literary functionary; allegedly Song Chin-p'a had been reluctant to publish Han Sŏl-ya's novel *The Taedong River (Taedonggang)*. Although it is impossible to say whether there were grounds for this accusation, Song Chin-p'a was dismissed from his job as chief editor and expelled from the party.[10] He subsequently applied for permission to return to the USSR, which was initially granted but later revoked by the Korean authorities, with Soviet approval. Instead Song was sent to the countryside for "labor reeducation." The sentence was not one of imprisonment; instead, Song Chin-p'a was required to do manual work at a factory for a month (obviously such punishment was yet another influence of Mao's China, with its belief in the redeeming power of hard unskilled labor).[11] This episode was one of the first indications that any critique of the personality cult in Korea was not going to be tolerated by the authorities.

In this minor but perhaps typical episode, we first encounter the name of Han Sŏl-ya, as well as the "literary theme" that was to play such a major role in the subsequent events. Indeed, the North Korean literature of the period was a rather sorrowful collection, even when compared with the fiction of other "people's democracies." It was not incidental that all attempts to sell translations of North Korean fiction in the Soviet Union and other Communist countries ended in failure; in spite of generous subsidies, North Korean literature was never taken seriously even in "fraternal countries," whose readers had been accustomed to consuming literature with a very heavy and overt ideology. Administratively, the North Korean literature and arts were organized and managed along the standard Soviet-type lines. A powerful Writers' Union, which was a kind of ministry for literature, ran publishing houses, provided writers with a living (occasionally a rather good living), and, together with official censorship agencies, was cautious about ideological correctness in literature. This whole system was run by Han Sŏl-ya, the chairman of the Writers' Union. His position made him the most powerful administrator of the North Korean cultural scene.

Han Sŏl-ya himself was a mediocre writer, but he proved to be a remarkably unscrupulous opportunist and careerist. Han originally came from the South, where, after a short period of flirting with leftist ideas in the early 1930s, he emerged as an eminent pro-Japanese writer during the Pacific War. Like many of his fellow intellectuals, he made a sudden about-face in 1945 and soon found himself at the helm of North Korean literary politics. Despite his "southern" background, Han had distanced himself from the Domestic faction from the beginning of his career in the North, and at an early stage he had become one of the first and most zealous adulators of Kim Il Song.[12] For a while, his dedication to Kim Il Song helped him not only to survive the slaughter of the domestic Communists but even to gain official recognition as "the greatest writer of modern Korean literature." This title he shared with Yi Ki-yŏng, a figure who was not particularly keen about politics and therefore posed no real threat in matters of power. Han himself was also purged in 1962, however, and then probably pardoned in 1969, just prior to his death.[13] Nevertheless, during the period 1955–1957, Han Sŏl-ya's influence was at its height, and he played an important role in the campaign against the Soviet Koreans.

Han Sŏl-ya and his entourage (which included the critic Ŏm Ho-sŏk and the writer Pak Si-yŏng, among others) had been running the North Korean literary bureaucracy from the late 1940s. They had had some competition, mostly from former South Korean writers who had some Communist connections and had moved to Pyongyang between 1945 and 1950. These writers, including Yim Hwa, Kim Nam-ch'ŏn, and Yi T'ae-jun, had a close relationship with the South Korean Communists, and this relationship eventually determined their fate. One of them, Yim Hwa, became a defendant at Yi Sŭng-yŏp's show trial in 1953 and received the death sentence, while others found themselves in increasingly perilous positions. Once Pak Hŏn-yŏng and other domestic Communists had been purged, their allies and personal acquaintances in the literary circles were exposed to the furious attack of Han Sŏl-ya and his henchmen. Although it is virtually impossible to detect any serious differences in style or ideology between the works of Han's adherents and the works of Han's foes, the latter group's fiction was thoroughly scrutinized and subjected to a crushing political critique after 1953.

The official critics discovered many "ideological mistakes" and even "subversive propaganda" in the texts of Kim Nam-ch'ŏn and other disgraced writers. These writers were now depicted as having been pro-Japanese elements before 1945 and associates of Pak Hŏn-yŏng the Spy after Liberation. These accusations were groundless, given that most of their post-1945 writing was essentially the same boring and highly politicized propaganda as the contemporary works of Han Sŏl-ya and his adherents (the only difference being that Yi T'ae-jun and Kim Nam-ch'ŏn were marginally more gifted). In regard to their political positions in the colonial period, the picture was also rather complicated. The accusations of collaboration with the Japanese contained a seed of truth, but they could have equally been applied to the other side as well. It is true, for example, that some works that Yi T'ae-jun had authored before 1945 were not free of pro-Japanese trends, but it is equally true that in Han Sŏl-ya's autobiographical novel, *Tower (T'ap),* and in his pre-1945 stories one could find glowing descriptions of selfless Japanese soldiers.

It is most likely that the entire conflict between the South Korean writers and Han Sŏl-ya's supporters resulted from a clash of personal ambition. The personal relations between some prominent South Korean writers and Han Sŏl-ya were poisoned from the early 1930s, and their competition for domination within the North Korean literary bureaucracy hardly made them friends. The purge of Pak Hŏn-yŏng and the domestic Communists provided Han Sŏl-ya with a convenient pretext for getting rid of his administrative rivals and personal enemies.

The public attack against the Soviet Koreans was launched in December 1955, but there is reason to believe that preparations for the attack commenced well beforehand. During a Central Committee plenum in April 1955, Pak Ch'ang-ok, who was the chairman of the State Planning Commission and the Soviet Koreans' unofficial leader, was criticized for providing wrong (excessively optimistic) data on the state of affairs in DPRK agriculture. Incidentally, the same plenum witnessed the disgrace of Pak Il-u, "Mao's man in Korea" and a prominent leader of the Yan'an faction.[14] In July, Pak Il-u was placed under house arrest.[15]

In August 1955, Kim Il Song ordered the collection of information critical of Pak Ch'ang-ok and his work.[16] On January 24, 1956, Vice-premier Pak Ŭi-wan reported to a Soviet diplomat that "for more than two months the CC [KWP Central Committee] and almost all party cells have been busy discussing the behavior of the Soviet Koreans."[17] If Pak Ŭi-wan's "more than two months" is accurate, then the campaign—or at least the preparations for it—was launched sometime in November 1955.

It appears that Pak Ch'ang-ok was the main target of the planned attack, probably because of his prominence among the Soviet Koreans and his obvious ambitions for the leadership. On November 21, Kim Il Song criticized the work of the State Planning Commission, which was headed by Pak Ch'ang-ok (Masao Okonogi suggests that this criticism was related to industrial policy).[18] Some days later Kim met Pak Ch'ang-ok for a personal discussion. According to a contemporary account provided by Pak Ch'ang-ok himself, Kim Il Song's tone was derogatory, and he did not address issues of economic planning but instead raised the relatively obscure matter of former "mistakes" in literary policy, a matter that did not directly concern either Pak Ch'ang-ok or the majority of Soviet Koreans. Pak Ch'ang-ok was accused of paying too much attention to ideologically suspicious writers from the South and lending insufficient support to "politically correct" writers such as Han Sŏl-ya.[19] This was an indication of the forthcoming campaign.

The main thrust of the assault took place in December 1955. On December 2 a plenum of the KWP Central Committee was convened in Pyongyang. The Central Committee, a group of some seventy people and the second most important body in the party, met a few times a year to discuss the most important problems of the political strategy. The plenum was by no means a place for free discussion, but behind the closed doors of the Central Committee a measure of frankness was possible. In addition, the Central Committee was a place where the party's top leaders could freely announce new policies and give their analysis of the current situation, something impossible to do in more open gatherings.

The plenum ran for two days, December 2 and 3, but reports of it were not officially released in *Nodong sinmun* until December 7. Such a delay was not uncommon in the secretive political culture of a Stalinist state—indeed, it was customary and followed the contemporary Soviet tradition. Both the brief official announcement of the plenum in *Nodong sinmun* and articles in later publications mention only two items on the plenum agenda: increasing agricultural output and an "organizational question" (*chojik munje*—in Communist bureaucratic jargon this vague expression was usually employed in relation to appointments and dismissals). Apart from discussions relating to agriculture, the plenum announced the convention of the Third KWP Congress the following year. In the next two months, official press references to the December Plenum consistently focused on agriculture-related subjects;[20] only in mid-February did the North Korean press begin to hint that other matters were also discussed.

Officially the plenum dealt with agricultural policy and was rather uneventful. However, much of the material from the Soviet Embassy reveals the December Plenum in quite a different light. In this material, agricultural issues are mentioned rarely if at all; instead the emphasis is on the plenum as a forum for discussion of the alleged "mistakes" committed by some high-level officials in regard to literary policy. All of the accused—Pak Ch'ang-ok, Ki Sŏk-pok, Pak Yŏng-bin, Chŏng Yul, and Chŏng Tong-hyŏk—were prominent members of the Soviet faction.[21] In addition, another member of the Soviet faction, Kim Yŏl, was accused of financial mismanagement and expelled from the Central Committee and the KWP. He was then made the subject of a criminal investigation.[22]

The main topic of the plenum agenda was an "incorrect policy" in literature, allegedly pursued by the Soviet Koreans. However, the attack was not confined to literature, and other more serious and sinister accusations were also directed toward the Soviet Koreans. From Pak Ch'ang-ok's remarks to a Soviet diplomat some months later, it is not difficult to imagine the substance of these accusations: "I have never fought factional struggles or criticized party policies; I have not distorted party politics concerning the United Front, nor have I trodden the path of reconciliation and agreement with [our] enemies."[23] Han Sŏl-ya attacked the Soviet Koreans with special ferocity, accusing them of "factional, splitting activity."[24] According to information obtained by the embassy from the plenum's participants, Kim Il Song himself was active in formulating these accusations.

It is not really clear why literary policy was chosen as the pretext for attacking the Soviet faction. The choice seems odd, even paradoxical, given that a majority of the Soviet Koreans had not received a proper Korean education and in some cases could not even speak standard Korean. Some of them were unable to read Korean fiction easily, and it is unlikely that many of them had any more than a vague notion of contemporary Korean literature. Their jobs were also mostly unrelated to cultural policy, which until 1953 had been the domain of the Domestic and Yan'an factions. Members of these latter factions had a good Korean educational background, whereas the Soviet Koreans had mostly graduated from Russian-language schools and the majority of the former guerrillas did not have a substantial education at all. Many Soviet Koreans were, however, engaged in "ideological work" and in this capacity had made some occasional forays into the field of literature. In 1952 and 1953 such "ideological workers" as Pak Ch'ang-ok (then head of the Central Committee's Agitation and Propaganda Department), Ki Sŏk-pok (a chief editor of *Nodong sinmun*), and Chŏng Yul did participate in a few discussions on literary policy. They either attacked Han Sŏl-ya and his supporters (including the famous dancer Ch'oe Sŭng-hŭi) or sought to protect opponents of Han Sŏl-ya from his wrath. On one occasion Ki Sŏk-pok attempted to justify the plot of "Honey," a much-criticized short story by Kim Nam-ch'ŏn that depicted a wounded KPA soldier forced to take shelter in a peasant home. The official criticism was that the glorious North Korean army would never abandon a wounded comrade.[25] However, the involvement of the Soviet Koreans in literary politics was limited. Although some modern histories of North Korean literature portray the Soviet faction as resolute supporters of Yi T'ae-jun, Kim Nam-ch'ŏn, and others, it is probable that the actual association between the Soviet Korean politicians and the South Korean writers was not particularly strong. Perhaps the affinity between these cadres and writers has been exaggerated by later historians —partly because connections between these two groups were later repeatedly emphasized by the official North Korean propaganda.

Even if the Soviet cadres were somehow involved in literary politics in the early stages, by late 1955 these clashes had been generally forgotten. This turn of events was alluded to by Pak Ŭi-wan in his conversation with Kim Il Song in February 1956: "These mistakes [by Pak Ch'ang-ok] have been much less serious in the last one and one-half to two years. It is strange to be reminded of mistakes [made] seven or eight years ago."[26] "Seven or eight years ago" was certainly an exaggeration, but it was true that by 1955 few of the Soviet Koreans in question had anything to do with literature or art. In December 1955, Pak Ch'ang-ok was chairman of the State Planning Committee; Ki Sŏk-pok was the commander of the military academy, and Kim Chae-uk was deputy minister of agriculture. As head of the Agitation and Propaganda Department of the KWP Central Committee, Pak Yŏng-bin alone was indirectly concerned with literature; he alone could be held responsible for problems in cultural and ideological policy areas. All of the others accused were now as far removed from contemporary Korean art as was possible.

The attack on the Soviet Koreans did not happen overnight; it had been in preparation for some time. For example, in October 1955, Kim Il Song suggested that Pak Ch'ang-ok deliver a speech about the activity of the North Korean Writers' Union. It is now apparent that this was a well-designed trap and that Kim Il Song intended to force Pak Ch'ang-ok to express his opinions on literature in order to use these pronouncements as a more solid basis for future accusations. That Kim Il Song made such a proposal in October again confirms that preparations for the attack on Pak Ch'ang-ok and other Soviet Koreans were launched several months before the December Plenum. In October, Kim did not succeed in luring Pak into the trap. Pak responded that he "[did] not know anything about the activity of the union" and that "his knowledge of Korean literature [was] inadequate."[27] It is unlikely that Pak Ch'ang-ok suspected the trap that Kim Il Song was setting for him, so his response was in all probability simply an honest confession of his own incompetence. It is possible that Kim Il Song's choice of alleged "mismanagement" of literary policy as a pretext for an assault was influenced by the noisy Soviet propaganda campaign of 1946–1948, which, while aimed at revealing and suppressing dissent among intellectuals, was disguised as a literary discussion. Kim Il Song and other prominent North Korean leaders still had vivid memories of that highly publicized campaign that was once supervised and directed by Andrey Zhdanov, a patron of the first Soviet ambassador to Pyongyang, T. F. Shtykov. Alternatively, the "rectification campaign" in Yan'an in China, again using literature and art as the pretext, could have influenced Kim's thinking and decisions. Taking into consideration the unusually active stance of Han Sŏl-ya, it is also possible that this "officially approved genius" of North Korea might have somehow influenced Kim Il Song's plans and the choice of the campaign theme. After all, Han had a vested interest in purging his rivals and their erstwhile protectors.

The December Plenum marked only the beginning of the campaign. According to the well-established tradition, the campaign was to be developed further. Kim Il Song obviously wanted to make a point by striking the Soviet faction firmly. Therefore the next step was a huge meeting of the North Korean top cadres, which, according to information received by the Soviet Embassy, was held in Pyongyang on December 27 and 28 and was officially considered an "extended presidium" of the KWP Central Committee. It is not really clear what was meant by "presidium" in some Soviet papers, but it was obviously a term for the KWP Standing Committee. Unlike the Soviet Communist Party, the KWP then had a three-tier structure of its leading bodies: the Central Committee was directed by the Standing Committee (13 persons in 1953), which in turn was supervised by the Political Council (just 5 persons in 1953). This system was abolished in 1956 by the Third Congress and was later reborn. In general it corresponds to the traditional Soviet division of the politburo into full and candidate members (even the above-mentioned proportions are roughly the same). The Standing Committee was normally a small body, but in some cases when its "extended sessions" took place, guests, including prominent party members, were invited on an individual basis. In December 1955 there were more than 420 participants, an unusually high number.[28]

It is common knowledge now that December 28 marked an important event in North Korean history. This was the day when the term *"chuch'e"* (the name of the future official North Korean ideology) was coined or, more precisely, radically reinterpreted.[29] On December 28, Kim Il Song delivered a lengthy speech entitled "About the Elimination of Formalism and Dogmatism in the Ideological Work and Establishing *Chuch'e."* The speech was not published immediately but was almost certainly distributed among cadres through the party's own channels of information exchange.[30] This can be surmised from the contemporary official press, where one can find vague references to unspecified "remarks by Kim Il Song" and even quotations that are now known to have come from the speech. It is also noteworthy that the term *"chuch'e"* of later fame was not yet used extensively in these early publications. The reinterpretation of the term as a more general political and ideological concept occurred later. For the first few months the key words used from the speech were "formalism" and "dogmatism," rather than *"chuch'e."*[31] It took quite a few years before *"chuch'e"* was reinterpreted as a ruling principle of North Korean ideology and policy and used as a name for a coherent ideological principle. In the *Popular Dictionary of Political Terms (Taejung chŏngch'i yŏng'ŏ sajŏn)*, published in Pyongyang in 1959, the term *"chuch'e"* is conspicuous in its absence, but in the large *Dictionary of the Korean Language (Chosŏn mal sajŏn, 1961–1962)* the present-day meaning of the term as a name for a political ideology is featured, though it still occupies a modest place as a secondary interpretation. It took a large and concerted effort on the part of Pyongyang ideologues in the late and middle 1960s to redefine *"chuch'e"* as a coherent ideology and the official philosophy of the DPRK.

The speech was remarkable in being the first authentic statement to enunciate explicitly the *chuch'e* principle—the future guiding philosophy of North Korea. The speech was subsequently published and has been republished a great many times (each time with changes that were deemed politically necessary at the moment). Despite its political significance, subsequent official publications for some reason remain silent on the precise details as to where and how Kim Il Song delivered the speech and only mention it as "a speech before party agitators and propagandists" *(tang sŏnjŏn sŏndong ilgun ap'eso han yŏnsŏl)*. Given that it is very unlikely that Kim Il Song simultaneously participated in two separate gatherings, we can confidently assume that the famous speech was in fact delivered to the extended presidium.

The content of the speech seems to confirm this hypothesis.[32] The speech was essentially nationalistic, with frequent appeals to national sentiment and patriotism, as well as calls to study Korean history and culture with greater enthusiasm. Kim Il Song, with great and open disdain, asserted that the glorification of all things Soviet and/or Russian was done at the expense of traditional Korean culture and history. These remarks, even when addressed to a closed meeting of the party's senior leadership, meant a break with the past, when the USSR had been unconditionally extolled by all Korean media. Apart from this, much of the speech is dedicated to the criticism of figures such as Pak Ch'ang-ok, Ki Sŏk-pok, and Pak Yŏng-bin, who were the main protagonists in the unfolding campaign. These men were accused of being insufficiently Korean and inadequately patriotic, of adopting too liberal an attitude toward bourgeois ideology and the arts, and, above all, of sponsoring "reactionary" writers such as Yi T'ae-jun. Kim Il Song stated that Pak Yŏng-bin, who was being influenced by the Soviet theory of "peaceful coexistence," had allegedly attempted to moderate the DPRK's staunch opposition to American imperialism. Kim did not yet dare criticize this theory itself but insisted it was not suitable for the unique conditions in Korea.[33] Pak Ch'ang-ok had allegedly "associated himself with the reactionary bourgeois writer Yi T'ae-jun," did not want "to learn the culture and history of our country," and could not properly use terms borrowed from classical Chinese *(hanmun)* because of a lack of schooling in the classics (the latter statement was true for the vast majority of foreign-educated Koreans then, as is the case now).[34] The speech also contained the standard set of accusations against the long-dead Hŏ Ka-i the Splittist and against the recently executed Pak Hŏn-yŏng the Spy, who had been eliminated approximately two weeks earlier, around December 15, 1955.[35]

Ostensibly a statement on literary politics, the *chuch'e* speech touched upon more important problems as well.[36] Apart from criticizing the Soviet Koreans, the speech contained an important new message directed at the party cadres: the North Korean party and state must be "nationalized" in conformity with national traditions. North Korean Communism would be redesigned as an essentially national—even nationalistic—ideology. The time had come to stop copying Soviet patterns; North Korea was to develop its own brand of Communist ideology to accommodate its own national interests above all other considerations. These ideas had great appeal for middle- and lower-level party cadres who, unlike their superiors, were "native-born" North Koreans with only moderate education and no overseas experience. They were therefore open to the allure of nationalism. By raising the question, Kim Il Song, a "local" North Korean by birth, artfully established himself as the chief exponent of the nation, a bold champion of "Korean-ness" against a backdrop of foreign pressure and its domestic agents. This position allowed him to further strengthen his dominance within the party while using the nationalist card to justify the curtailment of the dangerously liberal Soviet influence. It is not incidental that Kim Il Song began to play this nationalist card precisely when he did. The Soviet influence had come to represent not only a quite mindless Russification (as had been the case in the 1940s) but also a measure of liberalization and an easing of the political pressure on society.

Another important issue present in the speech was the attitude toward the "old revolutionaries," by whom Kim Il Song obviously meant the former guerrillas. Expressing great disapproval, Kim told about the discrimination they suffered on the grounds of their poor education and administrative inefficiency, as well as the resistance of bureaucracy to their promotions. We must suspect that this resistance had some justification, because the guerrillas were not known for their education and related virtues. In his speech, Kim demanded the elevation of the "veterans of the revolutionary struggle" to high positions within the party and the state. The past connections they had had with the armed anti-Japanese resistance were to be seen as sufficient grounds for promotion to the top administrative ranks. These remarks were another confirmation of the privileged status to which Kim's former subordinates were to be entitled from now on.

According to the Soviet Embassy documents, Kim Il Song had suggested that some of those criticized at the recent Central Committee plenum should address the meeting with "self-criticism." This task fell upon Ki Sŏk-pok, Pak Ch'ang-ok, Chŏng Yul, and Chŏng Tong-hyŏk. The only exception was Pak Yŏng-bin, who was in hospital at the time and had therefore not participated in the plenum or the extended presidium meetings. Pak Yŏng-bin was in fact not yet aware of the plenum's decisions.[37] At the presidium, Pak Ch'ang-ok was the object of a particularly ferocious attack and faced accusations from many participants, undoubtedly orchestrated by Kim Il Song and his immediate circle. In March 1956, Pak Ch'ang-ok recalled: "The conference was prepared in advance, and as the first [person to deliver a self-criticism], I had to face about one hundred questions. I was accused of wishing to become the national leader, if not the second in command. To this end, I had [allegedly] selected loyal cadres from among the Soviet Koreans. Pak Yŏng-bin and I employed the principle of collective leadership to promote ourselves and to belittle our leader, Comrade Kim Il Song. Some of the participants said we were the bearers of bourgeois ideology in the party."[38] Pak Ch'ang-ok persistently denied his participation in any "antiparty activities." Especially virulent in his attacks on Soviet Koreans was Han Sŏl-ya, the "living classic" of North Korean literature. His intense dislike of the Soviet Koreans was returned in kind. Han commented: "Pak Ch'ang-ok and Pak Yŏng-bin did not allow the party and the people to demonstrate their good feelings and love toward their leader."[39] To close the discussion, Kim Il Song delivered the concluding speech—the famous *chuch'e* speech.

As mentioned above, Kim Il Song's speech, originally unpublished, was nevertheless distributed among party organizations. In this way it became known to all members of the ruling Korean elite and probably to some lower-level functionaries as well.

The chain of official gatherings to "discuss and criticize" the alleged mistakes of the Soviet Koreans was to continue for some time. The December Plenum was followed by a conference on December 28 and additional official functions in January. On January 18, 1956, the KWP Central Committee issued a new resolution entitled "On Further Strengthening the Struggle against Reactionary Bourgeois Ideology in Literature and the Arts." At about this time, Pak Yŏng-bin was also expelled in absentia from the Political Council and the Central Committee, and other members of Soviet groups were subjected to various punishments.[40] In its spirit and tone, the resolution largely replicated Kim Il Song's speech. This resolution was neither published nor mentioned in the public press at the time. Even in the 1980s a dozen pages of *The General History of Korea* (an extensive official North Korean publication dedicated to the "struggle against formalism and dogmatism" in late 1955) mentions this resolution only briefly and fails to give its precise title.[41]

A standard feature of party operation was that decisions made at recent plenums, as well as speeches of party leaders, were "studied" at the lower levels. In January 1956 many meetings of lower-level party organizations were held throughout the country. The recently published official documents were interpreted as a signal for an all-round attack on the Soviet Koreans and provided their numerous rivals with a good excuse to settle personal and political scores. Lower-level party members actively criticized high-ranking Soviet Koreans, who were generally accused of creating "factionalism" and committing various ideological mistakes.

By the end of January the campaign against the Soviet faction was in full swing in the party cells. Throughout the month of January, many prominent Soviet Koreans were summoned to deliver self-criticisms in their party organizations or were subjected to interrogations about their various "mistakes," the greatest of these being their former connections with Hŏ Ka-i. The Pyongyang KWP City Committee, which was probably dominated by the Yan'an faction at that time, was particularly active in this campaign. Among other things, the City Committee ordered the party cells in different ministries to "investigate" earlier connections between some Soviet Koreans and the late Hŏ Ka-i, and a few Soviet Koreans were even required to testify to such connections.[42]

Kim Il Song summoned Pak Yŏng-bin, who had just been released from the hospital, and spent three hours insisting that he "recognize his mistakes." Pak Yŏng-bin initially denied all accusations leveled at him but eventually capitulated, submitting a forced repentance to the politburo on January 18. Meanwhile, Pak Ch'ang-ok stubbornly continued to deny any wrongdoing. At the close of the politburo meeting, Pak Ch'ang-ok requested permission to retire from his current position (chairman of the State Planning Committee), and a few days later his retirement was accepted by Kim Il Song.[43]

There is little doubt that the events of December and January were skillfully orchestrated. They were also politically well balanced. While engaging in the campaign, Kim Il Song adopted measures to conceal both the accusations against the Soviet Koreans and the entire campaign from the general public. The campaign was essentially a low-profile affair. As mentioned above, the December Plenum was officially convened to deal solely with agricultural issues, and at that time the December 28 speech by Kim Il Song remained unpublished. The alleged misdeeds of the Soviet Koreans were discussed only at exclusive meetings of party functionaries, without the participation or knowledge of the general public. It was impossible to prevent the leaking of some rumors, given that there were more than a million party members, and the cadres who had access to this information numbered in the tens of thousands. Outwardly though, from the point of view of the general populace, it was "business as usual."[44] This secrecy was probably aimed at preventing the Soviets from being disturbed, because an open attack could have been interpreted as an assault not only on the Soviet faction in the DPRK leadership but also on Soviet influence in general. It may also have been thought that open conflict within the party would be undesirable before the upcoming Third Congress of the KWP. Regardless of the reasons, the fact remains that the entire campaign was extremely low profile and was waged behind the closed doors of party offices.

In January 1956 several Soviet Koreans felt insecure enough to apply for permission to return to the USSR. According to the established procedure, permission to return to the USSR had to be obtained from both the Korean and the Soviet authorities simultaneously, although it seems that officials from both sides would normally make their decisions independently. These applicants numbered at least seven in total. Although the list is not available, it is clear that it did not include very influential figures such as Pak Ch'ang-ok, Pak Yŏng-bin, or Ki Sŏk-pok. This was not the first time that Soviet Koreans had left the DPRK for the USSR, but the number of applicants this time was unusually high—and a sign of things to come.

It appears that the Soviet Embassy was not particularly disturbed by the developments and chose to remain uninvolved, even though some diplomats were closely monitoring the situation (as confirmed by embassy archives). It is not clear whether this passivity was a conscious political choice or simply resulted from the reluctance of most Soviet diplomats to undertake anything particularly challenging or risky. Several Soviet Koreans (notably Pak Ch'ang-ok, Pak Ŭi-wan, and Pak Yŏng-bin) visited the embassy in search of support, but their attempts were completely unsuccessful. On the contrary, when the Soviet chargé d'affaires A. M. Petrov met Nam Il—the North Korean minister of foreign affairs, a former Soviet mathematics professor, and one of the few former Soviet Koreans who had distanced himself from the Soviet faction—on February 9, Petrov stated that the Soviet government "considers that Soviet Koreans who have committed offenses cannot cover [their faults] by going back to the Soviet Union." The following day Petrov repeated this statement to Kim Il Song, who then said that the North Korean authorities would not give the Soviet Koreans permission to leave the DPRK and would revoke the permission already granted. Petrov assented to this decision.[45]

Another interesting and seemingly typical indication of the Soviet position at that time was the behavior of I. S. Biakov, the Soviet Embassy's first secretary, during his meeting with Song Chin-p'a. The conversation took place after Song had returned from "labor reeducation," where he had been sent for the frank critical remarks he had made about Kim Il Song's personality cult. Song attempted to discuss the behavior of the Soviet Koreans and tried to draw Biakov's attention to the antagonistic attitude of the local officials toward the Soviet faction and toward Soviet influence in general. This was an important but extremely sensitive matter, so Biakov, who, like a majority of the Soviet diplomats, was extremely cautious, not only refused to discuss the matter further but actually silenced Song. Biakov even attempted to make a point about his position while reporting the conversation to his superiors: "I rebuked him [and said that] he should be more responsible with his words, especially after he had been rebuked by the CC [Central Committee] for the irresponsible conversations concerning the personality cult in Korea [he had had] with the head of the press department of the Ministry of Foreign Affairs."[46] The message was obvious—"Keep your opinions to yourself, and don't rock the boat!" Not all embassy staff behaved in this manner. Some of them were at least ready to listen to their interlocutors, but in the material available there are no signs that the embassy supported the Soviet Koreans' cause in any way or encouraged discussion of the personality cult problem in Korea.

The offensive against the Soviet Koreans continued. On February 15, 1956, the whole campaign appeared to take on a new dimension: it suddenly went public, in the most visible form possible. On that day,

Nodong sinmun, the official organ of the KWP and the voice of the North Korean government, published a front-page editorial condemning the accused officials. An editorial in a central newspaper of a Communist Party has always been a reliable bellwether in Stalinist political culture. This particular editorial was somewhat longer than normal (it filled three columns, a size comparable to only four of some sixteen front-page editorials published by *Nodong sinmun* between January 15 and February 15 of that year), and even more tellingly, it did not follow the standard pattern. Usually, "problems," "mistakes," "distortions," and their alleged perpetrators were only mentioned in a couple of paragraphs hidden somewhere in the middle of an article, which was otherwise dedicated to "glorious victories" or "great achievements." In this instance, however, even the editorial's headline sounded markedly menacing: "Let's Irrevocably Eliminate the Poisonous Consequences of Bourgeois Ideology from Literature and the Arts!" The editorial also broke with another established tradition of the official Communist press—not to mention the names of culprits unless the persons in question had already been purged or were on the verge of being purged. This editorial did name names. The accusations and wording were unusually straightforward, giving the impression that the persons mentioned were already "unmasked enemies of the people." According to the article, Pak Ch'ang-ok, Pak Yŏng-bin, Ki Sŏk-pok, Chŏng Tong-hyŏk, and Chŏng Yul had praised the "bourgeois writers" Yi T'ae-jun, Kim Nam-ch'ŏn, and Yim Hwa and had underestimated the Korean Artist Proletarian Federation (KAPF), the colonial-period left-wing writers' organization where Han Sŏl-ya and some of his henchmen had begun their careers. The editorial insisted that those named had "committed antiparty actions by being in ideological collusion with Yim Hwa, Yi T'ae-jun, Kim Nam-ch'ŏn, and other agents of Pak Hŏn-yŏng's gang" and that "by attacking the writers [who were] loyal to the party, [they] actively supported and protected the activity of Yim Hwa."[47] Among the culprits, the articles listed Hŏ Ka-i, the former leader of the Soviet faction. That a reference to Hŏ Ka-i appeared alongside a reference to Pak Hŏn-yŏng, a known "American spy and traitor," implied that the former was also guilty of subversive activity or even treason. In the editorial, Hŏ Ka-i was not explicitly labeled a spy, but he was posthumously accused of "antiparty activity" *(pandang haeng'ui)*. The article also appears to have been the first open publication to reveal to the general public that the December Plenum had discussed ideological questions.

The editorial seemed to be the first shot of a major campaign against the Soviet Koreans. This same issue of the newspaper, which was coincidentally published on the first day of the Twentieth Congress of the Soviet Communist Party, also carried a long article (one and a half full newspaper pages) authored by Han Sŏl-ya himself. The piece was a record of the speech Han Sŏl-ya had made three weeks earlier (January 23) at a "conference of literary, arts, publishing, and propaganda activists" in Pyongyang. The supervisor of North Korean literature used the opportunity to settle old scores with his fallen rivals Kim Nam-ch'ŏn, Yim Hwa, and especially the recently disgraced Yi T'ae-jun. Han Sŏl-ya commented on other figures as well, including Hŏ Ka-i and Pak Ch'ang-ok: "On several occasions our party has required that Comrade Pak Ch'ang-ok work toward strengthening the party spirit [*Tangsŏng,* a literal translation of the Russian *"partijnost"*] in the fields of literature and the arts. Furthermore, the party has repeatedly noted and criticized the nonparty activities of these comrades. However, Comrade Pak Ch'ang-ok did not obey the party instructions. Furthermore, these comrades refuse to reconsider their criminal acts *(choe'haeng)* in glorifying and protecting reactionary writers, and in spite of the certain harm [they inflicted] on our literature and arts [which are] inspired by party and class spirit, they still try to justify this [behavior]."[48]

For a reader versed in Stalinist political culture (as many readers of the newspaper indeed were), these publications must have looked like a signal for a general assault on the hapless officials and suggested an imminent purge. However, this was not the case. The articles proved to be not the first phase of an open attack but rather the last stage of a campaign less than three months old. The Han Sŏl-ya speech, although published on February 15, had in fact been delivered three weeks earlier at the climax of the campaign. Although *Nodong sinmun* continued to publish some articles that suggested a certain disquiet within the party, the offensive had come unstuck in mid-February. On the next day, February 16, *Nodong sinmun* carried a lengthy article written by Pak Kŭm-ch'ŏl (from the Yan'an group, but a longtime active supporter of Kim Il

Song), outlining various mistakes made by "some party cadres." The article warned primarily against factionalism but also against familism *(kajokjuŭi)*, bureaucratism *(kwanlyojuŭi)*, and, somewhat surprisingly, the personality cult. Although this last warning employed the term "personality cult," its significance was not made explicit; the warning was vaguely directed toward the often-criticized "worship of the individual." However, the article did not mention Pak Ch'ang-ok or literary issues, nor did several later articles against "factionalism" that appeared in *Nodong sinmun*.[49]

Later articles published in *Nodong sinmun* further reflected these new and surprising trends. On February 24 a front-page editorial again raged against the "bourgeois writers" Yim Hwa, Yi T'ae-jun, and Kim Nam-ch'ŏn but did not refer once to their alleged allies in the Soviet faction who had been so furiously attacked the previous week. On March 1 the vice-chairman of the North Korean Writers' Union, Hong Sun-ch'ŏl, wrote a lengthy article attacking this same hapless trio. Although he mentioned their alleged Soviet Korean supporters (probably because Hong was close to Han Sŏl-ya), shrewd readers—and many *Nodong sinmun* readers had become skilled at reading between the lines—would not have failed to detect two important and telling anomalies. First, two of the most influential members of the Soviet faction—Pak Ch'ang-ok and Pak Yŏng-bin—were not mentioned at all, even though they had until recently been considered the main culprits.[50] Second, other Soviet Koreans were mentioned only briefly. A similar pattern was again observable one week later in a virulent attack against "the three reactionary writers" by Ŏm Ho-sŏk, a notorious henchman of Han Sŏl-ya's. In his article, Ŏm Ho-sŏk wrote that the "bourgeois writers" had protectors, but he named only one culprit: Ki Sŏk-pok.[51] Pak Ch'ang-ok and Pak Yŏng-bin were again conspicuously absent, and thus Ki Sŏk-pok alone (who was a far less important figure in both the official establishment and the Soviet faction) was portrayed as the sole malefactor. Ki Sŏk-pok was also the only person forced to repent in an open letter to *Nodong sinmun*: "I trod an erroneous path when I praised Yi T'ae-jun's "Grandmother Tiger" and Kim Nam-ch'ŏn's "Honey" [short stories], [acting] contrary to the party line." His confession was not without reservation; he dared to remind his readers that for a long time both Pak

Ch'ang-ok and Pak Yŏng-bin had enjoyed official recognition, thus hinting that he was not solely culpable. The language used in his open letter was also a far cry from the self-humiliating standard public repentance, so common in Stalinist political culture.[52] In any event, Ki Sŏk-pok lost his position and became a humble "referent," a minor clerk in the Ministry of Culture (the capacity in which he is mentioned in the embassy papers of May 1956).

Ki Sŏk-pok's forced repentance represented the last phase of the campaign, which ended abruptly in early March. Following this, critical personal references to Soviet Koreans' alleged erroneous approach to literary politics totally disappeared from the press. Articles in *Nodong sinmun* on March 22 and April 4 referred to "certain mistakes of some cadres" in regard to cultural policy, but they named no one. [53] Even Han Sŏl-ya, who was at that time busy writing for *Nodong sinmun* (another indication of his high station), no longer mentioned the Soviet Koreans. On March 25 his article on the Korean arts made no personal attacks on any active political figures.

This sudden change in attitude, as reflected in the official publications, corresponds well with the same phenomenon observed in the Soviet Embassy papers. According to the papers, Kim Il Song began to tone down the campaign against the Soviet faction at the end of January. On January 24, Pak Chŏng-ae, one of Kim Il Song's most reliable lieutenants, met with Pak Ŭi-wan, a prominent Soviet Korean who had only recently been criticized, and told him of some new developments.

Pak Chŏng-ae conveyed to Pak Ŭi-wan the remarks made by Kim Il Song during a recent meeting of the KWP Political Committee and the North Korean Politburo, a body that in theory was subordinate to the party Central Committee but in reality was the supreme executive body of the party and therefore the entire country. The same day, Pak Ŭi-wan relayed these new developments to a Soviet diplomat. According to Pak Chŏng-ae (quoted by Pak Ŭi-wan), "Kim Il Song . . . spoke about the incorrect attitude of certain party officials toward Soviet Koreans. He proposed a meeting with the Soviet Koreans to reassure them [that their positions were secure] and also a meeting with Central Committee officials to explain to them the incorrectness of the behavior of certain cadres toward the Soviet Koreans."[54] This was the first indication of a new official political line toward the Soviet Koreans. Henceforth, the entire campaign against the Soviet faction was blamed on "certain" overzealous cadres, and Kim Il Song insisted that he had had nothing to do with the entire affair. According to Pak Chŏng-ae, Kim was even claiming to be "disturbed by the current situation."

This abrupt change in the political atmosphere became increasingly apparent in late February and early March 1956. Shortly after the above-mentioned articles appeared in *Nodong sinmun,* Kim Il Song, who was by then taking part in meetings of the heads of Central Committee departments and cabinet ministers, stated that the Soviet Koreans had contributed significantly to the development of the DPRK.[55] On February 28, Kim Il Song met with Pak Ŭi-wan and told him that "the people who came from the Soviet Union are good party cadres and we were too demanding of them."[56] Kim Il Song again blamed "certain cadres," in particular members of the Pyongyang KWP City Committee (read: Yan'an faction) who were overzealous and who had allegedly begun to investigate former connections between some Soviet Koreans and Hŏ Ka-i on their own initiative. Pak Ch'ang-ok, like many others, seemed to have been sufficiently naive to have accepted Kim Il Song's declarations at face value. At the beginning of March, Pak Ch'ang-ok told a Soviet diplomat: "During February, I had two conversations with Comrade Kim Il Song about the decisions of the presidium and twice expressed my disagreement. I can tell you that Kim Il Song himself is very upset by this affair and asks [us] to forget everything and return to work. He has ordered all officials from the Central Committee to cease discussion of these questions [relating to the Soviet Koreans]."[57] The signals were clear: the whole campaign was a mistake, an aberration. It was to be blamed on minor officials, and everything would soon be back to normal.

Publications of the contemporary official press and the embassy papers indicate that sometime in late February, just when everything seemed to indicate that the campaign against the Soviet Koreans was reaching its climax, it abruptly came to a halt. The campaign did not run out of steam but was deliberately stopped. Such a change was probably the result of a conscious decision—one most likely taken by Kim Il Song himself, as his statements to Pak Ŭi-wan and Pak Ch'ang-ok testify. What was the reason for this change in position? In the course of time, new materials may shed more light on this question, but in the meantime we might consider some possibilities.

The sudden end to the campaign undoubtedly indicated that from its very beginning the campaign had quite limited goals, and by late February these goals had been achieved. A lesson had been learned: the most prominent Soviet Korean leaders had been warned off, and the lower cadres had again been made to realize that Kim Il Song was the supreme authority within the party and that no foreign protection could save anyone from the Great Leader's wrath. It was a timely warning, because the de-Stalinization in the USSR had begun to escalate. Kim Il Song did not want to risk an open confrontation with Moscow or complicate the already uneasy domestic situation. The Soviet capital had just witnessed the Twentieth Congress of the Communist Party of the Soviet Union (CPSU), where Khrushchev had delivered his famous "Secret Speech," openly denouncing Stalin and his policies. This was a logical development in the de-Stalinization campaign waged by the Soviet reformers following Stalin's death, and the winds of de-Stalinization and reform blew everywhere in the Communist camp.

Kim Il Song had chosen not to participate in the Twentieth Congress, although Soviet diplomats were told that some prominent North Korean leaders (Pak Chŏng-ae, for example) had suggested that he attend the gathering. Kim Il Song explained this away by saying that he was intending to visit East Germany later that year and thought that "two foreign trips in one year would be one too many."[58] The Korean delegation to the Twentieth Congress was instead led by Ch'oe Yong-gŏn, who was by then firmly established as "number two" in the Pyongyang hierarchy (other members were Hŏ Pin, chairman of the party Committee of Northern Hamgyŏng Province, and Yi Hyo-sun, head of the Central Committee Personnel Department).[59] Kim's explanation could hardly be taken at face value, given that his summer trip would eventually include visits to not only Germany but all Eastern European Communist countries, as well as Mongolia, and that it would be exceptionally long (some seven weeks).

In halting his campaign against the Soviet faction, Kim Il Song almost certainly also had in mind the forthcoming Third KWP Congress, scheduled for late April. The startling news from Moscow strongly influenced North Korean officialdom. The open denunciation of Stalin was a major blow to the established worldview held by the majority of North Korean bureaucrats. Available contemporary remarks on the matter indicate that this is not merely informed conjecture. Describing the general feeling among the party elite, Pak Ch'ang-ok remarked to a Soviet diplomat in March 1956 that "the problem of the personality cult is discussed everywhere [in the North Korean establishment]." Pak Ch'ang-ok's impression was that a majority of those involved in these discussions preferred not to express a definite position on this sensitive question—a not unreasonable position, given the circumstances.[60] Given such a parlous situation, it would have been imprudent to continue the campaign against the Soviet Koreans, and Kim Il Song, who badly needed the Third Congress to proceed smoothly, may have wanted to calm the situation.

Kim Il Song took further steps to placate the situation. In February the North Korean leader, who for a long time had denied the obvious— the existence of his own personality cult in the DPRK—suddenly changed his mind and made a self-critical declaration, perilously close to repentance. On February 18 he delivered a speech to a meeting of vice-premiers and Central Committee departmental heads. According to Pak Ŭi-wan's later comments to a Soviet diplomat, Kim Il Song admitted: "Recently, spoken and written propaganda has exaggerated the role of personality in the development of human society. . . . [My] name is mentioned far too often in newspapers and magazines, and [I am] falsely credited with many achievements. This contradicts the Marxist-Leninist theory that guides the development of our party, and [it] leads to the misguided education of party members. All departmental heads must take all necessary steps [to correct] this phenomenon and to establish a correct understanding of the respective roles of the individual and the masses in the development of society."[61] However modest and reserved, this was an official recognition that a personality cult existed in Korea and that Kim Il Song was its focal point.

It is important, and hardly incidental, that this declaration and these maneuvers coincided with a major change in the tone and style of official publications. As mentioned above, the personal attacks against the Soviet Koreans came to a sudden halt soon after February

20. Kim Il Song's declaration on February 18 might also appear at first glance to be a major turnabout in policy toward the personality cult, but this was not the case. These remarks, delivered to a restricted group of top dignitaries, brought about no significant policy change. It is much more likely that his humble self-criticism did not reflect a genuine change of heart on the part of Kim Il Song but rather represented a shrewd maneuver aimed at easing internal party tensions. By criticizing himself, Kim Il Song was hinting that he was not invincible and that he was capable of recognizing and correcting his own shortcomings; in doing so, he forced his opponents to adopt a "wait and see" approach rather than to take immediate or direct action. Many cadres were uneasy about Kim Il Song's authoritarian style and personality cult. They wanted to use the changing international situation to make North Korea a more liberal and tolerant society. These cadres would prefer to wait, given that Kim Il Song was hinting that he would correct his own past mistakes himself. As we shall see, Kim Il Song employed these same tactics again later, with at least some measure of success.

We cannot be completely sure that this and other similar statements by Kim were only meant to win some time. Another possibility cannot be ruled out: that Kim Il Song may temporarily have thought about riding the rising tide of de-Stalinization. After all, in some of the Communist countries of Eastern Europe—notably in Czechoslovakia, Albania, and Romania—local leaderships survived the turbulent years of de-Stalinization almost intact: the strongmen made only moderate concessions to the new pressures and managed to retain their positions by paying lip service to new ideas and slogans. In the case of Albania and Romania, this was followed by a return to full Stalinism in the 1960s, but in the late 1950s the leaders of both countries professed their hostility to the personality cult and its attendant evils. Vulko Chervenkov adopted the same strategy in Bulgaria, although it did not save him from being eventually ousted by his marginally less Stalinist rivals. In any case, the leaders of these states made excellent use of this "new style" of demagogy and occasionally, as in the case of Chervenkov, publicly declaimed their personal responsibility and remorse, not unlike Kim Il Song's declarations behind closed doors in the spring and summer of 1956.[62] This tactic helped some Eastern European dictators survive the turbulent times, and such an outcome was not impossible in the case of the DPRK either. However, Kim Il Song, even if he had entertained such an idea, eventually chose another approach.

The publication in early April of several major articles on Stalin's personality cult in the North Korean press is probably connected with these maneuvers. Significantly, these were not articles written by Koreans but official translations of Russian and Chinese publications. This foreign authorship is entirely understandable, for an individual's expression of any specific opinion on such a sensitive subject would not have been prudent. It would be seen by any Korean Communist as an interference in the domestic policies of the "elder brother" state, which was still much feared (and respected) in North Korea at the time. Also, exploration of the problem of the "personality cult" could have been interpreted as a veiled attack on Kim Il Song himself, something no one was yet prepared to risk. The articles nevertheless made explicit reference to the "personality cult." They also offered to readers for the first time an opportunity to grasp the authentic meaning of the term.[63] Earlier, if the term had been mentioned at all, it had often been explained in deliberately vague terms that permitted and encouraged its confusion with the long-criticized and long-condemned "theory of individual heroism"; it is highly probable that these attempts to cloud the term's meaning were deliberate.[64]

The campaign against the Soviet Koreans was accompanied by other moves aimed at gradually undermining the once-powerful Soviet influence. Although the campaign was stopped in February, the restrictive measures against Soviet predominance were strengthened during the first half of 1956. These measures were very low profile at the time but were not unnoticed by the Soviet Embassy.

First of all, the North Korean authorities undertook measures to restrict the channels of Soviet influence in North Korean domestic policy. For a decade, intimate contacts between some Soviet Koreans and Soviet Embassy staff were seen as normal and even laudable. In the new atmosphere, such a close interaction was increasingly unwelcome and suspicious. At the beginning of May, the Soviet Koreans were unofficially discouraged from visiting the embassy. According to Pak Ŭi-wan, Kim Il Song, while addressing the Central Committee plenum in December

1955, had made the disdainful remark: "Some Soviet Koreans go to the Soviet Embassy as soon as they are criticized!"[65] In May 1956, Pak Kil-yŏng, the North Korean ambassador to East Germany, told a Soviet diplomat about recently introduced restrictions on contacting foreigners. According to the new system, if a Korean official wanted to meet a foreigner, he needed special permission from his superiors. One should remember that citizens of Western or other supposedly unfriendly countries were completely absent from the DPRK at this stage of Korean history, so the only people who could possibly fall into the category of "foreigners" in Pyongyang in 1956 were Russian and Chinese nationals. Hence these new regulations clearly had important political implications: they were introduced to hinder uncontrolled interaction and information exchange with Pyongyang's closest allies and sponsors. In addition, issuing permissions for meetings with foreigners was entrusted to Pak Kŭm-ch'ŏl, who was considered a hidden enemy of both the Soviet Koreans and the Soviet influence in general. Pak Kil-yŏng also mentioned that the Soviet Koreans were occasionally called "Soviet agents" by some members of Kim Il Song entourage.[66]There was a grain of truth in such a statement, but the expression of such a sentiment had been unthinkable just a few years before.

There were also other signs that the North Korean authorities were seeking to reduce the degree of Soviet influence in other fields. This was especially the case in the arts and the humanities, where the Soviet impact had been so considerable since 1945 and where all experiments were less potentially risky than in technology or science. The *chuch'e* speech provided some "theoretical foundations" for these changes in policy. On March 18, *Nodong sinmun* ran an editorial entitled "Against Dogmatism and Formalism," which was basically a synopsis of the *chuch'e* speech. The next day, on the same page as Ki Sŏk-pok's forced recantation, the newspaper ran an article on a "conference of art activists," which attacked unspecified "foreign cultural influence" with unprecedented vigor. The article chastised vocalists who preferred to sing arias and romances by "foreign composers" instead of native Korean songs.[67] To grasp the real meaning of this remark, we have to remember that Western influence was almost entirely absent from the 1950s North Korean cultural scene. Since Broadway musicals and French chansons were unlikely to be presented on the North Korean stage of 1956, in the DPRK cultural context "foreign" could mean only "Russian/Soviet." The Korean theater repertoire was, to put it mildly, overloaded with pieces by Russian/Soviet composers. This article was one of the first explicit attacks, if not the very first, by the official press on a perceived excessive foreign (read: Soviet) influence, a tangible sign of things to come.

This development of new, nationalistic trends was seemingly facilitated by Han Sŏl-ya, who in May became the minister of education. As mentioned earlier, this supreme boss of North Korean literature had been a staunch enemy of the Soviet Koreans. His approach possibly reflected his own hidden nationalism or was a side effect of his rivalry with some Soviet-backed writers, but it is more likely that such a position was just another indication of his uncanny political sense and ability to adjust to imminent change. In earlier times he had, after all, been eager to praise the country's "great Soviet friends, liberators of Korea."

In February 1956 a decision was made to reduce the airplay of Korean-language programs on Radio Moscow. These programs had been previously aired by local broadcasting services, but airplay time was cut by half after February. When the Soviet chargé d'affaires asked Ho Chŏng-suk, the North Korean minister of culture and propaganda, for the reasons for such a drastic cut, she replied that the North Korean broadcasting service would use this time for broadcasting propaganda programs to the South.[68] Obviously, the diplomat did not object.

The Korean Society for International Cultural Exchange was not immune from attack either. In spite of its name, from the outset the primary task of this organization had been the dissemination of Soviet culture rather than any kind of "international cultural exchange." The society was one of the principal channels of Soviet cultural influence in North Korea. In the late 1940s and early 1950s, far from being a humble "friendship society," it was one of the most influential North Korean institutions. By the end of 1955, however, "reform" of the society had greatly reduced its power and significance. Local branches were closed, the collection of personal membership fees was halted, and control of its profitable publishing section was transferred to the Ministry of Culture and Propaganda. As a result the society's income was reduced tenfold, and its influence shrank accordingly.[69]

It is also worth mentioning that in 1956 there was no "Month of Soviet-Korean Friendship," a lavish Soviet cultural festival that had been an all-important event in the Korean cultural and political calendar since 1949 and had not even been interrupted by the war. When Yi Ki-yŏng, the chairman of the Korean-Soviet Friendship Society, informed A. M. Petrov of this decision, he did not attempt to give the reasons for such a measure.[70] This tradition was soon resumed, however, albeit on a much smaller scale.

Although Kim Il Song made some attempts at reconciliation with the Soviet Koreans in late February, they did not significantly alter the new line in his cultural policy. Kim Il Song vowed eternal gratitude to the Soviet Union and Soviet Koreans and blamed the entire campaign on "certain officials," but his government continued its concerted efforts to thwart Soviet cultural influence. In the spring of 1956 the KWP Central Committee ordered a halt to the staging of Soviet plays in Korean theaters—something that would have been quite unthinkable only a year earlier. The College of Foreign Languages, where 80 percent of students majored in Russian, was also suddenly closed, and students were transferred to the Kim Il Song University. According to information provided to the Soviet Embassy by Minister of Construction Kim Sŭng-hwa, Han Sŏl-ya proposed the downgrading of Russian-language teaching in North Korean colleges. From the spring of 1956 onward, Russian was no longer taught to third- and fourth-year college students.[71] The number of articles about the Soviet Union in North Korean magazines and newspapers also began to decline, although by standards of the later decades it still remained considerable.

3 The Third KWP Congress

IT IS IMPOSSIBLE TO SAY with full certainty whether Kim Il Song, who in late February decided to halt the whole campaign against "literary deviations," actually feared possible complications during the forthcoming KWP Congress and, if so, to what degree those fears were justified. His main focus was international, rather than domestic, aiming to weaken the Soviet influence without risking direct confrontation with Moscow. Dissolving domestic tensions on the eve of a party congress might have been his second aim. If indeed it was, then Kim was successful.

The Third Congress took place in Pyongyang on April 23–29. According to the original KWP statute (1946), the party congress was supposed to convene once every year, but in 1956 the period was extended to four years. These regulations proved to be meaningless: in the entire KWP history no congress has ever met on time. Between 1946 and 2002 the average interval between congressional meetings was nine years (and not a single congress was held between 1980 and 2002). By 1956 eight years had passed since the previous, Second Congress, which was held in March 1948. These eight years were a time of great upheaval both inside and outside North Korea. The Korean War created an entirely new environment on the peninsula, as well as drastically changing the international standing of the North Korean regime. The gradual consolidation of Kim Il Song's power led to a considerable reorganization of the North Korean elite. Because the congress was officially considered to be the supreme body of the party, this convention was deemed necessary to provide legitimacy for new policies and new institutions.

There were times in Russia under Lenin (and also in some other countries) when party congresses had indeed discussed things of real importance and were a place for frank and heated debates, but by the 1950s this had become almost ancient history. By the late 1940s, when the DPRK borrowed the Stalinist state machinery, congresses had already lost all their original meaning and had been transformed into highly ritualized and pompous rubber-stamping conventions. All the real work was done by power brokers before the congresses, and then the delegates, handpicked by the party machine, anonymously confirmed all proposals and appointments. The functions of a congress were largely, if not exclusively, ceremonial. The provision for congresses was purported to be proof of the alleged "democratic legitimacy" of the party leadership, a confirmation of its support by the "masses." Congresses sometimes played another role as well: they often provided the leaders with an opportunity to make public official assessments of the current situation and to air important statements about future policy. Unlike the secretive meetings of the Central Committee, congressional sessions were public. All speeches and addresses were published in the official press, and the proceedings were often broadcast live on radio and, later, television.[1] Occasionally, the congresses provided convenient grounds for interparty and interstate diplomacy, since they were normally attended by delegations from dozens of "fraternal parties." During congresses, these delegations could easily meet to discuss various problems. For example, as we shall see later, some important discussions in regard to Korea took place in Beijing during a congress of the Chinese Communist Party in September 1956.

The tradition of meaningless, pompous congresses was to survive virtually unchanged until the final collapse of Leninist socialism in the late 1980s. This statement is made with the wisdom of hindsight, however. In the uncertain and exultant atmosphere just after the CPSU Twentieth Congress in the mid-1950s, nothing could be taken for granted. Kim Il Song would not have been able to exclude the possibility that an open attack against him and his policies might be launched during the upcoming congress. If Kim had entertained such concerns, they were not to eventuate. In general the Third KWP Congress turned out be yet another rubber-stamping convention.

According to the well-established ritual, Communist Party congresses began with an extensive report by the Central Committee. This report was usually delivered by the head of the party, and therefore it was Kim Il Song who did so at the Third KWP Congress. This report was so lengthy that in *Nodong sinmun* the complete text occupied seven full-size newspaper pages. Kim started with a general review of the international and domestic situations and proceeded to the specific problems of the party. A large part of the report was taken up by a lengthy sketch of KWP history. Kim stressed the special role of the North Korean party organizations after 1945 and vilified Pak Hŏn-yŏng and other South Korean leftists, as well as some victims of earlier purges, such as Hŏ Ka-i. According to Kim, their main sin had been factionalism—that is, opposition to the "correct" (read: Kim Il Song's) party line. Officially Pak and other South Korean Communist leaders were condemned to death as "American spies." It is surprising that the accusations of "spying" were mentioned by Kim only a few times and almost in passing, while the main emphasis was on the factionalism of the disgraced leaders. Kim Il Song may have chosen such a cautious approach because his audience still included many people who used to know Pak Hŏn-yŏng and his confidants personally. They might therefore have been skeptical about any espionage accusations, whereas factionalism might have sounded like a much more realistic crime.

In his speech, Kim Il Song employed a remarkable trick when dealing with the most dangerous problem of the day—the personality cult. Though Kim did use this expression, he did so in connection with the fallen "factionalists," who were allegedly promoting personality cults of their own leaders. He made it clear that if North Korea had ever had a personality cult, it was the personality cult of Pak Hŏn-yŏng and the like. These remarks were not completely unfounded: a personality cult had surrounded Pak in the late 1940s in the South Korean Communist Party (later the Workers' Party). The maintenance of a personality cult of the supreme leader was simply the standard practice for any Communist Party of that period. Nevertheless, the cult of Pak Hŏn-yŏng, even in the early stages of KWP history, was on a much smaller scale and of much less significance than that of Kim Il Song himself. In general Kim declined to use this explosive term too much and managed not to mention it even when he was talking about the recent CPSU Twentieth Congress. Another Soviet catchphrase of the period, "collective leadership," a frequent and equally explosive companion to the "personality cult," was not mentioned by Kim at all. From the Soviet point of view, these two key ingredients of the newly prescribed ideological assemblage were conspicuous in their absence from Kim's lengthy report.[2] It is also noteworthy that the next day the *Nodong sinmun* ran a prominent editorial in which the "personality cult" was again mentioned as something that had been promoted exclusively by the purged southerners and of course only applied to their leaders. The term "collective leadership" was, however, used in this editorial.[3]

Another important part of the speech, and of the congressional proceedings in general, was the special emphasis placed on the rapid development of DPRK heavy industry. The heavy-versus-light-industry controversy had been a part of Communist politics since the late 1920s at least. After a decade of unconditional preference given to heavy industry, the balance in the mid-1950s was obviously shifting toward light industry and consumption. This change was a reflection of the new perceptions and ideas that surfaced after Stalin's death. The late dictator's policy of the rapid growth of heavy industry at all costs and under any conditions had come to be seen—with some justification—as a costly mistake that adversely influenced the living standards of the populace and proved to be economically inefficient. The Communist countries of Eastern Europe therefore began to slow down their heavy-industry development programs and to relocate funds to light industry and agriculture. In such a new environment Kim Il Song's pledges to enforce high-speed industrialization looked anachronistic and even running against the current "line" of the "unbreakable Communist camp headed by Moscow."

Two other official reports to the congress were delivered by Pak Chŏng-ae and Yi Chu-yŏn, the then chairman of the Central Auditing Committee. The latter delivered the customary report dealing mostly with party finances and membership, while Pak Chŏng-ae briefed the delegates about proposed changes in the party statutes. The reforms were minor, such as extending the interval between KWP Congresses (not that they were ever held on time anyway). The previous three-tiered system (from Central Committee down to Standing Committee and Political Council) was abolished in favor of the more standard two-tiered system, with the Standing Committee as the supreme executive body of the party and, for all practical purposes, of the entire nation. The KWP Standing Committee—like its Soviet counterpart, the politburo—included both full and candidate members. Of course, the congressional delegates "unanimously" approved all of these proposals.

Usually there were few if any surprises during a congress. However, two important events occurred that were generally connected with the Third Congress, although they remained a secret to the majority of participants and the general public.

From the Soviet Embassy materials, it is known that some prominent members of the Soviet faction (including Pak Ch'ang-ok, Pak Ŭi-wan, and Pak Yŏng-bin) had hoped to meet L. I. Brezhnev. The future Soviet leader was at that time the head of the Soviet Party delegation attending the Third Congress. The Soviet Koreans wanted to discuss privately with the Soviet dignitary some issues in the North Korean domestic political scene, in particular the position of the Soviet Koreans. Pak Kil-yŏng, the then deputy minister of foreign affairs, was aware of these plans and relayed them to a Soviet diplomat. Pak remarked only two weeks later: "They could not do it [i.e., speak to Brezhnev], because of the current position of the Soviet Koreans in the DPRK. Nevertheless, Vice-premier Pak Ŭi-wan managed to inform Comrade Brezhnev on the situation in the DPRK, albeit very briefly."[4]

We do not know what Pak Ŭi-wan discussed with Brezhnev, because the records of this conversation remain beyond our reach. It is possible that even this limited and quasi-conspiratorial briefing influenced Brezhnev's position and the general content of his speech. The head of the Soviet delegation was the first foreign dignitary to deliver an address to the congress. He did so on April 24 and was followed by the Chinese delegate; other foreign guests appeared before the congress the next day. It was significant that Brezhnev, in his rather short address, specifically mentioned the personality cult and even hinted that such a problem might also exist in the DPRK. He declared: "The Third Congress will assist the KWP in establishing in [its] organizations the Leninist principle of collective leadership, which will protect [the party] from the dangers of the personality cult."[5] It is not difficult to guess how Kim Il Song and his entourage would have interpreted such a suggestion. It was akin to a challenge or even more so, given that Kim Il Song himself had virtually avoided mentioning the term "personality cult" in his speech.

We know that at the congress there was at least one more indication of the growing dissatisfaction with Kim's modus operandi. In late May, Ki Sŏk-pok (who had been embroiled in the literary discussion mentioned above) briefed a Soviet diplomat about another series of behind-the-scenes confrontations. According to Ki, during the party congress one of its participants, Yi Sang-jo, the ambassador to Moscow and a KWP Central Committee member, wrote two letters to the congress' presidium. In these letters Yi, a prominent member of the Yan'an faction who also maintained good contacts in Moscow, asked to discuss the personality cult problem and made explicit critical remarks about Kim's personality cult in the KWP. Of course, these letters were not discussed during the congress. This led to an open confrontation between Yi Sang-jo and Kim Ch'ang-man, another former Yan'an exile who by then had become Kim Il Song's zealous supporter. Kim Ch'ang-man insisted that Yi Sang-jo was going to apply the Soviet pattern, which was completely unsuited to the realities of the DPRK. Yi Sang-jo then accused Kim Ch'ang-man of attempts to ignore the Soviet Twentieth Congress' decision and new trends in world Communism. After their confrontation, Kim Ch'ang-man informed Ch'oe Yong-gŏn and several other former guerrillas of Yi's position. As a result, it was decided not to send Yi back to Moscow. Yi in turn consulted Kim Tu-bong, who was still technically head of the North Korean state. The Yan'an patriarch called Kim Il Song and expressed his support for Yi, so Kim Il Song gave his permission to send Yi back to Moscow. This decision, as we shall soon see, had some important consequences.[6]

It is possible and indeed highly probable that some other behind-the-scenes discussions and confrontations took place of which I am not aware. The question of the personality cult was certainly a major issue in the spring of 1956, although Kim Il Song managed to avoid any open discussion of this extremely sensitive question at the congress.

This was a major success for Kim. Meanwhile the international and domestic situations remained highly unstable.

When discussing the outcomes of the congress, we must remember that one factor of particular importance was the composition of the new Central Committee. In theory the Central Committee was elected by the party congress. In reality the congressional delegates simply voted for a prearranged list of candidates. The preparation of this list involved a long process of wheeling and dealing by the high-level cadres, and the leader (or in some more liberal Communist countries, a few of the more prominent leaders) had the final say. The Central Committee per se was not a permanent body—it met at more or less regular intervals, two or three times a year, but only for a few days each time. During the period of 1948–1961 (i.e., between the Second and Fourth KWP Congresses), plenums were held on average of 2.4 times a year, which is roughly similar to the number that were held in the contemporary USSR. In spite of the irregularity and relatively short duration of its formal meetings, the Central Committee also had a large permanent and very powerful bureaucracy—the so-called Central Committee apparatus. In North Korea in 1958 the Central Committee apparatus comprised 1,204 officials, excluding clerical and technical staff.[7] They were the most influential of all party apparatchiks (this term was coined in the Soviet Union to describe this group). This bureaucracy, actually controlled by the politburo rather than by the "elected" Central Committee, was the real central government of the Communist states in all but name. Under the constant guidance of the politburo and party leader(s), the Central Committee bureaucracy worked out strategy, to be later implemented by the Council of Ministers and other "normal" government agencies. In the Stalinist political tradition, which had been transplanted to North Korea, the Central Committee was a very secretive body. Even the information about its plenums was normally published long after the event. Being a Central Committee member was a privilege and also a sign of belonging to the inner (albeit not innermost) circle of power. It is noteworthy that in the Soviet Union, in compliance with Lenin's belatedly published political will, from the 1950s onward a share of Central Committee seats was allocated to the token representatives of the "working masses," and a certain number of these exemplary milkmaids or shock workers sat on the plenums. North Korea, on the other hand, never followed suit, so the KWP Central Committee remained a strictly closed circle of party elite. Nevertheless, its membership grew to reach 317 in 1980. From 1946 to 1960, however, it was still a relatively small and hence manageable body of fewer than 100 individuals.

Democratic or not, the Central Committee was a unique institution within the overall political machinery of a Leninist state. It was the body that had the right to elect and, if necessary, recall politburo members and even the party head (general secretary, chairman, first secretary—the title could differ in place or over time). In most ruling Communist parties, the party head himself was elected not by the congress but by the Central Committee. He could therefore lose his job if the Central Committee chose to vote him out. In reality the party oligarchy or party dictator seldom had to worry about being ousted one day by a majority vote of the Central Committee. Nonetheless, from time to time, such incidents did occur in the ruling Communist parties. Behind the closed doors of the Central Committee, some semblance of free discussion was occasionally possible. The expression of concern and even muted disagreement with certain aspects of current policy, when aired by a Central Committee member among his (seldom her) equals, would normally be tolerated. Nevertheless, even these top cadres had to be quite cautious and shrewd in their pronouncements or critiques.

Let us take a closer look at the new KWP Central Committee, "elected" in April 1956. This committee was particularly important, because it was this body that would devastate the opposition challenge four months hence. Its composition might provide us with some clues as to why the subsequent events unfolded as they did. In order to analyze the composition of the Central Committee, we will have to use the now not-so-fashionable "Kremlinologist" approach—an attempt to track down the factional affiliation of individual Central Committee members. In the case of the KWP this approach is entirely appropriate, given that in the North Korean context factional affiliations mattered enormously. Unfortunately, mistakes in determining the factional affiliation of the individual members are unavoidable—not because the borders between the factions or factional affiliations of a certain cadre were ill defined (they normally were clear-cut) but because biographical data about many early North Korean leaders are rare or nonexistent. Virtually nothing is known about certain obscure figures who appear almost from nowhere on the Central Committee roster in the late 1940s or mid-1950s, only to disappear without a trace a few years later, presumably but not necessarily the victims of purges. A little more information is available about those who lasted longer—into the 1960s and 1970s—but these survivors are mostly ex-guerrillas. If a North Korean politician was affiliated with the Guerrilla faction, this connection is normally quite well known. For the more obscure minor figures from other factions, their pre-1945 background (and hence their affiliations) is often uncertain. In this book I rely primarily on the data painstakingly collected and analyzed by Wada Haruki. Though these data must certainly contain some inaccuracies, which are unavoidable at this stage of research, they are by far the best compendium of such information available.[8]

According to the Soviet tradition, which had become a standard practice throughout the Communist parties, the Central Committee included two types of members: full members, who had voting power, and candidate members, who did not. In 1956 the KWP Central Committee had 71 full members and 45 candidate members. Here I will concentrate on the full members—partly because the candidate members, lacking the power to vote, did not play a decisive role in the "August incident" and partly because the full members' backgrounds are much better known. Of the 71 full members of the Central Committee, only 30 had been full members of the 1948 Central Committee; of the remaining 41 newcomers, 5 had been candidate members in 1948.[9] This was quite a significant turnover, considering that the overall number of full members did not grow much: in 1948 the Central Committee had 67 members, and in 1956 it had 71.

The new Central Committee included 11 former guerrillas (the 1948 committee had 8). Five of these (Ch'oe Hyŏn, Ch'oe Yong-gŏn, Yi Hyo-sun, Yu Kyŏng-su, and Yi Yŏng-ho) had not been members of the 1948 Central Committee. One of them, Ch'oe Yong-gŏn, was not even technically a member of the KWP until 1955. Another ex-guerrilla, Yi Hyo-sun, was promoted from among the candidate members. It is also worth noting that all ex-guerrillas who had been full members in 1948 and who were still alive in 1956 were reelected to the Central Committee (2 of the 1948 ex-guerrilla members, Kim Ch'aek and Kang Kŏn, had been killed in action during the war).

Predictably, it was the Soviet faction that suffered most. Instead of the 14 members it had in the 1948 Central Committee, it received only 9 seats in 1956. The Soviet faction also had by far the highest turnover— about 70 percent: of the 14 original members with a "Soviet" background, 10 were dropped from the Central Committee (including the deceased Hŏ Ka-i). These political casualties included the much-criticized Ki Sŏk-pok and Kim Chae-uk. Another target of the recent campaign, Pak Ch'ang-ok, retained his position and even moved slightly upward in the list, from number 11 in 1948 to number 7 in 1956. Apart from Pak Ch'ang-ok, 3 other "Soviet Korean" survivors from the 1948 Central Committee included Pang Hak-se, the ruthlessly efficient and much feared security chief who came to associate himself with Kim Il Song at a very early stage and, somewhat surprisingly, was to survive a few more decades; Kim Sŭng-hwa, minister of construction; and Han Il-mu, a rather apolitical general. Five of the "Soviet Koreans" were newcomers. Of them, General Nam Il, a negotiator of Panmunjom fame, was promoted from the position of candidate member, while 4 others (Ch'oe Chong-hak, Hŏ Pin, Pak Ŭi-wan, and Kim Tu-sam) had not even been candidate members in 1948.

The Yan'an faction fared much better: it had 18 full members on the Central Committee (in contrast to 17 members in 1948). The turnover was high in this group as well, about 50 percent: only 8 of the original 17 remained on the new Central Committee. Pak Il-u and (Kim) Mu Chŏng had been purged. Among the other political casualties were at least 2 other prominent veterans of the Chinese civil wars: Kim Ung and Pak Hyo-sam. They were replaced by some other cadres of Chinese background, including 2 persons who were to play a crucial role just a few months later: Sŏ Hwi, who had never previously been either a full member or a candidate, and Yun Kong-hŭm, who had been a full member of the Central Committee in 1946, lost his seat in 1948, and was now making a comeback.

An important sign of things to come was the first appearance of people who did not belong to any "traditional" faction. These were mostly young to middle-aged cadres whose rise to national prominence had begun after 1945. Some of them were technocrats or professional soldiers, but career party functionaries were not uncommon. Though they were not affiliated with any of the traditional pre-1945 factions, their outlooks had been influenced by the already well-established Kim Il Song regime and its propaganda. When they joined the party, it was already the party of Kim Il Song. Whether they were sincere or not, they were forced to participate in the official adulation of the Great Leader. They did not share memories of the time when Kim was an insignificant guerrilla fighter somewhere in the Manchurian backwater, while the "real events" were perceived as occurring in Yan'an, Seoul, or Moscow. These newly recruited cadres knew only one leader, and for all practical purposes they were Kim's people. Some of them could have been mistakenly seen as Domestic Communists, because they were from North Korea and some of them had had connections with the left-wing groups during the colonial period—or so they insisted after 1945. Unlike the "real" Domestic faction, none of them had been active in the Korean Communist underground of the 1930s and early 1940s.

It is quite difficult to estimate the number of these new cadres, especially since background biographical data are so scarce. However, it is known that the number of people who had not been in the Soviet Union, China, or Manchuria prior to 1945 was quite significant—at least some 20 persons. Wada Haruki includes most of them in the Domestic faction in his list, simply because they were "locals" by birth. Of the 25 persons Wada claims as Domestic faction members, only 3 (Pak Chŏng-ae, Han Sŏl-ya, and O Ki-sŏp) were members of the first 1946 Central Committee, were prominent in the North during the first months after Liberation, and had probably played some role prior to 1945. Of the other 22 supposed Domestic faction members, 7 are mentioned in the list of the 360 delegates who were allegedly "clandestinely elected" in South Korea as members of the DPRK Supreme People's Assembly in 1948. This fact might indicate that they had enjoyed some standing in South Korean Communist circles at that time (4 of these 7 were also members of the South Korean Workers' Party Central Committee in 1946).[10] These 7 can also be regarded as authentic Domestic Communists with a South Korean background. The remaining 15 were mostly people without much pre-1945 political fame. We can surmise that most of them belonged to the new generation of cadres and cannot be counted among the Domestic faction, despite their "local" origins. These people included some personalities who had remarkable careers later on, such as the future premier of the Administration Council, Yi Chong-ok; future vice-premiers Kim Hoe-il, Kim Hwang-il, and Chŏng Chun-t'aek; and Academy of Science chairman Kim Yŏng-ch'ang. The careers of these individuals continued to flourish into the 1960s, the 1970s, and in some instances the 1980s. Some of them died a natural death, but many nonguerrilla members of the 1956 Central Committee were swamped politically (or even physically) in the tidal waves of purges during the late 1950s and early 1960s.

The shift in the power balance within the party bureaucracy was even more obvious at the highest level, in the North Korean Politburo, which was renamed the Standing Committee at the Third KWP Congress. According to the post-Stalinist "collective leadership" concept, the politburo was supposed to be a collective dictator of sorts. In practice, hardly any of the ruling Communist countries ever had a politburo that was not to a significant degree dominated by the party headman. In Stalinist regimes the politburo resembled a "king's council," a board of advisers to an omnipotent dictator who could appoint or dismiss the politburo members at will. Unlike the Central Committee, the politburo was a permanent institution and met more or less on a weekly basis. As the supreme body, it ran the powerful Central Committee bureaucracy. In both Stalinist and post-Stalinist Communist countries, the politburo was an extremely important institution. Being a member of this body meant being a member of the innermost circle of power and privilege.

Like the Central Committee, the North Korean Politburo comprised both full and candidate members (11 and 4 in the 1956 KWP, respectively). In the 1956 Standing Committee, 5 of its 11 full members were former guerrillas. In 1948 only 2 of the 7 Political Council members were ex-guerrillas. Among the 6 nonguerrilla members of the 1956 Politburo, Pak Chŏng-ae and Nam Il, though technically Soviet Koreans, had joined Kim Il Song's faction at an early stage and had become his ardent supporters. Chŏng Il-ryŏng also boasted a similar reputation. Only

Kim Tu-bong and Ch'oe Ch'ang-ik, both from the Yan'an faction, could be considered more or less independent politicians. Among the 4 candidate members, Yi Hyo-sun was an ex-guerrilla, whereas Kim Ch'ang-man (despite his Chinese background) had attained celebrity status, or notoriety, as Kim Il Song's ardent eulogist. Yi Chong-ok, whose career was just beginning, belonged to the newly emerging elite of local technocrats strongly attached to and dependent on Kim Il Song and his policy. The only candidate member who could not be considered "Kim's man" was Pak Ŭi-wan. This outspoken Soviet Korean even arranged a clandestine meeting with Brezhnev during the Third Congress to complain about Kim Il Song's policy. It was quite clear that Kim Il Song was the absolute master of the Standing Committee: 9 of the 11 full members and 3 of the 4 candidate members were his devoted and unwavering supporters.

Kim Il Song did have a measure of success at the Third Congress. His faction, strengthened by defectors from other political groups, greatly increased its share of power in the party and the state. Kim might have had to deliver confused and ambiguous pronouncements about current developments in his lengthy address, but he achieved something more important than a political declaration: he greatly increased his grip over the Central Committee bureaucracy and the party machinery. In the space of a few brief months this grip was to prove decisive.

4   The Conspiracy

FROM 1955 TO 1956, domestic and international situations permitted the emergence of an opposition group within the North Korean party leadership. This window of opportunity was the only one in the entire history of Kim Il Song's DPRK. Before that, the possibility for such a situation to arise had been prevented by wartime conditions and the steel grasp of foreign control. After 1956 the more authoritarian nature of Kim Il Song's regime was the preventive factor. Until 1956, while North Korea was (to borrow J. Rothschild's expression) "in the grip of mature Stalinism," any challenge to the Soviet-backed and Chinese-approved Kim Il Song would have seemed—and most likely would have been—suicidal.[1] Even if some members of the leadership were not happy with his current policies or their own place within his system, they were forced to keep such views to themselves. The fate of Pak Hŏn-yŏng and other leaders of the Domestic faction, as well as the tacit approval of their purge by the Soviet authorities, convincingly demonstrated the likely fate of any potential opponent to Kim Il Song.[2] Between 1950 and 1953, North Korea was fighting a major war, and under the circumstances many party and government cadres might have felt that a challenge to Kim Il Song's authority was tantamount to treason to their country and to the cause of Communism, a cause that most of them still took quite seriously.

However, over the years 1955 and 1956, profound changes in the Soviet Union influenced the situation in other Communist countries and led to an outbreak of reform and pro-democracy movements. These movements are well exemplified by both the Hungarian revolution and the "Polish October"—a series of strikes and rallies that led to significant changes in domestic politics. The ferment was much more widespread, and North Korea was not just a passive backwater of undisturbed Stalinism. This movement in Korea did not spread to the population as a whole. It affected mainly the better informed and educated members of the party elite and some intellectuals. Rather than open riots or rallies, its manifestation came in an unsuccessful attempt to oust Kim Il Song, who was seen by some to personify the old Stalinist politics.

The high tide of de-Stalinization occurred during the spring of 1956. Khrushchev's "Secret Speech" was delivered to the CPSU Twentieth Congress, and although some halfhearted attempts were made to keep it actually secret, its content soon became widely known in the USSR and beyond. The speech and related decisions triggered a series of significant changes in the USSR. Within the next two years the overwhelming majority of political prisoners were released, censorship was relaxed, new trends in culture were tolerated and sometimes encouraged, and foreign exchanges increased. Soviet society responded to the changes with a noticeable—albeit short-lived—revival of enthusiasm for the Communist system. For a while it appeared that the system might be capable of transforming itself and correcting its former mistakes and crimes. The Soviet people and even the press began to discuss social topics with relative freedom, perhaps very moderate by democratic standards but unthinkable under Stalin.

It is also worth remembering that China, another major sponsor of Korea at the time, was not immune to these new ideas either. The eventual establishment of Mao's personality cult and the exceptionally irrational nature of the Chinese political system of the 1960s and 1970s have overshadowed the fact that the mid-1950s were a comparatively liberal period in Chinese history and arguably the most liberal period of the entire Maoist era. These liberalization attempts culminated in the Hundred Flowers movement, launched in May 1956 in the aftermath of Khrushchev's "Secret Speech." The movement's name was a shortened form of an ancient Chinese dictum: "Let a hundred flowers bloom together, let a hundred schools of thought contend." The initial idea of this movement was to encourage criticism from below. As John Fairbank and Merle Goldman state: "Mao estimated that among a total of at most 5 million intellectuals . . . not more than 3 percent were by this time hostile to Marxism."[3] These liberal experiments were even accompanied by a veiled critique of Mao's personality cult. Mao's deification had by then had a long history, but most Communist Party leaders had seen Mao's personality cult as a useful technical device. They considered it indispensable in a country populated by a traditional uneducated peasantry, accustomed to the idea of a ruling emperor. After 1949 and especially after 1953, Mao's leadership style came under attack by many top party cadres. Under pressure, Mao had to make some moderate concessions that were particularly visible from 1956 to 1957. These developments led to a considerable restriction of Mao's authority at the Eighth Congress of the Chinese Communist Party.[4] The changes were short-lived and soon reversed, but they nevertheless influenced the developments in Korea as well.

Kim Il Song anticipated trouble and perceived the unfolding de-Stalinization campaign in the Soviet Union and many other Communist countries as a major threat to himself. He guessed that the Soviet developments might lead to domestic political complications in Korea as well. This proved to be a correct estimation. At the same time, Kim Il Song made an understandable mistake when identifying the primary source of the danger. He perceived the Soviet Koreans as the most important potential troublemakers, and in an attempt to eradicate this latent threat, he launched a preventive strike against them in late 1955. He was proven wrong, however. Kim's power was challenged not by the Soviet Koreans, despite their predisposition toward the influences of the latest ideological fashions from Moscow, but by the Yan'an faction. It was the onetime "Chinese Koreans" who formed the core of an opposition group and openly attacked Kim Il Song. Though a few discontented Soviet Koreans also eventually joined the conspiracy, their roles were largely marginal, and the entire episode was essentially a "Yan'an group affair."

When did it all begin? The earliest direct evidence of the existence of a clandestine opposition group within the North Korean leadership does not appear in the Soviet Embassy papers until July 1956. The opposition leaders secretly established contact with the embassy and informed the Soviet diplomats of their plans. These contacts looked conspicuously like the deliberate actions of a well-organized group. It gives us ample reason to surmise that the opposition had already existed for some time, at least from May or June 1956.

The development of the crisis was probably facilitated by Kim Il Song's prolonged absence from the country. In the first half of the pivotal 1956 summer, from June 1 to July 19, Kim Il Song was undertaking an unusually extensive overseas trip. Throughout these seven weeks he visited nine Communist countries and stayed in Moscow twice—on his way to and from Eastern Europe. It was the longest overseas trip he ever undertook in his capacity as leader of the DPRK (his second-longest voyage was to occur much later, in 1984). Kim was accompanied on the trip by his deputy Pak Chŏng-ae, who was also useful as a fluent Russian speaker and an expert on Soviet politics; Nam Il, the minister of foreign affairs and another knowledgeable expert with a Soviet background; and Yi Chong-ok, who had recently been appointed chairman of the State Planning Commission to replace the dismissed Pak Ch'ang-ok. Yi's presence was relevant to the basic economic goals of the trip. The mission's main task was to solicit more aid and cheap loans in order to get resources for a recently approved Five-Year Plan, the first plan of its kind in Korean history. The economic achievements of the trip proved to be quite moderate, perhaps because no Communist country was ready to give much away while facing an unstable and unpredictable domestic situation. The team also included token representatives from two non-Communist puppet "parties," because North Korea was still serious about maintaining the fiction of a United Front at this stage. These representatives were very unlikely to have taken part in any confidential meetings or important decision making.[5]

The prolonged physical absence of a dictator from a country always provides favorable conditions for fermenting discontent. It is almost certain that Kim Il Song's extended overseas trip created a unique opportunity for the disaffected members of the North Korean elite. The situation looked even better for the opposition, since Kim's daily duties in Pyongyang were taken over by Ch'oe Yong-gŏn, whom the opposition initially mistakenly considered to be its own secret sympathizer.

By June–July 1956 the tensions within the North Korean ruling elite were rising. Not everyone who strove for change also wanted to replace Kim Il Song. As is clear from the embassy papers, some members of the Korean elite apparently hoped that the meetings and conversations with the Soviet leaders would influence Kim Il Song's policies and help achieve the changes they considered necessary. These officials did their best to ensure that the Soviet leaders spoke with Kim Il Song about his attitude toward the personality cult and other sensitive questions. Whether this activity was coordinated or was merely the result of several individual initiatives is unknown. The meeting between Pak Ŭi-wan and Brezhnev, discussed in chapter 3, was not the only occasion in which high-ranking Koreans attempted to use Soviet influence to force Kim Il Song to change his ways. On June 16, Yi Sang-jo, the North Korean ambassador to the Soviet Union, had a deliberately frank conversation with a high-ranking Soviet diplomat in Moscow. Yi spoke critically of Kim Il Song's personality cult and "distortions of socialist legality" (a standard Khrushchev-period euphemism for arbitrary arrests, tortures, and executions) in North Korea. Yi Sang-jo explicitly suggested that the Soviet leaders discuss these problems with Kim Il Song himself during Kim's visit to the USSR.[6]

These attempts were not in vain. In the summer of 1956, during his negotiations with the Soviet leaders, Kim Il Song was reprimanded for "improper behavior." At this time Moscow could still afford to lecture the heads of other Communist countries as if they were unruly boys. Although the minutes of the Moscow negotiations are still beyond the reach of scholars, there are enough hints in the embassy papers to reconstruct what might have occurred in Moscow. The "remarks of the Soviet Communist Party Central Committee" concerning Kim Il Song were mentioned by Nam Il and Pak Chŏng-ae, who were probably both direct witnesses of the meeting, as well as by Yi Sang-jo, who later explicitly stated that he was not a witness.[7] Although no names are mentioned in the documents, the reprimands were probably made by none other than Khrushchev himself. On July 24, Nam Il told the chargé d'affaires, A. M. Petrov: "The remarks of the Soviet Communist Party Central Committee about certain mistakes and shortcomings in the KWP's work are understood by Kim Il Song correctly and sincerely. Kim Il Song told Nam Il and some other members of the government delegation that he would do his best to fully and decisively correct these mistakes, including [those connected with] the question of the personality cult. In Kim Il Song's opinion these mistakes should be eliminated, not instantaneously through a full discussion in either the Central Committee or local party organizations, but gradually, without involving the party members as a whole in discussing the questions."[8] This reaction was part of the strategy that Kim Il Song had begun to use as early as February: behind closed doors, among high-level cadres, he would reluctantly recognize the existence of a personality cult, hinting meanwhile that he himself was not strongly opposed to the new spirit of reform and would solve the problems eventually. These hints, combined with moderate repentance and "self-criticism," were probably meant to pacify his critics and obviate potential attack. After all, if wrongs are recognized and are to be righted in due course, all obtrusive discussion is then nothing more than a sign of impatience, if not worse.

However, while Kim Il Song was being subjected to this unpleasant "friendly advice" from the Soviet leaders in Moscow, back in Pyongyang the opposition group was busy preparing an open attack on him. Using materials recently declassified, we can now acquaint ourselves with some of the more important details of their actions, because the opposition leaders decided to keep the Soviets informed of their plans.

The existence of a plot became known to the Soviet Embassy in July 1956, although it is conceivable that some information could have been delivered earlier. The first hint of something unusual was on July 10. Kim Sŭng-hwa, the minister of construction and a member of the Soviet faction, visited the Soviet Embassy to discuss some routine business—the ongoing construction of a new embassy compound. In the course of the talks, he changed the topic of conversation and, in the absence of the Soviet ambassador, informed the chargé d'affaires, A. M. Petrov, of "widespread dissatisfaction" among North Korean cadres who were allegedly critical of the Kim Il Song personality cult. Kim Sŭng-hwa, who, as we shall see, by that time was already a member of an anti–Kim Il Song group, certainly overstated the degree of this "dissatisfaction," but he nevertheless hinted that there were profound differences of opinion among the ruling elite of the DPRK.[9]

The crisis began to unfold the day after Kim Il Song's return from his overseas trip. A considerable amount of evidence shows that for some reason Kim Il Song's return and perhaps some information about his trip triggered the opposition activity. On July 14, Yi P'il-gyu, head of the Department of Construction Materials in the cabinet and a prominent figure from the Yan'an faction, went to the embassy to speak with Petrov.[10] Since the Soviet ambassador, V. I. Ivanov, was absent from Pyongyang, Petrov, as acting ambassador, was the top official in the Soviet Embassy. Yi P'il-gyu, Petrov's Korean interlocutor, was a man of considerable stature and background. At the age of sixteen Yi had taken part in the revolutionary movement in China; later in Korea his activities had led the Japanese to imprison him. After 1945, Yi initially worked in the security services and then held a succession of influential posts, mostly related to military or internal security, including deputy chief of general staff, commander of the Sixth Army, and deputy minister of the interior (under Pak Il-u). According to information that Yi P'il-gyu offered his Soviet interlocutor, Yi and Pak Il-u were close friends, and Yi's influence had waned significantly as a result of the Pak Il-u affair.[11] Pak Il-u's fall from grace caused Yi P'il-gyu to lose his positions, although ostensibly not his connections, at the Ministry of the Interior. Notwithstanding this, Yi P'il-gyu's influence inside the Yan'an faction probably remained considerable. Yi P'il-gyu also said that he had close personal relations with Yi Sang-jo and was aware of the latter's verbal attacks on Kim's personality cult during the Third KWP Congress. Being a Yan'an faction affiliate, Yi P'il-gyu had not been a frequent visitor to the Soviet Embassy (indeed, his name cannot be found in embassy papers prior to this conversation).

The subject of the conversation, which lasted one and a half hours, was extraordinary. From the very beginning, Yi P'il-gyu put diplomatic niceties aside and came down hard on Kim Il Song and his policies. Yi accused the North Korean leader of establishing a personality cult, of exaggerating the role of his guerrillas during the anti-Japanese struggle at the expense of the contribution of the Soviet Army and other resistance forces, of taking an "incorrect attitude" toward other members of the party leadership, and of other transgressions.

It must be noted that this important document exists in two quite different versions. One version is a draft handwritten copy, probably composed during the conversation or soon afterward, and the other is a later, typed text.[12] This was the normal procedure; notes taken during such a conversation were transformed into a handwritten draft, which in turn was then edited and typewritten by an embassy typist—normally a few days or even a week or two after the actual conversation. Customarily, the handwritten drafts were destroyed, and only the typed copies were filed and sent to Moscow. However, in this case the draft was not destroyed, and in early September it was discovered that the final typed text differed markedly from the handwritten draft. How this was discovered is unknown, but the result was a minor scandal in the Soviet Embassy.

These events and the probable reasons behind Petrov's futile attempt to falsify the document are of some importance. Petrov deliberately misdated the typed version as July 20, instead of the correct July 14. When the scandal began to unfold in September, Petrov sent Ambassador Ivanov a short memo in which he mentioned some other remarks that had allegedly been made by Yi but were not included in the handwritten copy.

The content of the handwritten and typed copies differs in some important respects. Many changes were simply the result of the understandable and, indeed, necessary editing process. However, some discrepancies were far more serious and the "corrections" made to the original notes followed a pattern. First, Petrov deliberately dropped some of the most critical remarks made by Yi P'il-gyu and, in doing so, presented Yi's position toward Kim Il Song as less hostile than it really was. Second, Petrov completely deleted from the edited copy all of Yi P'il-gyu's remarks on Yi Sang-jo, the then DPRK ambassador to the USSR. These deleted remarks indicated a close personal relation between Yi P'il-gyu and Yi Sang-jo and contained concrete evidence of Yi Sang-jo's attempts to protest the personality cult. Third, in the typed copy Petrov alleged that Yi had informed him of the existence of an organized opposition to Kim's regime, but remarks of this kind were completely absent from the handwritten original. According to the handwritten notes, Yi explicitly stated that resistance to Kim Il Song's policies was both desirable and necessary but that nothing had eventuated, whereas in the edited copy Yi is cited as repeatedly mentioning the existence of a clandestine anti-Kim group. In this narrative I will use the information from the handwritten original, unless otherwise specified. (Specific details of the more important discrepancies between the two documents are discussed in notes.)

After some introductory observations about a growing glorification of the Manchurian guerrillas and the related falsification of the history of the Korean Communist movement by Kim Il Song and his coterie, Yi P'il-gyu proceeded to his most important point—Kim Il Song's personal dictatorship over the country and the party: "Kim Il Song's personality cult has become quite intolerable. Kim Il Song's word is law. He is intolerant and does not seek advice. He has gathered sycophants and lackeys all around him in the Central Committee and the cabinet."

In the later, typed text, Petrov insisted that Yi P'il-gyu informed him of a plan to remove Kim Il Song that had matured among the North Korean leadership. Yi had allegedly told the acting Soviet ambassador: "A group of cadres considers it necessary to undertake certain actions against Kim Il Song and his closest associates at the earliest possible opportunity. . . . The group sets itself the task of putting new persons in charge of the KWP Central Committee and government." However, these statements are absent from the handwritten original and therefore may be a later insertion.

It is clear from the handwritten notes that Yi did say something about the urgent need to get rid of Kim Il Song, although he probably did not say that the preparations for such an action were already taking place. In the handwritten text, Petrov described Yi P'il-gyu's response when asked what might be done to repair the situation in the party: "There are two ways of achieving this. The first is to replace the current leaders of the KWP Central Committee and the government. This would require a sharp and decisive [campaign of] criticism and self-criticism. This is the first method. However, Yi P'il-gyu said that he doubted whether Kim Il Song would ever do this. In his opinion, the crimes committed by Kim were [already] so great that he would not do this. The second [method] is forcible upheaval. He said that this path would be difficult and protracted and would probably call for sacrifice. However, this was the revolutionary path. In order to achieve it, according to Yi P'il-gyu, an underground action must be instigated." In the edited typed text, the remark about "Kim's crimes" was omitted, and the entire text made more insipid.[13]

According to information that Petrov later provided to the ambassador, Yi also said: "If a change in the DPRK leadership is not achieved peacefully, it [will be necessary] to switch to underground work and launch [underground] activity." Petrov added, "Since he [Yi] and his supporters are acting as revolutionaries, they will be supported by the revolutionary elements and the Chinese People's Volunteers." It is remarkable that Petrov initially omitted this passage even from his handwritten record of the conversation, let alone from the typed copy. Nevertheless, these remarks can be found in a short memo sent by Petrov to Ambassador Ivanov, after the falsification of the text had been discovered. The decision to write this additional short memo was likely made under the pressure of evidence provided by the embassy interpreter. The remarks imply the existence of Yi's "supporters," a notion that accords with the typed copy but differs from the handwritten original.[14]

According to the typed version, Yi mentioned to Petrov that a resistance group existed within the ranks of the KWP cadres. Yi was quoted as saying: "There are people in the DPRK who are ready to embark on such a course [of resistance] and are currently making appropriate preparations."[15] The typed text also states that Petrov asked Yi P'il-gyu who the members of this group were, but that Yi evaded the question. Subsequently, Petrov allegedly asked Yi about his "attitude toward the above-mentioned underground group" and that Yi was again evasive. However, Petrov writes in relation to this conversation: "I was under the impression that he definitely played an important role in this group."[16] According to the typed version, another of Petrov's questions was why Yi had decided to inform the Soviet Embassy about the situation. Yi P'il-gyu allegedly replied: "They [the opposition] would like to alert the Soviet Embassy to the possibility of certain forthcoming events in the DPRK."[17] All of these important exchanges and statements are conspicuously absent from the handwritten copy and are likely to be Petrov's later inventions or, at the least, his deliberate misinterpretations of Yi's remarks.

Toward the end of the conversation, Yi P'il-gyu began to speak about certain Korean dignitaries. These remarks about top KWP cadres are quoted in essentially the same way in both the handwritten and the typed copies (aside from some minor stylistic editing) and are unquestionably authentic. Understandably, Yi held some members of the Yan'an faction in high regard—with the notable exception of Kim Ch'ang-man, a fervent supporter of Kim Il Song's who might be considered one of the earliest adulators of the future Great Leader. At the same time, Yi offered quite unflattering estimations of the leading Soviet Koreans Pak Chŏng-ae (at the time, Pak was also one of Kim Il Song's closest associates) and, somewhat surprisingly, Pak Ch'ang-ok, who, as we shall soon see, was also a prominent member of the opposition. Yi asserted that Pak Ch'ang-ok had been directly responsible for the creation of the Kim Il Song cult: "Pak Ch'ang-ok will have to do much to atone for his guilt. After all, he was the first to name Kim Il Song as an indispensable person, praising him to the skies. He is the originator of Kim Il Song's personality cult."[18] This pronouncement might have been true, but it also indicated that rivalry between the Soviet and Yan'an factions had not died out, even under such exceptional circumstances. Yi's harshest criticism was of the former guerrillas and other members of Kim Il Song's inner circle. The worst language was reserved for Han Sŏl-ya: "Han Sŏl-ya—he should be killed. He deserves it even only for just one book—*History*. He is a very bad and harmful man; he is Kim Il Song's sycophant, a bootlicker." However, Yi made an important and quite surprising exception in his criticism: Ch'oe Yong-gŏn, de facto "number two man" in the Pyongyang hierarchy, was mentioned quite favorably, despite his long-standing reputation as one of Kim Il Song's most trusted lieutenants.[19]

Yi P'il-gyu's visit, important and controversial as it was, was neither incidental nor isolated. Indeed, it was a sign of things to come. On July 21 a new meeting, between counselor S. N. Filatov and Pak Ch'ang-ok, took place in the Soviet Embassy. After the death of Hŏ Ka-i, Pak Ch'ang-ok had become the de facto leader of the Soviet Koreans, although his reputation among them was never as strong as Hŏ Ka-i's. As has been mentioned, Pak had to retire in January 1956 in the midst of the campaign against the Soviet Koreans. When the campaign ended, Pak Ch'ang-ok received a new appointment, but his pride had probably been deeply wounded. Pak told Filatov that the attack on Kim Il Song would take place during the next plenum and that Pak himself was going to play a hand in it.[20]

Two days later, on July 23, yet another meeting took place at the Soviet Embassy. This time counselor S. N. Filatov received Ch'oe Ch'ang-ik, vice-premier and a member of the Standing Committee of the KWP Central Committee (i.e., the North Korean Politburo). Ch'oe Ch'ang-ik was one of the most prominent leaders of the Yan'an faction. In China he had been one of two vice-chairmen of the Korean Independence League (a Korean left-wing organization in China that formed the nucleus of the future New People's Party and Yan'an faction). It was Kim Tu-bong who in the mid-1950s remained the supreme authority among the former exiles in China, but he normally did not intervene in practical politics. After the fall of Pak Il-u, Ch'oe Ch'ang-ik had replaced Kim Tu-bong as the acting leader of the entire Yan'an faction. The purpose of their visits to the embassy was identical to that of the visits by Yi P'il-gyu and Pak Ch'ang-ok—to outline their plans for Kim Il Song's removal and to inform the embassy of their scheme.

First, Ch'oe Ch'ang-ik briefly reviewed the recent session of the Standing Committee (on July 21), at which Kim Il Song spoke at length about his visit to the Soviet Union and the countries of Eastern Europe. Then Ch'oe Ch'ang-ik moved on to the main subject: "I am becoming more and more convinced that Kim Il Song does not understand how harmful his behavior is. He paralyzes the initiative of members of the Standing Committee and other executives of the party and the state. He intimidates everybody. Nobody can voice an opinion on any question. People are subjected to repression for the slightest criticism. He has gathered around himself sycophants and mediocrities." Kim Ch'ang-man and a number of former guerrillas were also the objects of Ch'oe's invective.[21]

True to the spirit of the new times, Ch'oe Ch'ang-ik reproached Kim Il Song chiefly for the propagation of his personality cult in its various forms: "Kim Il Song . . . does not wish to change [his] forms and methods of leadership. He does not wish to subject the mistakes he has made to criticism and self-criticism. This kind of behavior by Kim Il Song cannot facilitate the development of our party activity nor contribute to strengthening its ranks. Kim Il Song's personality cult has infiltrated our party. It has spread and continues to spread on a large scale. Democratic legality in our country is distorted, and the Leninist principle of collective leadership is not adhered to." Ch'oe Ch'ang-ik explained the reason for his visit to the embassy as a wish to inform the Soviet authorities that "at the next plenum of the Central Committee, Kim Il Song will probably be subjected to sharp criticism."[22]

These visits were followed on the next day, July 24, by a meeting between Kim Sŭng-hwa and counselor Filatov. Kim Sŭng-hwa, then minister of construction, was a Soviet Korean and a close personal friend of Pak Ch'ang-ok's, as well as a victim of the attack against the Soviet Koreans in late 1955. He came to report his recent conversations with Kim Tu-bong, the famous scholar and leader of the Yan'an faction, concerning the political situation in the DPRK and the possible attempt to censure Kim Il Song.[23]

On August 2 yet another member of the Yan'an faction—Minister of Commerce Yun Kong-hŭm, who was to play a major role in the forthcoming events—visited the embassy. Yun also met Filatov and told him in detail about an important meeting that had been organized by the KWP Central Committee on July 30 (discussed below).[24] This was to be the last of these extraordinary visits, which apparently stopped just as suddenly as they had started. No further records of such meetings exist among the declassified documents.

We can assume that the visits of the opposition leaders to the Soviet Embassy during July 21–24 were quite deliberate and indeed constituted an integral part of their strategy. This suggestion is supported by the fact that these meetings took place almost simultaneously and their subject and content were largely the same. It seems highly probable that, in so doing, the conspirators tried to secure Soviet neutrality, if not support, and to avoid the impression that they were doing something behind the Soviets' backs. (The opposition leaders can be called conspirators because their organization was necessarily clandestine or semi-clandestine, although, as we shall see, they hoped to achieve their goals within the framework of existing institutions and by legal means.) Moscow was still perceived as the supreme arbiter of North Korean politics and, more broadly, of the entire Communist movement. Thus we can assume that the conspirators feared that an unexpected and covertly prepared attack against Kim Il Song conducted without prior Soviet approval would set off a negative reaction in Moscow, which in turn could doom the attack to almost certain failure.

This remarkably intense flurry of contacts began the day after Kim Il Song returned from his overseas trip. The timing might indicate that the basic decision to act during the next plenum was approved by the opposition leaders only after they had received some feedback from Kim's trip and probably learned something about his meetings in Moscow as well. As we shall see, until at least July 26 the next plenum had been officially scheduled to take place on August 2. Therefore, the conspirators probably felt pressed for time and wanted to fix everything within the few remaining days—hence the remarkable frequency of their contacts with the embassy.

However, not everyone who met with the Soviet diplomats during those hot July days belonged to the opposition. On July 24, Petrov was invited to speak with Nam Il, the then minister of foreign affairs and a former Soviet college teacher. Though initially a member of the Soviet faction, Nam Il—along with Pak Chŏng-ae and Pang Hak-se, the influential and reclusive chief of the secret police—had very early and decisively gone over to Kim Il Song and become his staunch supporter, rivaling the ex-guerrillas in his consistent devotion. Nevertheless, when the situation in the North Korean ruling circles became more delicate, Nam Il considered it necessary to contact the Soviet Embassy, though it is not clear whether he was soliciting advice or just probing the possible Soviet reaction to the looming crisis. Being the minister of foreign affairs, he did not go to the embassy but instead invited Petrov, the acting ambassador, to his office on July 24.

Nam Il told Petrov that on July 20, the first day of the opposition's feverish activity, Pak Ch'ang-ok had visited Nam Il's home, something he had never done before. Nam Il had just returned from the overseas trip with Kim Il Song, and Pak Ch'ang-ok, perhaps counting on factional solidarity, hoped to draw Nam Il into a conspiracy or, at the very least, to ascertain his position. Pak Ch'ang-ok had told Nam Il that a group of Central Committee members was going to organize a move against Kim Il Song at the next plenum. Kim Il Song would be accused of incorrect leadership methodology, the propagation of a personality

cult, and the persecution of Soviet Koreans. Pak Ch'ang-ok had suggested that Nam Il take part in this action.[25]

Nam Il was extremely hostile to the idea. He remarked to Petrov:
"Such a sharp propounding of the problem of the personality cult in the
Korean context . . . would lead to undesirable consequences; it could
undermine the prestige of the party and government leaders, discredit
Kim Il Song in the eyes of the party masses and the people, and cause
considerable discussion within the party." Echoing Kim Il Song's own
reasoning, Nam Il added that there was no particular need to criticize
Kim Il Song himself, so long as the latter tried to correct his mistakes. As
Nam Il put it: "Although he is a little too sensitive about the comments
of the leaders of the Communist Party of the Soviet Union Central
Committee regarding himself, his attitude in general is quite correct,"
emphasizing that "in spite of all Kim Il Song's shortcomings and mistakes, there is nobody in the DPRK who could replace him." Afterward
Nam Il asked Petrov point-blank if he should report his meeting with
Pak Ch'ang-ok to Kim Il Song. Petrov answered that this, of course, was
a matter for Nam Il himself, but that if a conversation with Kim Il Song
were to take place, it would be better to refrain from mentioning the
names of the participants in the proposed action.[26] It is not clear (and
indeed is doubtful) whether this advice was heeded, nor whether it
could have possibly been heeded.

It is probable that something serious also took place on July 28,
when Petrov met with Nam Il and Pak Chŏng-ae. In his diary, Petrov did
not detail anything of this conversation, merely mentioning that "the
information about the conversation was sent to Moscow by telegraph."
A similar entry, mentioning a new meeting with Nam Il, is found in his
diary for August 1. Because the telegrams have not been declassified, we
can only guess at the purpose of these meetings. However, they almost
certainly were somehow connected with the developing crisis.[27] Later
on, we shall have cause to return to these two still mysterious meetings
with leading pro–Kim Il Song members of the Soviet faction.

Kim Il Song was undoubtedly well aware of the opposition's plans
and did everything possible to engineer their eventual failure. On
August 31, just a few hours after the conclusion of the plenum that had
thwarted those plans, one participant, Ko Hŭi-man, remarked to the

first secretary of the Soviet Embassy, G. Ye. Samsonov: "The intention of this group to use the plenum for antiparty attacks against some executives in the party and government was known before the plenum."[28] Indeed, there is no doubt that the opposition leaders were unable to keep their plans secret and that Kim Il Song had ample information about their schemes. Kang Sang-ho, then deputy minister of the interior, recalled that in the summer of 1956, while Kim Il Song was still overseas, Ch'oe Yong-gŏn had called him in. Ch'oe said that some former members of the ML group, a Marxist-Leninist group that had existed in Seoul in the 1920s and became the foundation for the Yan'an faction, had decided to use Kim Il Song's foreign trip to hatch an antiparty plot and planned to speak against Kim at the next Central Committee plenum. Ch'oe had issued instructions, first of all, that measures for the safety of Kim Il Song be initiated and, second, that Pang Hak-se, the minister of the interior, and Sŏk San, the chief of military security, be summoned urgently from abroad.[29]

The most effective and shrewd of Kim Il Song's countermeasures was undoubtedly the postponement of the plenum. In September 1956, while speaking with a Soviet diplomat in Moscow, Ko Hŭi-man boasted: "Having been informed that the attack would take place at the Central Committee plenum, the leaders of the Central Committee kept delaying the plenum to confuse the [opposition] group. The date of the plenum was announced on the very eve of the first day of the plenum, thus disorganizing their [the opposition members'] actions."[30] This report appears to be true. As late as July 26, Kim Il Song had told Petrov that the plenum would take place on August 2.[31] The same date was also mentioned on July 23.[32] It is probably significant that Kim Il Song lied to the Soviet diplomats. He obviously tried to use the Soviet Embassy to mislead his enemies, and he probably hoped to get some insight into which side the Soviets would support. However, at the last moment, the plenum was postponed, for the reasons explained so well by Ko Hŭi-man above, and it did not take place until late August. This gave Kim Il Song precious time to thwart the opposition's plans. During this critical month, Kim Il Song secured the support of a majority of Central Committee members, while the opposition, kept in the dark until the very last day of August, was forced into passivity. Perhaps the sudden break in contact between the opposition and the embassy reflects this delay, for the opposition had no option but to await developments.

One of Kim Il Song's foremost concerns must have been to reduce the number of potential troublemakers to as few as possible. Not much is known about "individual work" (that is, political bribes and blackmail) used against less reliable members of the Central Committee, though undoubtedly such things occurred. However, information is available about some measures aimed at winning more general support from the party cadres. On July 20, Kim Il Song met a group of high officials—the vice-premiers and deputy chairmen of the KWP—to tell them about his visit to Moscow and other Communist capitals. The next day, the same information was delivered to the KWP Standing Committee. A quite detailed picture of these meetings was reported by Ch'oe Ch'ang-ik to Filatov on July 23. Among other things, Kim Il Song had mentioned the current crisis in Poland. (The Poznan riots of late June had precipitated a mass antigovernment movement that was on the point of erupting.) The Polish crisis had been stimulated, Ch'oe insisted, by three main mistakes of the Polish leaders: "They told people too much about the decisions of the Twentieth Congress [of the Soviet Communist Party] regarding the personality cult," they had not exercised "rigorous leadership," and they had not paid attention to the "dangerous ideological trends" among the intellectuals. According to Ch'oe, Kim Il Song thought that the best leadership style was to be found in Romania and Albania—two countries that had managed to avoid even moderate de-Stalinization and were soon to begin distancing themselves from Moscow.[33] Obviously the message that Kim Il Song wanted to deliver to the North Korean ruling elite was simple: de-Stalinization would probably spell dangerous political instability and might put their collective position in jeopardy. To avoid trouble, great caution should be taken when dealing with "dangerous ideological trends," and the present "rigorous leadership" strategy should be followed.

Kim Il Song did not confine himself to exposing the probable perils of de-Stalinization, however. Not only did he try to terrify the North Korean elite with the dire consequences likely to follow hasty reforms, but, for the more liberal-minded part of his audience, he also did not reject reform outright and signaled that he himself was going to right all wrongs. This had been one of his favorite tactics since at least February, one that was probably employed not only with the North Korean inner circle but also in Moscow with the Soviet leaders as well.[34] On July 30 there was a meeting of the heads and deputy heads of the departments of the KWP Central Committee, as well as some ministers. This meeting is known from the record of Filatov's conversation with Yun Kong-hŭm, which took place two days after the meeting. The speeches at the meeting were delivered by the deputy chairman of the KWP Central Committee, Pak Kŭm-ch'ŏl, and by Pak Chŏng-ae. Both were considered close to Kim Il Song, and therefore their speeches were understood to be an indirect statement by Kim Il Song himself. The two speeches were more or less identical in ideas and structure and were conciliatory, even penitent, in tone.

Pak Kŭm-ch'ŏl recognized that there were "serious shortcomings" in the work of the KWP Central Committee: "First of all, there was and still is a Kim Il Song personality cult within our party. But this has not [presented], nor does it present, the danger that Stalin's personality cult did within the Communist Party of the Soviet Union. Therefore the leaders of the KWP Central Committee decided to overcome the personality cult and its consequences gradually, without submitting the question to wide discussion among the party membership."[35] Pak Kŭm-ch'ŏl also declared that "the KWP Central Committee had committed some mistakes in selection and dismissal of personnel," promising that these errors would eventually be corrected.[36] This was an obvious hint that some cadres who had recently lost their positions would have the chance of being restored and that some others could also hope to get a promotion.

Pak Chŏng-ae spoke much in the same manner. She also reluctantly admitted that the personality cult existed in the DPRK, but she appealed for a calm, discreet solution to the problem: "During the visit of our delegation to Moscow the problem of the personality cult was discussed at the meeting with the leaders of the Communist Party of the Soviet Union. In view of the fact that Kim Il Song's personality cult is not a danger to our party, we decided not to discuss this question too widely, and to overcome step by step all the shortcomings in our work connected with it. However, when Kim Il Song was absent, some prominent party members . . . demanded a full-scale discussion of the problem of the personality cult and spoke of the necessity of struggling to overcome the personality cult within the party. The leaders and the party would not permit any schism that could weaken the party." She added: "The leaders of the Soviet Communist Party will not interfere in the actions of the KWP."[37] Pak Chŏng-ae also promised that the people responsible for the purge of the Soviet Koreans in early 1956 would be punished—an obvious attempt to win the support of the Soviet faction while facing the "Yan'an threat," since everyone knew that the "cadres responsible for the persecution" mainly belonged to the Yan'an faction.

There is little doubt that both speeches were written to a set of guidelines that in all probability had been approved by Kim Il Song himself. The general mode of both speeches was certainly in accordance with Kim Il Song's latest tactic. The speeches again admitted that the accusations (even of the existence of the personality cult in North Korea) might not be completely groundless, but they promised that Kim Il Song himself would gradually put everything right. The obvious goal of this strategy was to quell any discontent and to show the would-be dissenters that there was no necessity for any precipitate action. The conciliatory remarks about the Soviet Koreans would seem to have been equally intentional. After a recent campaign against the Soviet Koreans, Kim Il Song had striven to neutralize discontent among them and thus prevent them from participating in any possible alliance with the opposition. Kim was eventually quite successful with his appeasement strategy, for a month later only a handful of the Soviet Koreans decided to support the challenge of the opposition. At the same time, Kim Il Song, speaking through Pak Chŏng-ae, had made it clear that any direct intervention by the Soviets in support of an opposition push would be unlikely.

As often happens, some indications of the new line can be found in the official press. On August 1, *Nodong sinmun* published a lengthy editorial explaining the recent Soviet ideological developments and newly introduced official concepts: peaceful coexistence, multilinear roads to socialism, collective leadership, and so on. All of these concepts were soon to be anathema to the Pyongyang ideologues, but in the editorial they were presented in quite a favorable light. It is particularly remarkable that special attention was given to the most troublesome part of the new Soviet ideological assemblage—the personality cult. The main message of the editorial was fairly similar to the announcements Kim himself had recently made on his meetings with the top cadres. The difference was in the degree of openness. Because the authors of the newspaper could not be too frank while addressing such a disparate audience, they had to wrap the ideas in a more traditional code, one transparent to an experienced reader. First of all, the editorial writer basically agreed that a personality cult was wrong: "It is clear to everybody that the ideology of a personality cult has nothing to do with Marxism-Leninism." The editorial also hinted that the KWP and Kim Il Song himself were doing everything to fix the problem: immediately following critical remarks about Stalin's personality cult, the editorial quoted at length those parts of Kim's speech to the KWP Third Congress in which he promised to follow the "historic decisions" of the Twentieth Congress. However, the main emphasis of the article was on the attempts of "enemies of the working class" to use the new trends to divide and weaken Communist movements and undermine the great achievements of the socialist countries. The ostensible conclusion was the same as other official pronouncements on the topic: the personality cult might be erroneous, and the struggle against it might make sense, but it must be done in an orderly and controlled manner, lest enemies use it for their own purposes.

5 The "August Group" before August

IT APPEARS THAT, with the help of newly available materials, more definitive answers can be offered to some questions relating to the intraparty opposition in the summer of 1956. Some new questions may also be posed that unfortunately cannot be answered at the present time.

The material available does not provide any information regarding the early history of the conspiracy. However, we can be certain that the opposition existed and was well organized by June 20, when, just after Kim Il Song returned from his trip, the conspirators began to frequent the Soviet Embassy. Yi Sang-jo, for example, in spite of being the ambassador to Moscow, certainly stayed in touch with the opposition and began to criticize Kim Il Song openly in early June.[1] In late June or early July, Kim Sŭng-hwa met Kim Tu-bong to ascertain his position in the event of a possible move against Kim Il Song.[2] Even if in the unlikely event that Yi Sang-jo and Kim Sŭng-hwa had initially acted independently of each other, the opposition must have existed from June at least, for it would have taken its leaders some time to organize themselves to the degree that was obvious by late July. At the same time, it is unlikely that the opposition could have appeared any earlier than 1955, when the accelerating anti-Stalinist campaign in the USSR began to influence North Korean politics. In the final analysis, any attempt to identify a precise date might be unrealistic, given that the development of the opposition was most probably a gradual occurrence. Most members of the opposition belonged to the Yan'an faction; thus the whole plot might have developed gradually in the course of informal but nevertheless influential networking among these former Korean immigrants in China.

After August a great many people—the vast majority of the members of both the Yan'an and the Soviet factions—were either purged or had to leave the country. They were all accused of being proponents of the opposition. In most cases the accusations were barely justified, and the majority of the later purge victims had little to do with the people really responsible for the "August incident." The contemporary (that is, pre-August) embassy materials identify with certainty a half dozen members of the opposition, namely, Ch'oe Ch'ang-ik (vice-premier), Yi P'il-gyu, Yun Kong-hŭm, Sŏ Hwi (chairman of the trade unions), Pak Ch'ang-ok (vice-premier), Kim Sŭng-hwa (minister of construction), and Yi Sang-jo (ambassador to Moscow). They all belonged to the top echelon of the North Korean establishment. In fact, all were full members of the Central Committee except Yi P'il-gyu and Yi Sang-jo, who were candidate members. Undoubtedly this list of conspirators is not complete, but it is possible that among the highest levels of the DPRK leadership—that is, among the Central Committee members—the opposition had few other active supporters. With the sole exception of Kim Sŭng-hwa and Yi Sang-jo (both of whom were overseas in late August), the above-mentioned politicians were the only people to deliver anti-Kim Il Song speeches during the August Plenum.[3]

Later, Pak Ŭi-wan, an outspoken and straightforward Soviet Korean official, was also often listed among the conspirators.[4] However, it is likely that he was included in the list after the fact. His name did not appear in pre-August embassy papers, and it was not until late 1957 that he was accused of being a conspirator. Taking into consideration the remarkable intensity of his contacts with the embassy, it would have been strange had he not contacted the Soviets, if indeed he was a member of the conspiracy. Therefore Pak Ŭi-wan was probably not among the original members of the "August group," although he might have known something about their plans. If that was the case, he would hardly have been unsympathetic toward them, as his earlier contacts with Brezhnev and some conversations with the Soviet diplomats testify.

The recognized leader of the Yan'an faction, Kim Tu-bong, aged and apparently disillusioned with politics, might also not have been a member of the opposition in the strict sense, although he was later purged for being variously a supporter or the secret mastermind of the action. There is contemporary corroborative evidence to show that Kim Tu-bong was at least aware of the existence of the opposition and was probably sympathetic toward its cause. On July 24, Kim Sŭng-hwa told Filatov about his two recent meetings with Kim Tu-bong, when they had lunched together. According to Kim Sŭng-hwa, during these meetings Kim Tu-bong had spoken of the economic difficulties and hardships endured by the people and of the unrestrained extolling of Kim Il Song: "Kim Tu-bong indicated that the Kim Il Song personality cult was widespread in the KWP and that although after the Twentieth Congress of the Soviet Communist Party all Communist parties have been seriously engaged in an attempt to overcome the personality cult and its consequences, nothing has been done in our party so far. . . . [Kim Tu-bong said that] Kim Il Song does not want to rectify his mistakes."[5] Kim Sŭng-hwa asked Kim Tu-bong what his reaction would be if a group of cadres rose up against Kim Il Song at the next plenum of the Central Committee. Kim Tu-bong indicated that he would look favorably on such an undertaking but added that "the current circumstances are so difficult that only a few will make up their minds to speak against Kim Il Song."[6] Kim Tu-bong's prophecy proved correct. Nevertheless, the available records of conversations show Kim Tu-bong to be a sympathizer rather than an active participant in the opposition maneuvers. Such a position was not surprising; Kim Tu-bong's aversion to practical politics had long been an open secret. In May 1956, Pak Kil-yŏng said: "Kim Tu-bong, a wise old man, respected by everybody, prefers to grow flowers in his garden and is not interested in state and party affairs."[7]

Among the members of the group mentioned in the embassy sources, only two were Soviet Koreans—Pak Ch'ang-ok and Kim Sŭng-hwa. Given that most of the Soviet faction tended to discuss all sensitive problems with the Soviet diplomats (a tendency well demonstrated a few months earlier, during the campaign against the Soviet Koreans in late 1955), we can be fairly certain that few, if any, other Soviet Koreans of rank were initial supporters, at least actively, of the opposition.

Even Pak Ch'ang-ok himself was not among the original founders of the "August group." Until the spring of 1956 he had been quite critical of the Yan'an faction and of Ch'oe Ch'ang-ik personally. For example, as recently as March 1956, Pak Ch'ang-ok, while talking with a Soviet diplomat, had accused Ch'oe Ch'ang-ik of bias toward the Soviet Koreans and was openly hostile toward him.[8] The mutual dislike between the Yan'an and the Soviet factions was well known, and Ch'oe Ch'ang-ik was believed to be a staunch enemy of the Soviet Koreans.[9] However, when Kim Il Song launched a campaign against the Soviet Koreans in late 1955, Pak Ch'ang-ok, along with Pak Yŏng-bin, were its primary targets, and it is probable that Pak Ch'ang-ok's support of the opposition's cause was in no small measure fueled by his desire for revenge. It is not incidental that during talks with a Soviet diplomat Pak Ch'ang-ok, rehearsing his future speech at the plenum, concentrated on his own personal and factional grievances. "First of all," he declared, "I'll criticize Kim Il Song for avoiding acknowledging openly that he and his circle created the personality cult. I am also responsible for this, and I am going to speak of it at the Central Committee plenum. I'll dwell on Kim Il Song's incorrect attitude toward the Soviet Koreans. The drive organized by him against the Soviet Koreans, and against myself and Pak Yŏng-bin in particular, did not contribute to strengthening the party ranks. On the contrary, it spread unhealthy sentiments, a lack of mutual confidence, suspicion, and so forth."[10]

The notion that it was mostly the attacks on his person that drew Pak Ch'ang-ok to the opposition seems also to have held currency among Korean officials soon after the "August incident." In February 1957 the then deputy minister of communications, Sin Ch'ong-t'aek, remarked to two Soviet journalists: "Pak Ch'ang-ok had not initially belonged to that group. They recruited him, using the injuries that had been inflicted on him by the leadership."[11] Kim Sŭng-hwa's actions, on the other hand, were probably motivated by a feeling of solidarity with Pak Ch'ang-ok, for Pak was his close personal friend.

The main goals and methods of the opposition emerge fairly clearly from the newly released materials. First of all, the opposition leaders wanted to replace Kim Il Song and his coterie with new leaders, predictably themselves. The opposition members were quite frank about this. On July 14, Yi P'il-gyu said that "the [opposition] group sets itself the task of putting new people in charge of the KWP Central Committee and government."[12] On August 9, Yi Sang-jo, who a couple of months earlier had suggested that the direct intervention of the Soviet leadership might be sufficient to "reform" Kim Il Song, had by now changed his tack and even named likely future leaders following Kim Il Song's fall.[13] One of the leaders Yi mentioned, Ch'oe Ch'ang-ik, was not so forthright during his meetings with a Soviet diplomat and insisted that his main task was to rectify the situation within the party. However, he also hinted that it might eventually be deemed necessary to oust Kim Il Song.[14]

Why did they start all this? What were the main reasons and motives behind their decision to take the extremely dangerous step of joining a conspiracy? These questions are open to speculation and, at least partially, will always remain so; the innermost motives of the people who dared challenge Kim Il Song in 1956 may never be fully understood. Nevertheless, information in the documents available makes possible some reasonably plausible suppositions about the motives of the opposition leaders and participants.

The "August group" were not incorruptible idealists fighting for a noble cause—there was a great deal of factional hatred and power struggle in their motivations. An indication of this is the high incidence of personal assault on politicians from other factions. Though officially the opposition's concern was to get rid of inefficient cadres, there is little doubt that personal political interests were the main reason behind much of the invective. The opposition members vehemently criticized Kim Il Song's coterie—mostly former guerrillas but also those members of the Soviet (e.g., Nam Il and Pak Chŏng-ae), Yan'an (e.g., Kim Ch'ang-man), and Domestic (e.g., Han Sŏl-ya) factions who from early on had allied themselves with Kim Il Song. Lengthy diatribes against these Kim supporters were an integral part of all conversations between the opposition members and the Soviet diplomats. During these meetings the dissenters mentioned (very critically) up to a dozen members of Kim Il Song's inner circle, including Han Sŏl-ya, Kim Ch'ang-man, Kim Il, Yim Hae, Pak Kŭm-ch'ŏl, Han Sang-du, Yi Chong-ok, and Chŏng Chun-t'aek.[15] The Yan'an members also often attacked two Soviet Koreans—Pak Chŏng-ae and Nam Il, although Pak Ch'ang-ok explicitly protected the former from widespread accusations that she once saved her life by collaborating with the Japanese police. It is also worth reiterating that some opposition members initially appeared to consider Ch'oe Yong-gŏn a secret supporter, although later developments proved them wrong.[16] If we consider Kang Sang-ho's remarks about Ch'oe's role in thwarting the opposition plans, and Ch'oe's subsequent political rise to the political heights, we might even speculate that Ch'oe Yong-gŏn deliberately tried to win the trust of the dissenters for the sake of Kim Il Song, either to get more information about the opposition plans or to lure Kim's enemies into committing foolhardy mistakes. (Later, during the plenum, Ch'oe was to be one of the main targets of their attack.) The opposition paid a lot of attention to matters of personnel appointment and dismissal, which no doubt reflected the harsh reality of the permanent factional struggles among the KWP elite.

However, it would be an oversimplification to assume that the opposition consisted merely of position seekers who were anxious to use the new international and domestic situation to remove their political and personal enemies (who, it should be noted, never hesitated to use every opportunity to return the favor). The dissenters obviously had some personal agendas to fulfill. Although they wanted to gain more power, there is reason to believe that the lust for power or revenge was not the only significant motivating factor. They also had the desire to create a more humane, prosperous, and, in a certain sense, more democratic North Korea. They wanted to practice de-Stalinization in North Korea, a desire perfectly in line with the contemporary trend in the rest of the international Communist camp.

The main reason for dissatisfaction was the personality cult, a fact cited by the opposition supporters at virtually every meeting with the Soviet diplomats. Another oft-stated problem was that of "distortions of socialist legality," which, as noted above, in post-Stalinist Soviet political jargon stood for arbitrary arrest, mass execution, and torture. Apart from Kim Il Song's personality cult and "distortions of socialist legality," the opposition figures frequently described the sufferings of the common people as stemming from an overzealous drive for heavy industrialization and the consequent disregard for human life. This subject was raised by Kim Sŭng-hwa during his conversations with Kim Tu-bong, was briefly mentioned by Ch'oe Ch'ang-ik and Yi Sang-jo during their encounters with the Soviet diplomats, and was discussed at length by Yi P'il-gyu. The words of Yi P'il-gyu are worth quoting at length because they show how a well-informed official viewed the general situation in the DPRK: "Farmers compose 80 percent of the population of [North] Korea. After Liberation they were offered an excellent opportunity for a better life; however, they remain very poor. The government has been following an incorrect taxation policy. During the past ten years, instead of 23–27 percent tax, they have been taking more than 50 percent from the farmers. Such a policy continues to this day. It is not necessary to recount the methods employed in 1954–1955 to gather taxes. Tax collecting was accompanied by beatings, murders, and arrests. The party's activities are based on violence, not persuasion. The cooperative movement is based on violence. The workers live poorly; [they] do not have enough grain or soybeans. The intellectuals and students live in difficult conditions."[17]

Such worries were fairly common among the opposition members. In May 1957, Pak Kil-yŏng, the Korean ambassador to East Germany, told a Soviet diplomat: "The country's economic situation remains exceptionally difficult. Nearly half of the population has no food, clothing, or footwear. . . . Korean people are very stoic and are used to hardships, but this cannot last forever. It is time to do something to improve the people's situation." Pak Kil-yŏng, himself a Soviet Korean, was not a member of the opposition in any sense, but these remarks indicate that a substantial number of North Korean officials were uneasy about the desperate economic conditions of the country's population.[18] The revolution was expected to improve the lot of the common people, and since this was not happening, its lifelong supporters had reason to worry.

These statements echoed a discussion of North Korean industrial policy that took place in 1954–1955 and was studied by Masao Okonogi.[19] At that time, Pak Ch'ang-ok insisted on paying more attention to light industry and improving living standards, although this line was eventually rejected by Kim Il Song. During his meeting with a Soviet diplomat, Pak Ch'ang-ok returned to this question, observing that the North Korean leadership was indifferent to the hardships of the common people.[20] As we have seen, Pak Ch'ang-ok expressed a commonly held view of the Korean cadres, many of whom were skeptical about Kim Il Song's policy of heavy industrialization at all costs. The rationale behind Kim's decision to industrialize is fairly clear: the forceful development of heavy industry meant both a reduction in the DPRK's economic dependency on the USSR and China and, more significantly, an increase in the potential military capabilities of the North Korean government. The significant reduction in the amount of Soviet aid in the mid-1950s also encouraged this approach, as the Soviet Union began to appear to be a less generous and reliable sponsor. This line was supported by the common wisdom of Stalinist (and Leninist) ideology, which unequivocally equated classical, iron-and-coal heavy industry with progress and development. However, not everybody was happy to support this "guns, not butter" policy, especially given that the wounds inflicted on the suffering population by a headlong rush to industrialization were visible everywhere.

There is no reason to believe that the opposition had ever planned to challenge the Leninist conception of state socialism and its basic principles, such as the one-party system. Their own background as lifelong Communist cadres in the harsh environment of Mao's "liberated areas" or in Stalin's Soviet Union, as well as the general situation in and around Korea, would have precluded this. All assertions to the contrary, which were later spread by the official North Korea propaganda machine, can be rejected as groundless and deliberate falsifications. The August conspirators were by no means "counterrevolutionaries"—or, as they might be styled in our post-Communist times, "democracy fighters"—and it would be ahistorical to expect them to be "closet anti-Communists" or "closet democrats" of any kind.[21] In all their conversations with the Soviet diplomats, the conspirators criticized policies but not strategic principles. They did not question Leninist state socialism but intended to improve it, along the lines of what was being done in the USSR and some of the more liberal "people's democracies," to make it more viable and compassionate, more sensitive to the needs of ordinary people.

Whatever one may think of the applicability or otherwise of such terms as "democracy" or even "legality" to political institutions in a Stalinist state, it is worth emphasizing that the opposition intended to act within the institutional framework of the party's statutes and declared political rules. It might be said they planned to achieve their goals through legal means, though these means were not exactly "democratic" (nor could they be, since the North Korean state was not "democratic" in any sense either). The dissenters wanted to criticize Kim Il Song during the forthcoming plenum and hoped they would win over a majority of Central Committee members to their side. According to paragraph 36 of the party statutes, adopted in 1956, the party chairman was technically elected by the Central Committee, and therefore the Central Committee also had a right to reelect him. This was hardly a democratic procedure, given that the Central Committee was a tiny, secretive, and basically self-appointed body of oligarchs. However, it was a strictly legal procedure.

Kim Il Song later insisted that his enemies intended to replace him by force, if necessary. Suh Dae-sook in his well-known study came to the conclusion that this accusation was implausible, because by 1956 the Guerrilla faction was firmly in control of the military and "any serious military move by any group other than the partisans would have been suicidal at that time."[22] I can only agree with this conclusion and add that in the embassy papers there is no mention of any such plans. With the exception of some remarks by Yi P'il-gyu, who indeed hinted at the possibility of a "forcible upheaval," all other opposition members spoke of peaceful and legal means of achieving their goals. The informants of "Lim Ŭn" (a pseudonym of Hŏ Chin) also remarked that it would have been better had they decided to use military force against Kim in 1956. "Lim Ŭn," though not without some regret, stated that the opposition did not contemplate any military actions, although he (or his informants) obviously considered it feasible.[23] However, these remarks were made in the late 1970s and more than likely constitute belated wishful thinking. Suh Dae-sook is obviously correct: even if the Yan'an faction had at some time in the past had sufficient influence in the military, this was certainly not the case in 1956. Suh's opinion appears even more plausible if we take into consideration that no such accusations appeared during the initial stage of the purges, in the months immediately following the plenum. A year went by before the opposition was accused of plotting a mutiny; the first such accusations were aired in December 1957. The accusations were made public during the First KWP Conference in March 1958, but they were never really substantiated.

It is not clear whom the opposition would have liked to see as the new North Korean leader in place of Kim Il Song. No names were mentioned during the meetings with the Soviet diplomats. However, rumors circulating after the crisis (that is, in late 1956 and 1957) insisted that the opposition fancied Ch'oe Ch'ang-ik as the new party chairman and Pak Ch'ang-ok as the new premier.[24] These choices would seem to be reasonable enough, especially since Pak had already been a vice-premier, and Ch'oe, by virtue of being the opposition leader, would have been an ideal candidate for the highest position in the party. The only contemporary information (that is, information preceding the August affair) about the opposition plans in this respect is a remark by Yi Sang-jo, the North Korean ambassador to Moscow.

Yi seems to have been in close contact with the opposition members and later that year, after their failure, defected to the Soviet Union. On August 9, while briefing a high-ranking Soviet diplomat about the ongoing preparations for an attack on Kim Il Song's policies, Yi Sang-jo asserted that the opposition would like to appoint Ch'oe Ch'ang-ik as the new party chairman and Ch'oe Yong-gŏn, at that time mistakenly perceived as a sympathizer, as commander in chief of the North Korean armed forces. No other names were mentioned.[25] At a new plenum a year later, Ko Pong-gi, an official accused of collaboration with the opposition and made to deliver a repentance, argued that the opposition wanted to appoint the disgraced Yan'an leader Pak Il-u as the new chairman of the party, while Ch'oe Ch'ang-ik, Pak Ch'ang-ok, and Kim Sŭng-hwa were to be his deputies.[26] However, this latter statement was delivered well after the opposition had lost its bid, and the text was obviously written by the authorities as part of a deliberate propaganda campaign; hence it is unreliable. We must remember, though, that, like any propaganda, it might well contain a grain of truth—if it were considered beneficial to the authorities. The same statements are found in a testimony given by Pak Ch'ang-ok in 1959, during a secret investigation of the "August affair." According to his statement (a copy of which was shown to a Soviet diplomat by the North Korean minister of the interior), Ch'oe Ch'ang-ik was to be made the new party secretary, and Pak Ch'ang-ok himself was to be appointed the new premier.[27] This statement resembles the remarks of Yi Sang-jo and therefore, despite its being obviously forced, might be accurate.

Thus it appears quite plausible that Ch'oe Ch'ang-ik was viewed as the future leader of North Korea in opposition circles. It is noteworthy that the conspirators did not mention Ch'oe's name or any other names to the Soviet diplomats, for they had apparently decided to keep silent on this important question. Yi Sang-jo's assertions do not really count here; he was in Moscow and could have been unaware of some of the tactical decisions made by the opposition in Pyongyang (for example, the possible decision not to mention names while talking to Soviet diplomats). We can speculate that the conspirators remained silent either because they did not want to alienate the Soviets by suggesting an obviously pro-Chinese candidate or because they did not want to look like a power-hungry group of office seekers who had already distributed the political spoils among themselves.

How did Moscow and the Soviet Embassy react to the situation? This is a question of great significance, but it is essential to remember that as long as such important materials as the telegraphic exchanges between Moscow and the embassy in Pyongyang remain classified, as well as the majority of the Soviet party documents, the answer to this question will be necessarily speculative and inconclusive. From the embassy papers currently available, the Soviet reaction seems to have been cautious, even reluctant. It appears as if the Soviet diplomats neither tried to talk the discontented figures out of their proposed action nor expressed direct support for them, although the diplomats frequently urged the opposition members to be "cautious."

Such neutrality is understandable. By 1956, Kim Il Song was no longer the direct protégé or even puppet of Moscow that he had been in 1945 or 1949, and consequently the Soviet diplomats were no longer willing to display a determination to defend him against all domestic challenges. Nor were the Soviets in principle opposed to leadership changes. After all, 1956 was a time of great change in both the politics and the ruling circles of many socialist countries, resulting in the dismissal of a significant number of Communist leaders: Chervenkov in Bulgaria (April), Rakosi in Hungary (July), and Ochab in Poland (October, although this case was somewhat different because Ochab was not a Stalinist but a reformer, albeit less radical than his successor, Gomulka). Most of these changes were encouraged, or at least approved, by

Moscow. Everywhere in the Communist world "little Stalins" who had established their cults in line with the old Soviet pattern were becoming an endangered species, and few people doubted that Kim Il Song belonged to this group. The ideas of the Twentieth Congress and its various interpretations—exploited and supported sometimes by blatant opportunists, sometimes by national Communists, and sometimes by surviving Marxist idealists—were spreading from Prague to Pyongyang. The actions against Kim Il Song did not seem at all extraordinary; on the contrary, they fitted perfectly well into the general pattern of events in the Communist camp over the turbulent summer of 1956. If the Soviets did not object to the replacement of Chervenkov or Rakosi, why should they object to the removal of Kim Il Song?

On the other hand, the political stability of the DPRK could not but be of concern to the Soviet diplomats. Replacing Kim Il Song with somebody who might have more support within the KWP, though politically feasible and even desirable, would be tolerable only as long as such actions did not jeopardize the stability of this easternmost Communist citadel. For the Soviets the DPRK formed a kind of protective buffer between the American troops stationed in South Korea and the vital industrial regions of Chinese Manchuria and the Soviet Far East. Therefore, irrespective of their attitude to Kim Il Song, the Soviet diplomats had to be cautious, and many conversations ended in much the same manner as the discussion between Filatov and Pak Ch'ang-ok on July 21. This is how Filatov himself described the conversation in his report: "At the end of our conversation I once more called Pak Ch'ang-ok's attention to the gravity of the situation that had arisen and warned him against hasty decisions. I asked him to study attentively the situation in the party and not to permit his actions to be used by those who were dissatisfied with Kim Il Song's policy."[28] The same attitude was shown by Petrov during his meeting with Nam Il on July 24: "I stated my personal opinion that Nam Il's troubles over the sharp criticism of Kim Il Song deserved a great deal of attention and that Pak Ch'ang-ok's position on this question was evidently incorrect. I said that the initiative of sharp criticism of Kim Il Song by Soviet Koreans might be misinterpreted and this could cause undesirable repercussions both within the country and abroad."[29]

Some people, however, believed that the Soviet diplomats might have taken sides with Kim Il Song. Such a view was quite widespread in Pyongyang political circles soon after 1956. For example, Hŏ Chin (writing as "Lim Ŭn") in his pioneering study of North Korean history, stated: "One of the causes [of the opposition's eventual failure] was that the councillor of the Soviet Embassy breached the faith. When he spoke to Ch'oe Ch'ang-ik, the councillor took an affirmative attitude, but he later made a formal report to the Ministry of Foreign Affairs in North Korea regarding their talks. This might have been cautious behavior by a diplomat, but it constituted a dishonorable breach of faith from the standpoint of a politician and a revolutionary."[30] Hŏ Chin (also known as Hŏ Un-bae) subsequently wrote that Kim Il Song, having learned about the opposition's schemes, rushed back home to prepare a political counteroffensive. Hŏ Chin, himself a North Korean student in Moscow during the incident, wrote his book in the 1970s, on the basis of secret interviews with many North Korean exiles in Russia (notably Yi Sang-jo), and the book largely reflects their opinions and data. They might have been mistaken, but Hŏ Chin's inclusion of this information in his book indicates that it was widely believed by the exiles in the Soviet Union in the 1970s. Similar accounts can be found in many publications on North Korean history. This story probably originated with the South Korean government and intelligence sources, since they often mentioned it from the late 1960s onward (perhaps reflecting the rumors common among North Korean officialdom).

Basically, the story consists of two elements: (1) Kim Il Song learned about the conspiracy from the Soviets while he was overseas and then rushed back home to do something about it; and (2) the information about the conspiracy was provided to Kim Il Song or his supporters by a Soviet diplomat in Pyongyang (Hŏ Chin mentions "a councillor") via the North Korean Ministry of Foreign Affairs. The first element of this account must be rejected. The embassy papers give no indication of any unusual activity during Kim Il Song's overseas trip. The situation began to develop only after he had returned. Even though it is still possible to argue that information could have been obtained earlier by the Soviets through other channels (the KGB, for example) and then sent to Moscow by telegraph (and again there is no hint of such a thing in the declassified papers), a rather persuasive commonsense counterargument has already been suggested by Suh Dae-sook. Suh's argument is that Kim Il Song stopped off in Mongolia for three days during his return trip. Mongolia was not exactly a country of the greatest strategic and economic importance to Korea. Had Kim really been rushing home, such a prolonged stay in such a politically irrelevant city as Ulan Bator would have been out of the question.[31]

The second element—the betrayal of the opposition by the Soviet diplomats—deserves more attention. If we take this information at its face value, who could the "councillor" mentioned by Hŏ Chin's informants be? From the embassy papers, we now know that Ch'oe Ch'ang-ik indeed visited the embassy on July 23 and that he met with counselor Filatov. This occurred after Kim Il Song had returned home, so the information received from the Soviet diplomat could not have facilitated Kim's return, as has already been noted. However, it is not known whether Filatov or any other Soviet diplomat reported the affair to the North Korean authorities. On the one hand, Filatov, as his former colleagues recalled, had the reputation of being a very cautious person. He was a career party functionary with Stalin-era experiences and afraid of any unusual or risky action. Furthermore, none of the available documents mentions Filatov's meetings with anybody in the North Korean Ministry of Foreign Affairs during the pivotal days of late July. But the information could have been forwarded by someone else—for example, by Petrov during his meetings with Nam Il and Pak Chŏng-ae, which are mentioned, but not described, in the declassified papers. In any event, it is certain that rumors rightly or wrongly blaming Soviet double-dealing for the failure of the opposition were widespread among the North Korean party elite.

However, there is reason to be suspicious of these accusations. Irrespective of their veracity, Kim Il Song himself later had good reason to spread such rumors. By insisting on alleged Soviet backing, Kim Il Song showed the potential dissenters that they could expect nothing from their efforts, because without Soviet support all challenges to Kim's power would be doomed. Thus, whether the Soviets really provided him with information or not, Kim Il Song had a vested interest in insisting that they did. And this was Kim's strategy. In September 1956, Ko

Hŭi-man met a Soviet Foreign Ministry official, S. P. Lazarev, in Moscow. They talked about the recent August Plenum, and during the meeting Ko Hŭi-man indicated that records of the conversations at the Soviet Embassy, which ostensibly had been received by the North Korean leaders from the Soviet Central Committee, had been shown to the members of the opposition group. However, Lazarev did not take him at his word and considered it necessary to make the following remark: "Of special interest is the fact that Yi Sang-jo [the then Korean ambassador to Moscow] informed the Communist Party of the Soviet Union of a statement [made] by some executives of the KWP Central Committee at the last plenum. This statement noted that the CPSU Central Committee had not ostensibly recommended that the current situation in the DPRK be spoken of in a critical manner. Ko Hŭi-man's statement confirms that the reference to the 'instructions' [Lazarev's own ironic quotation marks] of the [Soviet] Central Committee situation was probably used at the plenum."[32] Thus Lazarev in September 1956 did not believe this version of events (which was to appear much later in Hŏ Chin's book) and even considered it necessary to attract the attention of his superiors to such statements. Of course, it is possible that Lazarev—who even in dry official papers did not conceal his apparent sympathy toward the "August group," as well as his malevolence toward Ko Hŭi-man and his "reciting of memorized speeches"—might have been unaware of the actions of other diplomats or top political leaders.

In addition, the visit of Anastas I. Mikoyan to Korea in September would be more difficult to interpret if Soviet diplomacy had sided decisively with Kim Il Song against his opponents, for the main task of the Mikoyan trip was to make Kim Il Song rehabilitate the participants of the opposition action. It is also worth remembering that Petrov had explicitly recommended that Nam Il not reveal the names of the conspirators to Kim Il Song.[33]

In December 1957, while making a secret speech to a new plenum of the Central Committee, Kim Il Song specifically dwelled on the Soviet attitude toward the opposition: "Certain people wanted to use the authority of the Soviet Communist Party against us. Nevertheless the [Soviet] Central Committee believed in us, rather than in certain other persons. The splittists wanted to use certain officials in the Soviet

Embassy against us. However, the embassy officials revealed all to us when we sent Nam Il and Pak Chŏng-ae there. . . . At the same time, when Comrade Mikoyan came [in September, to press Kim Il Song into a decision to stop the purges against the opposition], we told him that at the embassy there were some undesirable elements, and they were re-called [to the Soviet Union]."[34] The records of the conversations be-tween Nam Il and Petrov contain no indications that Petrov "revealed all." However, at least two other meetings took place at which these matters might have been discussed. At the same time, Kim Il Song could have been bluffing in both August 1956 and September 1957, trying to strengthen his position by hinting at Soviet support of himself. After all, claims of alleged Soviet support still mattered significantly at this time. And, finally, with respect to Kim's remarks on "undesirable elements" in the embassy, the only persons of importance who had left the Soviet Embassy between August 1956 and June 1957 were Petrov and Filatov— that is, the only two Soviet diplomats who had direct contacts with the conspirators in July and early August. If Kim Il Song's declaration was not entirely a bluff, then it would appear that these diplomats had sup-ported the opposition rather than betrayed it.

Hence, we can neither confirm nor disregard the widespread view that the Soviet Embassy played a crucial role in thwarting the opposi-tion plans. A definitive answer to this question will not be possible until researchers gain access to all the relevant materials—something that is not likely to happen in the foreseeable future.

In this regard we must return to the above-mentioned mysterious incident, which is probably related to still unknown intrigues and clashes within the Soviet bureaucracy. As mentioned above, the impor-tant meeting between Petrov and Yi P'il-gyu—the first contact between the conspirators and Soviet officials—took place on July 14. However, for some unknown reason Petrov deliberately misdated his record of the conversation, which, according to the standard procedure, was sent to Moscow. This document was dated July 20, six days after the actual con-versation. In addition, Petrov edited the original in a way that significantly distorted Yi's statements (at least, as they had been reported in the earlier version). As a result of these changes, Yi's position came to appear less radical. Another probable goal of the considerable "editing" (if such a term is not too mild) was to create the impression that Yi had mentioned some kind of organized resistance to Kim Il Song's domination. This fabrication was, however, soon discovered—how it was discovered is unknown, but presumably some internal intrigues within the embassy were responsible. On September 28 the Soviet ambassador, V. Ivanov, dispatched the original handwritten draft to Deputy Foreign Minister N. T. Fedorenko. In an attached short memo, Ivanov attracted his superior's attention to the fact that the handwritten notes were initially dated July 14, not July 20, and only later had Petrov "corrected" the date. Ivanov also informed his superiors that this earlier date had been confirmed by Kim Chu-bong, an ethnic Korean Soviet diplomat who had been interpreting the Yi-Petrov conversation.[35] This was a very severe breach of protocol and discipline, and the likely result was the recall of Petrov, whose name is not to be found in the embassy papers from late 1956 onward. This baffling incident undoubtedly reflects some contradiction within Soviet officialdom, but at this stage we can only surmise the motives of its participants.

There is a great temptation to look for a political motivation behind this unusual event. For example, we may note that in the typed text Petrov consistently played down Yi P'il-gyu's frequent remarks on the necessity of "upheaval" in the DPRK (Petrov omitted Yi's remarks about "underground action" and the probable support of such activities by "revolutionary elements" and the Chinese People's Volunteers).[36] This omission may be seen as an indication of Petrov's attempts to present the conspirators as a lesser threat to North Korean political stability and thus can be seen as an expression of his hidden sympathy for the conspiracy. At the same time, it is known from a Hungarian source that even before the meeting with Yi P'il-gyu, Petrov had expressed his dissatisfaction with the current state of things. A Hungarian document, compiled in early 1956, stated: "Though the armistice had been concluded almost three years ago, the wartime work style remained substantially characteristic of political and economic life. How did this manifest itself? Primarily in the excessive cult of the individual, and in one-man leadership, and the consequences that flowed from this. According to the opinion of Comrade Petrov from the Soviet Embassy, the excessive cult of the individual was explainable and acceptable to a certain extent during the war, but now it becomes more and more an obstacle to development. As a consequence, there are sycophants around the highest leadership who accept everything uncritically and do not dare to oppose [the leadership]. No appropriate atmosphere of criticism and self-criticism has developed, and only the positive developments are reported for the higher leadership."[37] These remarks by Petrov sound suspiciously similar to his records of the meeting with Yi. Either Petrov had been exposed to the same opinions earlier, or to some extent he worded Yi's statements in accordance with his own perception of the DPRK situation. In any event, the Hungarian document makes it clear that Petrov had been sympathetic to the opposition cause.

However, taking into consideration the situation at the Soviet Embassy at the time, a different explanation may be offered—one that has much more to do with the individual career concerns of Petrov than with his ideological sympathies, although the Hungarian document cited above confirms that Petrov did have such sympathies. It is possible that Petrov did not want to commit the customary record of conversation to paper because he was afraid of probable complications for himself. Yi's verbal attacks on Kim Il Song were sharp indeed, and documenting such explosive comments would be dangerous for Petrov. In the uncertain atmosphere of the summer of 1956 he could be blamed, for example, for not rebutting Yi or, on the other hand, for not providing him with support. In any event, the uncommon nature of the talk demanded extraordinary measures—and these measures were by definition risky. Hence it is probable that Petrov decided to await further developments, possibly hoping that a further clarification of the situation would emerge. After all, if the handwritten notes are to be believed, Yi did not mention the existence of any organized opposition to Kim Il Song on July 14, so Yi's words could be plausibly perceived as the opinion of just one dissenting individual, outraged and perhaps politically insignificant. Hence, Petrov had some rationale for taking a wait-and-see approach. When a week later the situation began to unfold and its possible implications became evident, Petrov finally decided to compile the document but misdated it to cover up his initial reluctance to draft it; inserted into the text a few remarks about some organized anti-Kim opposition, which by then had been known to exist and be active; and watered down some of Yi's sharper remarks. Personally, I prefer a combination of career worries and political sympathies as the most likely explanation for Petrov's action, but in general this entire incident still remains somewhat mysterious.

Hence, at this stage we cannot be certain about the Soviet attitude toward the "August conspiracy." An even more important and equally unclear question is the role of China in the affair. Unfortunately in this case too the lack of relevant materials is the greatest obstacle to any research. It will probably be at least decades before the corresponding materials from the archives in Beijing will be made accessible to scholars, so only a cursory and tentative answer to the question can be attempted at the present time.

It looks highly probable that the August opposition received some support from the Chinese Embassy even prior to the August Plenum itself. Actually, it is possible that the entire affair was instigated by the Chinese. The core of the opposition consisted of the Yan'an faction, which always maintained close connections with the Chinese Embassy. After the failure of the opposition attempt, the more fortunate of the unsuccessful conspirators fled to China, where they had no difficulties in securing asylum. There is little doubt that even if the Chinese leaders were not the immediate initiators of anti-Kim action, they were nevertheless aware of it well in advance. If members of the opposition (Ch'oe Ch'ang-ik, Yi P'il-gyu, Yun Kong-hŭm, and others) considered it appropriate to inform the Soviet Embassy about their plans, then there is no reason to doubt that they had also met with Chinese diplomats, especially considering that their relations with China were much closer. Kang Sang-ho, who at that time was the deputy minister of the interior and hence had reliable sources of information, told me that there was a secret connection between the conspirators and the Chinese Embassy.[38] It would even appear highly probable that the whole strategy was formulated after initial suggestions from Beijing or, at the very least, that Beijing's approval was conveyed to the opposition. Had China not approved of the opposition plans, it would have had ample opportunity to prevent the actions of the group. Under the circumstances of the period, approval from Beijing would have been a necessary precondition for any action.

What might have caused the Chinese leadership to harbor such ill feeling toward Kim Il Song? The deep and mutual dislike between Kim Il Song and the Chinese wartime commander in Korea, Peng Dehuai, was no secret. Furthermore, the recent purge of Pak Il-u, who had been Mao's personal protégé, hardly endeared Kim Il Song to Beijing. In addition, Kim Il Song's disregard of Mao's instructions during the Korean War had not been forgotten by Mao. In August 1956, Yi Sang-jo had evoked this fact in Moscow as a sign of Kim Il Song's tendency to ignore the "wise suggestions of fraternal parties."[39] This disregard, in turn, reflected hidden tensions between the North Korean and Chinese agendas: although the Chinese forces saved the DPRK from certain annihilation and restored the line mostly along the 38th parallel, Beijing was not going to sacrifice lives and resources to achieve Kim's "domestic" goals. Nevertheless, these factors would hardly be sufficient to instigate such a drastic measure as the forced removal of Kim Il Song.

However, there might be an additional reason—the still hidden but steady deterioration of relations between Beijing and Moscow. In 1955–1956 the Chinese leaders undertook some actions directed at undermining the Soviet domination of the Communist camp, and the North Korean affair might have been just another link in this chain of events that eventually led to the dramatic Sino-Soviet rift of the 1960s and 1970s.

Some possible clues for interpreting Chinese behavior before the "August incident" in the DPRK can be found if we take into consideration the almost simultaneous developments in Poland. In 1956, Poland witnessed a dramatic confrontation between the reformers (led by Gomulka) and the Stalinist conservatives. The programs and goals of the Polish reformers were similar to those of their North Korean counterparts: they sought to remove the vestiges of Stalinism and to make Polish society less repressive and more prosperous, while remaining firmly within the established framework of a Leninist social and political structure. The reformers' actions seriously alarmed Moscow, not the least because the movement's ideology had a palpable nationalistic bent, which in Poland, the traditional enemy of Russia, could not help but be essentially anti-Soviet. The reformers, indeed, were widely supported by the population, and the mass slogans were occasionally quite radical and openly hostile to Moscow. From the Kremlin's point of view, the situation seemingly warranted a large-scale Soviet military intervention, and in mid-October Moscow began to prepare the Soviet troops in Poland for possible action. This action did not eventuate, because the reformers not only enjoyed near universal and active popular support but also managed to negotiate an agreement with their opponents. The Polish conservatives, who were also moderate by the Stalinist standards, did not want bloodshed and were not willing to pay a huge price in human lives for clinging to power. The result was a negotiated compromise and the subsequent establishment of a reformist Communist government in Poland. Given that the new Polish leaders promised to remain good Soviet allies and to keep the popular anti-Soviet feelings at bay, Moscow reluctantly confirmed the promotion of Gomulka. However, in mid-October Soviet intervention looked very likely, the necessary preparations were well under way, and Beijing, as Moscow's major ally, was informed of these plans.

In this situation Mao saw a good opportunity to demonstrate to the world his ability to act as the champion and protector of smaller countries and minor Communist parties. Thus the Chinese took a remarkably harsh stance. They expressed their deep concern about the Soviet interventionist plans and stressed that the Polish people and the Polish party would have to be allowed to sort out their problems themselves. A special meeting of the Chinese Politburo, convened to discuss the possibility of Soviet military action in Poland, condemned such an action as an unjustified intervention in Polish internal affairs. On October 23, the day after the politburo meeting, Mao summoned the Soviet ambassador and asked him to urgently inform Moscow that China would protest any Soviet military action in Poland.[40] Under the circumstances, this support was decisive to the Polish anti-Stalinists. On a somewhat less official level, the Chinese—not completely without reason—blamed Soviet "Great Power chauvinism" for the entire Polish crisis and took care to make this opinion known in both Moscow and Warsaw. Obviously, in this particular case Mao was striving to present himself as a champion of national autonomy against the Soviet pressure—a theme that was widely employed by the Chinese propaganda machine in the 1960s. This stance contributed to the final decision of Moscow to refrain from violent military action in Poland.

All this may appear logical enough, but hindsight shows that semi-democratic reform and the promotion of de-Stalinization were not high on Mao's agenda. His real goal was to establish himself as a new leader of the Communist movement. As authors Chen Jian and Yang Kuisong noted: "[B]y late 1956, China's relations with the Soviet Union experienced a significant change: although in public Mao continued to maintain that Moscow remained the center of the socialist camp, he really believed that it was he who was more qualified to dictate the principles underlying relations between and among socialist countries."[41] Whenever necessary, China would support de-Stalinization (as was the case with Poland), while elsewhere it would endorse quite conservative, Stalinist actions. A good example of the latter approach occurred regarding Hungary, where an anti-Communist revolution was crushed by Soviet troops with the full support and encouragement of Mao.

This understanding offers some clues for explaining the Chinese support of the North Korean reformers in the summer of 1956. As the Polish example indicates, the anti-Stalinist stance of a particular group within the leadership of a Communist country did not necessarily rule out Chinese support, if Beijing believed that the group's eventual victory would be conducive to its main goal—asserting its own leadership in the world Communist movement. In such circumstances it would not be surprising if in 1956 Mao considered replacing Kim Il Song. After all, Kim was a former Red Army officer whose rise to power was once engineered by the Soviet military. Hence he might have been perceived as too pro-Soviet, whereas his enemies were predominantly politicians with lifelong connections to China. From Mao's point of view it made sense to replace Kim with Ch'oe Ch'ang-ik or some other member of the Yan'an faction who would be more sympathetic to Beijing and less connected to and dependent on Moscow (a good asset in case of a major breakdown with this tiresome "elder brother"). It would not really matter that this replacement would be done under slogans of de-Stalinization and pro-liberalization. In this particular case the Soviet ideas about the eradication of the personality cult created a convenient ideological justification for the entire affair, which was ultimately directed against Moscow and its dominion over world Communism.

At that stage, however, even those reformist slogans and ideas were not yet anathema to the Chinese leaders. In the summer of 1956, China was passing through what was perhaps the most liberal stage of Mao's entire rule. As mentioned above, in May 1956 the Hundred Flowers campaign began. The campaign lasted for only about a year, but it was the closest that Mao ever came to tolerating any kind of political dialogue. Like Khrushchev's "Secret Speech," this campaign, which was certainly well known among the former Yan'an exiles, formed a background to the entire August crisis in the DPRK. Therefore in the summer and autumn of 1956 the Chinese Communist leadership was probably not against the radical reform that the Korean opposition was suggesting —indeed, it was probably even ready to support the reformers, if this was advantageous to China's own agenda. Whatever the reasons, Beijing in 1956 could rival and even occasionally surpass Moscow in its willingness to embrace the reforms and change of leaders.

To a large extent, all of this is guesswork. The Chinese position, the reasons that China permitted or perhaps even encouraged the North Korean opposition, remains an open question—and an important one. We can only hope that future studies by Chinese or foreign historians will throw more light on it.

Kim Il Song *(left)* and Soviet General Ivan Chistiakov *(right)*, 1947.

Pyongyang Street, March 1950—three months before the start of the Korean War.

Street scene during U.S. air raid, Pyongyang, October 1950.

A bus stop in Pyongyang, January 1954.

Display of sacral images during a mass rally in Pyongyang to commemorate the tenth anniversary of Korea's Liberation, August 15, 1955.

The face of the enemy: anti-American posters, 1956.

Postwar reconstruction: the building of Kim Ch'aek Technological College *(right)*, Pyongyang, 1956.

The old and the new: downtown Pyongyang, 1956.

Anti-American rally in Pyongyang, 1957.

Stalin Street, Pyongyang, 1958. In defiance of Moscow, the name of this street was kept for the next two decades.

6 The August Plenum

AFTER ALMOST A MONTH of delays, the plenum opened on August 30 and continued for two days. On the official agenda were two items: the results of Kim Il Song's recent visit to the USSR and Eastern Europe, and the situation of the national health service. However, on this occasion as on many others, the official agenda was quite misleading. These two items, especially the second one, were of minor importance in comparison with the main event at the plenum: an opposition assault on Kim Il Song. The opposition mounted its attack and was immediately defeated—everything was over within just a few hours.

The August Plenum has been described, at least briefly, in most books dealing with North Korean history. The data provided by North Korean official publications are remarkably nebulous. In 1957–1959 the North Korean press produced a barrage of publications on the alleged conspiracy by Ch'oe Ch'ang-ik, Pak Ch'ang-ok, and their "henchmen," who were accused of a great—and ever increasing—variety of crimes and, eventually, of high treason. Nevertheless, these statements do not provide much factual information about the August confrontation. Instead they contain a standard set of high-pitched but vague accusations against the "counterrevolutionary, factionalist elements" and their "treachery."[1] From these publications it is impossible to learn what actually happened during the August Plenum, what "the splittist attack that the factionalists undertook" really means.

The plenum is also mentioned in a number of research works on

121

North Korean history. Among the more well-known examples are an early study by Koon Woo Nam, Suh Dae-sook's classical political biography of Kim Il Song, and the more recently published general reviews of North Korean history by Kim Hak-jun and Ch'oe Sŏng,[2] as well as earlier South Korean official and quasi-official publications, dating back to the late 1960s (though the latter are for the most part, as Suh Dae-sook pointed out, "highly unreliable").[3] The main source for these works was information obtained from defectors who in turn relied on everything from rumors to the party's classified periodicals. There is also a brief description of the plenum (just one paragraph) in Hŏ Chin's book.[4] This description is based primarily on testimonies of North Korean exiles in the Soviet Union, collected by Hŏ in the late 1970s. Fortunately, some original and reliable, albeit brief, contemporary documents are now available, as well as the manuscript of Kang Sang-ho's memoirs and records of interviews with him. These new materials shed some additional light on what happened on August 30, 1956, in the North Korean capital, although many questions remain that can be answered only when additional materials are declassified.

At that time, Soviet officials perceived the particular sensitivity of the situation, so most of the important Soviet materials relating to the plenum were classified as highly secret and remain so to this day. Hence most official contemporary Soviet accounts of the August Plenum are inaccessible. There is little doubt that such materials were once compiled by the Soviet Embassy, but they are beyond reach at the time of this writing and are likely to remain so in the foreseeable future. However, among the declassified documents is one extremely interesting account—an official record of a conversation between Ko Hŭi-man and G. Ye. Samsonov that took place on August 31, the last day of the plenum. Ko Hŭi-man—then a departmental head of the KWP Central Committee and a former Soviet Korean (yet a devotee of Kim Il Song's)—met the Soviet diplomat by chance at the Moranbong Theater. Protocol had dictated that the diplomats attend a performance by a visiting Hungarian group.[5] According to the record, Ko Hŭi-man was rather agitated by the recent confrontation at the plenum and, on seeing the Soviet diplomat, rushed to tell him about it. Given that this is probably one of the earliest accounts of the "August incident," related by a witness just a few hours after the event, it is worth quoting at length:

> The main body of the plenum agenda was not these questions [the official agenda items] but the eradication of an antiparty group, which consisted of Ch'oe Ch'ang-ik, Pak Ch'ang-ok, Sŏ Hwi, Yun Kong-hŭm, Yi P'il-gyu, and some others.
>
> Even before the plenum it had been known that this group was going to use the forthcoming plenum for their antiparty attacks against some leaders of the party and the government, including Pak Chŏng-ae, Chŏng Chun-t'aek, and Han Sang-du, who were considered [former] pro-Japanese elements [by the opposition], and against Ch'oe Yong-gŏn, Chŏng Il-ryŏng, and Kim Hae-il, who were seen as mediocre and unworthy. . . .
>
> Furthermore, Ch'oe Ch'ang-ik attacked Kim Il Song on the Standing Committee, [insisting that] the latter had concentrated the entire state and party power in his hands. [Ch'oe Ch'ang-ik] said that it had become difficult for himself and others to work with Kim Il Song. . . . Ch'oe Ch'ang-ik also sharply criticized the party line on industrialization while the overwhelming majority of the population is starving. According to Ch'oe's opinion, it would be better to use the aid from fraternal countries to improve the life of the working people. Kim Il Song objected to this suggestion, pointing out that this very policy was being pursued in South Korea, where aid from America and other places was spent on alms for the population. We do not want this, [Kim continued,] nor do the people. The party cannot base its policy merely on the needs of the day, as Ch'oe Ch'ang-ik insisted. In this respect he will not be supported by the people. . . .
>
> [T]he Central Committee foresaw the possibility of a salvo from the antiparty group attacking the party leadership. Indeed, this is exactly what occurred. The first speech was delivered by Yun Kong-hŭm, who stated that a police regime exists within the party [and] that there are many unreliable persons within the leadership, citing Ch'oe Yong-gŏn [as an example]. The plenum deemed Yun's speech to be an antiparty [act]. On the first day of the plenum, Yun was expelled from the Central Committee and the party. . . . Ch'oe Ch'ang-ik, Pak Ch'ang-ok, Sŏ Hwi, and Yi P'il-gyu also made speeches, and they were also rebuffed.[6]

Another source of information is Kang Sang-ho's memoirs. Kang Sang-ho himself was not a participant in the plenum. However, being a highly placed member of the Pyongyang hierarchy at the time (deputy minister of the interior), he had many opportunities to discuss the events with direct participants. According to his memoirs, the first to rise and speak at the plenum was Yun Kong-hŭm. In his short speech, drowned out by cries of protest, Yun stated that "Kim Il Song's personality cult has taken root" and "irresponsible persons are permitted to join the leadership." To make things clear, Yun Kong-hŭm specifically named Ch'oe Yong-gŏn and, according to Kang Sang-ho, even posed the rhetorical question, "How did it happen that the former leader of a petty-bourgeois party has suddenly turned out to be one of the KWP's leaders?"[7] However, Yun Kong-hŭm's speech did not achieve the effect that the conspirators had anticipated: practically no one supported Yun Kong-hŭm's accusations. Kim Il Song's supporters, who were in full control, immediately branded his speech an "antiparty sally" and rejected all the accusations as groundless.[8] According to Kang Sang-ho, Ch'oe Ch'ang-ik and other opposition members also attempted to speak, but they too were unable to win over the plenum, and indeed their speeches were almost incomprehensible amid the noise and shouting.

Yet another, somewhat surprising account of this confrontation exists. On September 7 an Albanian delegation led by Enver Hoxha visited Pyongyang and Kim Il Song. During meetings of these two most prominent would-be "national Stalinists," Kim Il Song related to his colleague Hoxha the recent events. Although this conversation does not reveal many new details, it makes sense to reproduce it in full, because Kim's omissions, as we shall see, may be more important than his inclusions. According to Hoxha:

> The revisionist wasp had begun to implant its poisonous sting there, too. . . . Kim Il Sung told us about an event which had occurred in the plenum of the Central Committee of the Party held after the 20th [CPSU] Congress.
>
> "After the report which I delivered," Kim Il Sung told us, "two members of the Political Bureau and several other members of the Central Committee got up and raised questions from the 20th Congress,

and stated that the question of the cult of the individual had not been properly appreciated amongst us, here in Korea, that a consistent struggle against the cult of the individual had not been waged and so on. They said to the plenum: 'We are not getting economic and political results according to the platform of the 20th Congress, and incompetent people have been gathered around the Central Committee.'

"In other words, they attacked the line and unity of leadership," continued Kim Il Sung. "The whole Central Committee rose against them," he said in conclusion.

"What stand was taken against them?" I asked.

"The plenum criticized them and that was all," replied Kim Il Song, adding: "Immediately after[,] the two of them fled to China."[9]

It is worth noting that the participants in the opposition's "offensive," according to Ko Hŭi-man, were Yun Kong-hŭm, Ch'oe Ch'ang-ik, Pak Ch'ang-ok, Sŏ Hwi, and Yi P'il-gyu. Ch'oe Ch'ang-ik and Pak Ch'ang-ok were the "two members of the Political Bureau" who were mentioned by Kim Il Song. The main accusations were the personality cult, the policy of development of heavy industry at the expense of light industry (and, ultimately, living standards), and Kim Il Song's attempt to promote personally loyal yet allegedly incompetent cadres, notably Ch'oe Yong-gŏn. Obviously, by then the conspirators had lost their original hope of having Ch'oe's support. The accusation of a personality cult was quite understandable in the atmosphere of the summer of 1956, while the personal attacks on the "incompetent" cadres, mostly from the Guerrilla faction, probably reflected the factional clashes, so endemic and frequent within the North Korean political elite. The industrial policy issue was a return to a discussion that took place in 1954–1955. Pak Ch'ang-ok, at that time chairman of the State Planning Commission, and several others had supported a more consumer-oriented policy, while Kim Il Song had chosen a more classical Stalinist line on rapid heavy industrialization.[10] Generally, the concern about extremely low standards of living, sincere or not, seems to have been a common consideration among the opposition; in July and early August it was articulated by Yi P'il-gyu and Kim Sŭng-hwa (in conversations with the Soviet diplomats and elsewhere), as well as by Kim Tu-bong (as relayed by Kim Sŭng-hwa). The published accounts of the incident, regardless of their sources, agree that the low living standards of the North Korean population and the lack of government effort to raise them were major issues during the August Plenum.

If we compare the above-mentioned accounts of the incident by Ko and Kang with the depiction found in published works, some minor inconsistencies are notable. For example, most scholars, using the South Korean government publications as well as some later North Korean official accounts, state that in his speech Sŏ Hwi demanded that the trade unions be made independent from the state and, particularly, from the party. This account occurs in works by Ch'oe Sŏng and Kim Hak-jun, as well as in North Korean publications (the latter probably influenced the former). The first accusations of this kind appeared soon after the plenum. In July 1957 the KWP official monthly published a lengthy article on Sŏ Hwi's alleged "subversive activity" in the trade unions. Among other things, this article insisted that Sŏ Hwi had wanted to relinquish the "party's guidance" in the trade unions.[11] These accusations were repeated later as well. For example, in 1981 the voluminous *General History of Korea* credited a "factionalist" (obviously Sŏ Hwi, since he was the only prominent opposition leader related to the trade unions) with saying: "The party cannot guide the trade unions. The trade unions have more members than the party; they are a bigger organization than the party. Since all party cadres are trade union members, they must be guided by the trade unions."[12] It would appear extremely unlikely that Sŏ Hwi would have ever said anything remotely like this nor, indeed, anything about wresting the trade unions from party control. Such an opinion might not look particularly outrageous to a modern Western reader—indeed, it might even look reasonable—but for any Marxist-Leninist (be they Stalinist or not) this pronouncement was a sinister heresy. Worse still, it was an old, well-known, and long-condemned heresy. In the early 1920s the Russian Communists discussed the role of the trade unions in the newly established Communist state, and some Soviet cadres expressed opinions identical to the above remark, so improbably attributed to Sŏ Hwi. For raising these questions, those people were promptly and severely rebuked by Lenin himself. In the late 1930s the "trade union discussion" was described at some length in the official

Stalinist *History of the Communist Party of the Soviet Union (Bolsheviks): Short Course,* the principal textbook on Stalinist Leninism both in the Soviet Union and in North Korea, as well as in countless official publications of party history. Since then this topic had remained staple fare for Communist indoctrinators. Every party cadre who had conducted any course of political study was expected to know about the "trade union discussion" and could easily identify this heresy. It is more likely that Sŏ Hwi said something mildly critical about excessive official control over the trade unions, because this control in North Korea was excessive indeed even by the standards of other Communist states.[13] Later these remarks by Sŏ Hwi might have been deliberately misinterpreted to present him to the party as an apostate and anti-Leninist revisionist. That Ko Hŭi-man did not mention such an outrageous—from an orthodox Leninist point of view—declaration to Samsonov on August 31, just after the fateful confrontation, also indicates that Sŏ Hwi most likely did not make such a statement. It is also noteworthy that Kim, while talking to Hoxha, his sympathetic listener, on September 7, did not tell him that the trade union question was mentioned during the plenum. Of course, had Sŏ Hwi's remarks about trade unions even marginally deviated from the commonly accepted ideological norms, Kim would certainly have reported such a heretical view.

Another accusation, later leveled against the "factionalists," was their alleged attitude toward "peaceful coexistence," the new and then much-debated Soviet term. In a strict sense, the "peaceful coexistence" doctrine implied that wars between Communist and capitalist worlds, heretofore believed to be unavoidable, could and indeed must be prevented. This notion—and it was Khrushchev's—highly irritated Beijing, where mindless revolutionist militancy ruled supreme (at least, in propaganda statements). Nor was it welcome in Pyongyang, where it was seen as a likely obstacle to the KWP's major policy goal: the eventual unification of the country under the auspices of the North. From the DPRK point of view, "peaceful coexistence" meant that the Soviet Union, in order to escape a major military confrontation with the West, might avoid committing itself to the unconditional support of the North Korean cause of unification, which might require military means. Hence North Korean officialdom had been uneasy about this concept since the very beginning, although for a while Pyongyang avoided direct criticism of its powerful sponsor.

Kim Hak-jun mentioned in his book additional allegations later made by Kim Il Song himself. According to these accusations, Ch'oe Ch'ang-ik had cited "peaceful coexistence" in support of his supposed insistence on the neutrality of the Korean Peninsula and had suggested the abolition of the Communist system in the North to create conditions for such neutrality.[14] The same accusations can be found in some North Korean statements of the late 1950s—for example, in the remarks by Kim Yŏng-ju, Kim Il Song's brother and a senior KWP functionary, to a Soviet diplomat in April 1958.[15] However, these allegations must be regarded with skepticism. The first part of the statement (i.e., plans to establish the neutrality of Korea) might possibly be true, although that is highly improbable. But the second part (abolition of the Communist system in the North for the sake of neutrality) would have been an abominable heresy, even worse than Sŏ Hwi's alleged declaration on the trade unions' independence from the party, and therefore it sounds quite fantastic. It is unthinkable that any sane party functionary, especially if backed by an increasingly militant Maoist China, would ever say anything remotely like this. Almost certainly, this is again a later insinuation made by the North Korean propagandists, designed to illustrate to party members just how far from the true revolutionary path Ch'oe and his coterie had deviated. I agree with Kim Hak-jun's skeptical approach to this accusation, which can probably be safely disregarded. Furthermore, had Ch'oe indeed said something remotely in this vein and had Kim Il Song been able to present any proof of this, it would be unthinkable for the joint Soviet-Chinese delegation to insist on Ch'oe's political restoration in September. There would have been no pardon for such a reactionary who was even ready to give up the hard-won revolutionary achievements of the North Korean people.

In the course of the plenum, the opposition did not win a majority in the Central Committee. Indeed it would appear that it did not even manage to win to its side a single member of the Central Committee who had not already been a member of the group in July. This failure was probably a result of Kim Il Song's thorough preparations for the plenum. His tactics of promising to right old wrongs, to give the discontented officials their due, to downsize the personality cult, to revise old policies, and so on won many neutral figures to his side. Kim's position also gave him opportunities to bribe and blackmail high-level cadres individually. The outcome of the crisis indicates that Kim Il Song was successful in his maneuvering and that he was ready for the decisive battle when the plenum began. According to "Lim Ŭn" (Hŏ Chin), even the seating arrangements were carefully prepared, so seats of the known opposition supporters—and there were quite a few of them—were surrounded by Kim's most reliable and aggressive henchmen.[16] The cacophony of yelling and whistling prevented the opposition members from delivering their speeches in any persuasive manner, and the plenum was quickly transformed into a shouting competition in which the sheer number of throats decided the outcome. Perhaps there might have been some other plenum participants who were ready to support the opposition's cause, had the situation taken another turn. However, facing the apparent predominance of the better-organized Kim loyalists, any such people probably chose to be prudent and remain neutral, if not joining in the chorus. For example, nobody mentioned that Kim Tu-bong, who had been sympathetic to the opposition, voted against Kim Il Song or otherwise expressed his support for the opposition acts during the August confrontation. His restraint did not save him from eventual disgrace and death, however.

Thus the majority supported Kim Il Song, literally silencing the opposition and obediently voting for repressive action against the rebels. As a result, Ch'oe Ch'ang-ik was expelled from the presidium and the Central Committee, and Pak Ch'ang-ok from the Central Committee. However, because both of them were preeminent politicians, neither was expelled from the party at that stage. Nevertheless, on the evening of August 31, Ko Hŭi-man told G. Ye. Samsonov that "the KWP Control Committee was asked to consider the question of their party membership,"[17] hinting at the likely fate of the rebels (expulsion from the party, followed by arrest, interrogation, and perhaps a show trial, and finishing with imprisonment or execution, according to the traditional Stalinist sequence). The somewhat less prominent Yun Kong-hŭm, Sŏ Hwi, and Yi P'il-gyu were expelled from the party instantly, at the plenum. All these events did not take more than one day, since on August

31, the second and final day of the plenum, Ko Hŭi-man said that Yun Kong-hŭm and others "had disappeared." Therefore we can conclude that the bold escape of the opposition leaders (discussed below) that followed the plenum debacle took place late in the evening of August 30. A former interpreter at the Soviet Embassy, Kim Chu-bong, recalled that "on the day of the plenum, at lunchtime," he and G. Ye. Samsonov by chance met Yun Kong-hŭm on the street. Yun tried to get out of his car, in the hope of striking up a conversation with the diplomats, but Samsonov, who obviously knew something about the recent developments, avoided the encounter and pulled Kim Chu-bong away from this likely source of danger.[18] If Kim Chu-bong's memory is correct—that is, if this incident indeed took place on August 30—it might mean that for a few hours Yun Kong-hŭm and others remained free.

The concluding speech of the plenum was delivered by Kim Il Song himself. According to Ko Hŭi-man, Kim expressed his regret for having been "too gentle" to the factions and their advocates, particularly to Ch'oe Ch'ang-ik.[19] This statement did not augur well for the opposition members (both real and alleged) or for their friends. At the same time, while talking to Hoxha one week later, Kim obviously tried to play down the seriousness of the purges, perhaps in order not to attract too much foreign attention to the events, which obviously contradicted the current trends in the Communist movement (perhaps this caution was prompted by the escape of the two conspirators, Yun Kong-hŭm and Sŏ Hwi, to China).

As was customary at the time, the information about the plenum was not published in the newspapers for some time. When it eventually appeared in *Nodong sinmun* on September 9, the report revealed only the official agenda (apart from a concluding sentence that mentioned "an organizational question"—a traditional euphemism for dismissals, promotions, or both).

Thus the attempt to change the North Korean political line and replace the country's leadership through legal means, as permitted by the North Korean constitution and party statutes, ended in complete failure. The scenario that under different circumstances succeeded that year in Bulgaria, Hungary, and Poland—where conservative Stalinist leaders eventually succumbed to the pressure of the local opposition (sometimes supported and encouraged, sometimes opposed and contained, by Moscow)—was not and probably could not have been realized in the North Korea of 1956. As was to be expected, purges of opposition participants followed. A lesson would be drawn from the attempt, and a lesson would be given to every North Korean: nobody should dare challenge the Great Leader and hope to get away with it.

The supporters of the unsuccessful opposition group were proclaimed "splittists" and "factional elements" (the latter term—*chongp'a punja*—was to be used by all official North Korean publications to define them throughout the following decades), although accusations of more heinous crimes like spying, sabotage, and mutiny, which had previously been routinely applied to fallen politicians, were set aside or postponed for a while. Some of the key figures, as we will see later, through their boldness or sheer luck, managed to escape Kim Il Song's wrath, despite a campaign against the opposition that was launched immediately after the plenum. Nevertheless this time Kim Il Song, at least initially, seems to have acted in a more restrained manner than he had during the purges of the Domestic faction in 1953–1955. Perhaps he was afraid of the reaction of both Moscow and Beijing at the persecution of "their men in Pyongyang." It is also possible that Kim was afraid of the discontent that a large-scale purge, especially one undertaken in a rather uncertain political environment, might trigger among the party elite as well. There is indeed some evidence of such a latent discontent. For example, in October 1956, Ye. L. Titorenko (probably the most perceptive and insightful Soviet diplomat in Pyongyang at the time) met Ch'oe Sŭng-hun, the deputy chairman of the KWP committee in the remote northern province of Ryanggang. Ch'oe asserted that the expulsion of Ch'oe Ch'ang-ik, Pak Ch'ang-ok, and others was "a serious distortion of intraparty democracy."[20]

For whatever reason, the campaign against the participants of the Ch'oe Ch'ang-ik–Pak Ch'ang-ok group and their supporters was kept very discreet for a while; it was not even accompanied by the customary diatribes in the official press. Even the lengthy articles on problems of Marxist-Leninist theory and party history, which had been frequent in the *Nodong sinmun* in late 1955 and early 1956 during the campaign against the Soviet Koreans, almost disappeared after August. For a year or so the North Korean press apparently shunned the more sensitive subjects of domestic politics, restricting itself to much safer pursuits, such as the glorification of the heroic labor feats of the enthusiastic masses, or venomous verbal attacks on the "South Korean puppets" and "their American masters."

Both of the disgraced leaders of the opposition were temporarily left at large and were even given new posts, although their new offices were not exactly of critical importance: Pak Ch'ang-ok became deputy director of a sawmill, while Ch'oe Ch'ang-ik, in a rude and presumably quite intentional gesture, was appointed manager of a state-run pig farm.[21] Nevertheless, this was but a temporary postponement of the inevitable. Their fate resembles that of many of Stalin's former opponents in the early 1930s, before the launch of the really large-scale purges in the Soviet Union. At that time an obscure post for a fallen politician more often than not was the prelude to a torture chamber and firing squad some years later (N. I. Bukharin, for example, in the last years before his trial was made editor of a newspaper and director of a small research institute).

Fate nevertheless smiled kindly on the opposition, for an unusually high proportion of their number managed to escape persecution. Of the eight initial conspirators whose names had been mentioned in the embassy papers compiled before the incident (Ch'oe Ch'ang-ik, Yi P'il-gyu, Yun Kong-hŭm, Sŏ Hwi, Pak Ch'ang-ok, Kim Sŭng-hwa, Yi Sang-jo, and perhaps Kim Tu-bong), five escaped Kim's wrath and fled to safe asylum in China or the Soviet Union. Rarely after any purge among party bosses in a Stalinist country have so many of the accused succeeded in fleeing danger. In Hungary, Bulgaria, Czechoslovakia, East Germany, Romania, and, earlier, the Soviet Union itself, no person of prominence (say, a Central Committee member, let alone a politburo member) had managed to escape abroad during the terror. However, if we concentrate on lesser cadres—rank-and-file of the Yan'an and, later, Soviet factions—rather than the top echelon, the "casualty rate" increases (even if, as we shall see, many Soviet Koreans were allowed and even encouraged to leave the DPRK between 1959 and 1961). However, most of the low- and middle-level cadres had nothing to do with the conspiracy. They were only later portrayed as opposition supporters, and on the flimsiest of evidence.

From any perspective, the initiators of the "August incident" were lucky. Kim Sŭng-hwa, for example, avoided the usual fate of a purge victim; sometime before early September 1956 (probably in late August, just before the plenum) he had left the country for Moscow to study at the Academy of Social Sciences and, understandably, never went back.[22] Much to the displeasure of Pyongyang officialdom, Kim Sŭng-hwa even published a lengthy article on the history of Korean Communism in a Soviet journal. The article itself was quite academic in content and politically could be described as safely orthodox. It did not touch any sensitive or controversial subjects, but Kim Il Song's entourage was quite upset by the very fact that a runaway minister not only had been granted asylum in Moscow but also had been given an opportunity to publish material on the Korean problems. They made some attempts to prevent the publication, but their efforts predictably found little sympathy in the Soviet Academy of Sciences—an institution where the new de-Stalinization policy found its most enthusiastic welcome. The Academy of Sciences bureaucracy successfully sabotaged the North Korean efforts.[23]

Kim Sŭng-hwa was not the only fortunate one. Yun Kong-hŭm and his friends also escaped an almost certain death by managing to flee the country. According to Kang Sang-ho, who was a direct participant in these events, on the night after the plenum Sŏ Hwi and Yi P'il-gyu went to Yun Kong-hŭm's home. We know that it was the night of August 30, for Ko Hŭi-man told Samsonov on the evening of August 31 that the culprits had "disappeared somewhere and cannot be found at the moment."[24] The Ministry of the Interior had kept the home under surveillance and placed its guards near the entrance, though technically neither Yun Kong-hŭm nor the other participants had yet been arrested (apparently arrest was deemed unnecessary). After some discussion, Yun Kong-hŭm, Sŏ Hwi, and Yi P'il-gyu decided to flee to China—partly, one must presume, because of their lifelong connections with the Chinese Communists and partly because of the relatively lax security on the border with this "fraternal country." Since the license plates of their cars were known to the police, they called another member of the Yan'an faction, Kim Kan, who agreed to join them and suggested the use of his car to effect their escape.[25] Kim Kan made a wise decision, given that all acquaintances of the opposition leaders were soon to be purged as well. The four fugitives (Yi P'il-gyu, Yun Kong-hŭm, Sŏ Hwi, and Kim Kan) left via a back door that had been left unattended by the police and promptly departed Pyongyang. Luckily, Korea was a small country, and the next morning the runaways arrived safely at the frontier river Amnok (better known by its Chinese name of Yalu). Their audacity aided the fugitives once again. As Kang Sang-ho recalled, "They had arrived early in the morning, saw a fisherman in a boat, and called to him. The fisherman explained later that he had seen some high-ranking cadres near the car. They approached him and asked if he could sell them some fish and give them a boat for a while. He agreed, and they rewarded him handsomely and sailed to a small islet situated between the Chinese and Korean borders in the middle of the Amnok. They pretended to have a little picnic. Indeed, they remained there for quite some time until the fisherman noticed them cross the Amnok and proceed to the Chinese side."[26]

Kang Sang-ho was sent to check if the fugitives were making their way to the Chinese border, while some other high-ranking police officers did their best to block all roads to the South, since a majority of the security officials thought the fugitives would try to cross the 38th parallel. Kang Sang-ho also crossed the Yalu and met the chief of the state security board of the Chinese county of Andong. Kang Sang-ho tried to persuade the Chinese to extradite the fugitives, but he was predictably unsuccessful. Yun Kong-hŭm and his comrades had already proceeded well beyond the border to Beijing, where they had a lot of influential friends from their Yan'an days.[27]

While Yun Kong-hŭm and his friends were making their bold escape, back in Pyongyang the inevitable purges were already in full swing. As usual, the results of the Central Committee Plenum were to be "studied" at provincial and city-level party conferences where not only the official agenda but also more sensitive information about the real events at the plenum were provided. A Hungarian report gives us some insight into the information provided to chosen party cadres during these closed briefings. The cadres were told that several Central Committee members had been expelled from the body. Their transgressions, according to the report, were manifold. First of all, they had stated that the KWP had not done anything to increase the living and cultural standards of the people in the three postwar years. Second, they had stated that the Japanese-trained intellectuals (e.g., the minister of the machine-building industry) were reactionaries and should not have been given important positions. Third, they had stated that the KWP Central Committee had not done anything to eradicate the personality cult, although such a cult did exist in the DPRK. Fourth, they had stated that it had been the Koreans fighting in China who had played the largest part in the Korean movement of national liberation, denying that Kim Il Song's guerrillas fighting in Korea [*sic*] had played the vanguard role in the struggle. The list of crimes was accompanied by commentaries that showed that all of these statements were completely groundless.

Within a couple of weeks of the "August incident," many members of the Yan'an faction were dismissed from their posts. For instance, in Pyongyang the city party secretary, Yi Song-un, told a Soviet diplomat that three high-level officials of the City Committee (including two deputy chairmen) had been relieved of their duties, on the charge of having connections with Ch'oe Ch'ang-ik.[28] Even official information about the party conference in Pyongyang menacingly mentioned "enemies among us," "splittists," and "factionalists." According to an article in *Nodong sinmun,* the participants in the conference were reminded that "enemies are engaging in all types of conspiracies in order to destroy our party."[29]

The great purge of the Yan'an faction was under way, but the Soviet Koreans appeared to be safe for the time being. Some members of the Soviet faction tried to use this situation to their own advantage and to settle old scores with the Yan'an faction that had accumulated in the period 1954–1956. At least one member of the Soviet faction even sought the support of the Soviet Embassy, blaming Ch'oe Ch'ang-ik for all his personal misfortunes and asking for redress.[30] They did not understand that their turn was to come soon.

7 The Soviet-Chinese Delegation and the September Plenum

IN EARLY SEPTEMBER the fortunes of the Yan'an faction were rapidly deteriorating, and a rising tide of purges was swallowing the Yan'an officials one after another. However, in September 1956 the purges were abruptly (albeit temporarily) interrupted when the Chinese and Soviet authorities decided to mount a direct intervention in the political struggle being waged in Pyongyang. Unfortunately, our knowledge of this affair is still very sketchy—much more so than our knowledge of the August Plenum—and for similar reasons. The key event of the September crisis was the visit of a joint Sino-Soviet delegation to Pyongyang, but primary data about this important event remain inaccessible for the moment. Because the team of Anastas I. Mikoyan and Peng Dehuai was officially a party delegation (as opposed to a state delegation), its documentation is held in the Communist Party archives that have yet to be declassified. And the Chinese side of the story is even more unlikely to be told anytime soon.

Therefore this part of my narrative is based mainly on interviews— above all, an interview with V. V. Kovyzhenko, a former high-ranking official in the Soviet Communist Party Central Committee who dealt with Korean problems in the mid-1950s—as well as on some remarks in the Soviet Embassy papers. That I have to rely so heavily on secondary sources at this stage in the narrative is indeed regrettable, but under the present circumstances it is also unavoidable.

On September 15, only two weeks after the August Plenum, the

Eighth Congress of the Chinese Communist Party (CCP) gathered in Beijing. It was, by the way, the same congress in which Mao's policy was subjected to veiled but serious critique and in which his power was temporarily curtailed through a set of institutional reforms. Among other things, the congress deleted "Mao Zedong Thought" from the party's new constitution. The congress also redesigned the structure of the party's top bodies in a way that restricted the power of its chairman (Mao) and placed special emphasis on the regular meetings of party committees, and in general it emphasized the importance of collective leadership.[1] These reforms, soon to be reversed, were obviously inspired by the contemporary Soviet developments. For this narrative, they are a reminder of how attractive the new ideas were throughout the Communist camp at that time.

According to an established tradition, the Soviet delegation, led by an eminent dignitary (this time it was Anastas I. Mikoyan), arrived in China to take part in the congress and deliver the customary address, as well as to discuss the current situation. The congress was attended by delegations from all other major Communist parties as well. The Korean delegation at the congress was led by Ch'oe Yong-gŏn, the same person who a few months earlier had attended the Twentieth Congress of the Soviet Communist Party. Perhaps Ch'oe was sent to demonstrate and stress Korea's equal distance from (or equal proximity to) both Communist Great Powers. Ch'oe Yong-gŏn participated in a reception hosted by Mao that was held on September 16 for foreign delegates. However, it was Yim Hae, a much less prominent politician, who delivered the customary address to the congress on September 19. This was a significant breach of the long-established tradition that required the top dignitary present to deliver the address. Hence we can assume that Ch'oe Yong-gŏn had had to rush back to Pyongyang sometime between September 16 and 19 because he, a trusted champion of Kim's policy, was badly needed there on the eve of the new confrontation.[2]

During the CCP Congress, which continued until September 27, Mikoyan met with Mao Zedong several times. By then, Yun Kong-hŭm and the other Korean runaway cadres had arrived in China, and it is quite conceivable that one of the topics discussed in Beijing was the domestic situation in North Korea and the recent crisis there. According to

V. V. Kovyzhenko, during a meeting with Mikoyan, Mao Zedong expressed his deep concern about the North Korean situation and condemned the recent actions of Kim Il Song and the new purges.[3] Incidentally, Mao and Mikoyan also had consultations with the delegation of Polish Communists, who wanted to discuss the rapidly deteriorating domestic situation in Poland, where mass discontent was looming and the situation was spiraling out of control.

Unfortunately, I have been unable to locate any direct participants in these Mao-Mikoyan talks or the minutes of their talks. However, it was during these talks that Mao and Mikoyan decided to send a joint Sino-Soviet delegation to Korea to investigate the situation. V. V. Kovyzhenko told me that the purpose of this mission was not only to study the situation in the DPRK after the August Plenum and to stop the purges but also possibly to replace Kim Il Song with another person considered more suitable by China and the USSR. Kovyzhenko, who was not a participant in the talks between Mikoyan and Mao, insists the initial thrust came from the Chinese side: "During the conversation between Mikoyan and Mao Zedong, the latter began to complain about Kim Il Song, saying that he was such and such a person, that he had launched that idiotic war, that he was a mediocrity, and that it was necessary to dismiss him. We had already learned that the August Plenum took place at this time and that some members of the Central Committee had strongly criticized Kim Il Song. Mao Zedong and Mikoyan decided to send a joint delegation to Pyongyang in order to study what was going on there and, if necessary, to replace Kim Il Song with a more acceptable figure."[4] If Kovyzhenko was correct and the decision to replace Kim Il Song or at least (to borrow the apparatchik jargon of the day) "to study the question" is indeed a fact (and this author is inclined to believe it to be so), such an option must have been approved by none other than Khrushchev himself. Regardless of whether such a drastic option as Kim's replacement was discussed or not, the delegation was definitely supposed, upon its arrival in Pyongyang, to convene a new plenum of the KWP Central Committee. This plenum would nullify the decisions of the August Plenum and halt the purges, as well as discuss the situation in the country.

The joint delegation was to be led by Anastas I. Mikoyan and Peng

Dehuai. Anastas Mikoyan, brother of the famous MiG (Mikoyan-Gurevich) warplane designer, was reputedly the most cunning and cautious politician in the Soviet leadership. He accomplished the not insignificant feat of being the only person to serve as a politburo member under Lenin, Stalin, Khrushchev, and Brezhnev while avoiding serious trouble and eventually dying of natural causes in his old age.[5] Throughout 1956 it was Mikoyan who frequented the "hot spots" of the Communist camp and became Moscow's de facto chief "crisis manager." In July, Mikoyan had helped to oust the ailing Stalinist regime of Rakosi in Hungary; in October he was back again, unsuccessfully trying to reach a peaceful compromise; and just a few days later it was he who accompanied Khrushchev to Poland, where the Soviet delegation reluctantly had to confirm the elevation of Gomulka and the disgrace of the Polish Stalinists.[6] Although the Pyongyang affair falls between these better-known episodes of the 1956 crisis, it seems that in this particular case Mikoyan was given this mission by accident, simply because he happened to be a Soviet leader visiting Beijing at the time of the sudden crisis in China's neighborhood. Mikoyan had not dealt with Korea before, did not know Korea or East Asia, and, as many people have noted, was rather chauvinistic toward Korea despite his own Middle Eastern origins. On the other hand, the Chinese minister of defense Peng Dehuai, a famous general who had commanded the Chinese troops during the Korean War, knew Korea extremely well and was himself quite popular among the North Koreans, especially among the military. However, since the war he had little respect for Kim Il Song (a feeling that was perhaps mutual). His appointment as the Chinese head of the delegation was therefore a bad omen for Kim.

Excluding technical personnel, the Soviet members of the joint delegation were Mikoyan himself, secretary of the Central Committee, politburo member, and at that time one of the highest Soviet leaders; B. N. Ponomarev, chief of the International Department of the Central Committee; V. V. Chistov, Mikoyan's assistant; V. V. Kovyzhenko, an official of the International Department of the Central Committee who was then responsible for Korean problems; and V. Ja. Sedikhmenov, an official of the same department who specialized in China (being a fluent Chinese speaker, he was invited as interpreter).[7] I have met both

Kovyzhenko and Sedikhmenov and discussed the events in detail with them (the former became a high-ranking diplomat, and the latter a well-known scholar of traditional China).

Kovyzhenko recollected that when the delegation arrived in Pyong-yang by train, Kim Il Song did not appear at the railway station to meet the "foreign guests," as would normally have been expected. Apparently he had decided to show his displeasure toward these uninvited "guests." His attitude became clearer a year later when a triumphant Kim Il Song related his recollections of the affair to high-ranking officials and said, obviously trying to conceal both his past embarrassment and present ex-ultation, "When Comrades Mikoyan and Peng Dehuai came . . . , how could we send them back, even though they had arrived without an in-vitation? We had to respect the dignity of their parties."[8] The members of the delegation proceeded to their residences (the Soviets and the Chinese were housed separately), and Kim Il Song visited them there the next day.

The delegation insisted that a new plenum of the KWP Central Committee be convened as soon as possible. Consequently, prepara-tions were begun forthwith under the full control and supervision of Anastas Mikoyan and Peng Dehuai. A day before the plenum there was a meeting of the joint delegation leaders in which Ponomarev and Mikoyan represented the Soviet side. Kovyzhenko observed that after this meeting Mikoyan and Ponomarev began to draft (in Russian) a reso-lution to be adopted by the plenum. This draft is presumed to have been distributed among the participants at the plenum. According to Kovyzhenko, Mikoyan's draft of the resolution not only blamed Kim Il Song for the purges that began after the August Plenum but also sug-gested his resignation. Mikoyan was certain that the Central Committee members, and particularly the members of the Soviet and Yan'an fac-tions, would obediently vote for the draft offered them by a representa-tive from Moscow. In general, this was Mikoyan's (as well as Stalin's) style. Despite Mikoyan's well-deserved reputation as a shrewd politician, everyone who recalls his visit to Korea mentions his arrogant treatment of the Koreans. G. M. Plotnikov, a Soviet military officer, historian, and Korean expert who was in Korea at the time of Mikoyan's visit, remi-nisced: "Mikoyan looked down on the Koreans, spoke disrespectfully of

them, and always claimed, 'I gave them a reprimand,' 'I explained everything [to them],' 'I ordered [them].' His lack of respect for Korea could be
detected in his every word."[9] V. D. Tihomirov, a Soviet diplomat and a
prominent expert on Korea, recollected that this attitude of Mikoyan's,
together with his conduct throughout the entire affair, later earned
Mikoyan in Korea the less than honorable nickname of "Mit'kunyŏng"
(asshole).[10]

In September, Mikoyan was preparing to play in Pyongyang a role
reminiscent of his recent actions in Budapest, where in July he had supervised the opposition's replacement of the current leader, Rakosi
(who was considered to be too Stalinist and too unpopular), with a more
suitable and less Stalinist figure, Gero. However, the situation in Pyongyang was very different. When the political storm was gathering in
Hungary, the Stalinist old guard had realized they had little support not
only among the general population but even among the party faithful.
In Korea there was no indication of a looming mass protest. As we shall
see, some discontent existed in North Korea, but it was a far cry from the
situation in Hungary or Poland.

What happened next? We have only Kovyzhenko's version of events.
"I was not present at the meeting with the Chinese," he stated in his interview, "but when Ponomarev returned, he declared, 'We'll compose a
draft of the resolution.' I replied, 'That's impossible.' Ponomarev in-
quired, 'Why?' I responded, 'Maybe it's possible to make oral suggestions,
but we must not leave any papers, and certainly not in Russian.' Ponomarev complained to Mikoyan, and he [Mikoyan] called me. Our conversation lasted for two hours or even longer, and eventually I convinced
him that on no account should we draft any written proposal on the
overthrow of Kim Il Song, because if Kim Il Song were to hold his ground
(and I had no doubt he would), he would never forgive us. Mikoyan then
gave his opinion: 'All right. Since the Chinese insist on it, let them do it
themselves, if they need to do it so desperately.' Thus it was settled."[11]

Certainly this is only one version of the incident (unfortunately, the
only version available for the present), and it must not be taken as a ver-
itable record. Alas, the official records of Mikoyan's visit remain classified.[12] Kovyzhenko says that after this discussion the general line of the
Soviet delegation was quite passive, and they did not especially insist on

Kim Il Song's removal. The Chinese side seemed to give up the idea as well. Thus the task was confined to party rehabilitation of the purged victims. The unexpected passivity of the Chinese delegation could have been the result of some other long-term considerations. In 1956 an open break between the Soviet Union and China seemed to be out of the question, but the tensions between the two countries were gradually rising and Mao Zedong, with his distrust of the "elder brother," did his best to place himself in a stronger position on the eve of a possible (or even calculated) conflict with Moscow.[13]

Given that the official documents on the visit are still beyond our reach, we can only guess whether Mikoyan met with some members of the Soviet faction. On the other hand, the Chinese members of the joint delegation certainly did meet with some officials of the Yan'an faction, including Kim Tu-bong himself (this fact was disdainfully mentioned by Kim Il Song in December 1957, when Kim Tu-bong was officially accused of collusion with the opposition).[14]

The Central Committee Plenum opened on September 23 and lasted just one day. Under Soviet-Chinese pressure, Kim Il Song agreed to rehabilitate the participants of the August events and their supporters and promised not to undertake any wide-scale purges of high-level functionaries. This time an official newspaper report (as usual, published after the fact, September 29) not only mentioned that Ch'oe Ch'ang-ik, Yun Kong-hŭm, Sŏ Hwi, Yi P'il-gyu, and Pak Ch'ang-ok (in that order) had been restored within the party but also for the first time referred to their earlier expulsion during the August Plenum. The same day and on the same front page, alongside the report, *Nodong sinmun* ran a huge editorial entitled "Explanation, Persuasion, and Education Are the Main Methods of Our Party's Leadership." The editorial tried to explain why so recent a decision had been reversed: "Even if [some people] commit a serious mistake, the party, by helping them correct this mistake, educates them [and transforms them into] even more loyal party members."[15] The editorial also repeatedly mentioned "intraparty democracy" and the "spirit of criticism and self-criticism." Its general tone was well in accord with the de-Stalinization mantras. It seemed that Kim Il Song had bowed to the foreign pressure and decided to follow the instructions of his foreign patrons once again.

8 The Purges

WHEN ANASTAS MIKOYAN and Peng Dehuai left Korea, it looked like they had successfully accomplished their task. The purges were stopped and even reversed. Kim Il Song promised he would not move against the August faction and its supporters. All the victims of the recent campaign were formally restored to their positions. Kim Il Song's conciliatory speech and the complete text of the resolutions of the September Plenum were distributed among party organizations. Sessions of local party committees and cells were held to provide lower-level officials and party members with information about the new policy.

The very presence of the Soviet-Chinese delegation was originally concealed not only from the KWP rank and file but probably from middle-level party functionaries as well. This concealment is understandable, given that the delegation's visit was rather humiliating for North Korean pride. Nevertheless, everybody could see the clear divergence, even contradiction, between the resolutions of the two plenums that had taken place within a short period of two weeks. As the deputy chairman of the KWP Central Committee, Pak Kŭm-ch'ŏl, noted to Counselor Pelishenko: "A number of party members have been puzzled at the difference between the resolutions on organizational questions ['organizational questions' was a common Communist euphemism for personnel appointments and dismissals] at the August and September Plenums and expressed their bewilderment."[1] A similar remark was made in November by Yi Song-un, a secretary of the Pyongyang City Committee of the KWP.[2]

The few months after the September Plenum was indeed a period of relative relaxation. For a brief while it looked as if North Korea was going to follow the example of other "fraternal countries" and embark on a moderate course of de-Stalinization. That autumn, Kim Il Song's name was mentioned in the official press less frequently, and tributes to his greatness and wisdom were somewhat muted. There were other signs of ideological and cultural relaxation. In October, *Nodong sinmun* ran an editorial entitled "For Active and Free Study and Discussions in Culture and Science," which stated: "There is no greater wisdom than collective wisdom. Opinions of any 'authority' or individual find it difficult to avoid subjectivity and bias. Is it not clear that the opinions of an individual, however great he may be, are narrower than the opinions of the masses?"[3] However reasonable, such remarks were an abominable heresy, a severe ideological crime by later Korean standards, because they cast doubt on the infinite wisdom of the Great Leader.

The general change of mood was reflected in literature and the arts, two fields that serve as good indicators of ideological trends in a Leninist state. From spring 1956 onward the general tone of the North Korean literary critique underwent a profound change, echoing and emulating similar changes in the Soviet literary politics. The issue of the day was the struggle against "schematism" *(tosikjuŭi)*. "Schematism" in this case was a euphemistic expression for slavish dependency on the ideological prescriptions that transformed works of art into mere illustrations of the current political slogans and propaganda exercises. As in the post-Stalinist Soviet Union, from whence this catchphrase originated, so in North Korea the "struggle against schematism" for all practical purposes meant that the writers and art managers were encouraged to limit the use of literature and art for propaganda purposes, while officialdom was expected to be more tolerant of politically "unsound" works. This new trend did not herald a real creative freedom for the arts, but it did mean that the ideological pressure was relieved to some extent. Works that would have been described as "reactionary" or "revisionist" in the early 1950s—or, for that matter, after 1959—could be published during those halcyon days. In most cases these works were aesthetically superior to the boring propaganda that North Korean artists had to produce in other periods of the regime's history.[4]

However, this relaxation was only temporary. Kim Il Song was not going to carry out resolutions or follow policies that had been imposed on him by unceremonious foreign pressure. His compliance was a trick, and he was quite determined to rid himself of these rivals who had dared to challenge him so openly. This began to become clear in the first few months after the September Plenum. Faced with the Sino-Soviet pressure, Kim Il Song agreed to rehabilitate "the splittists" who had been expelled from the party in August. However, their formal rehabilitation as party members did not mean that their former political influence would be restored. As was noted earlier, Pak Ch'ang-ok and Ch'oe Ch'ang-ik were left to manage a sawmill and a pig farm, respectively. Yet their freedom was short-lived. At the beginning of September 1957, Yu Sŏng-hun, the rector of Kim Il Song University, revealed to a Soviet diplomat that Pak Ch'ang-ok and Ch'oe Ch'ang-ik were in prison.[5]

Some less important supporters of the opposition were indeed reinstated to their former posts, but only for a short while. From November 1956 on, Kim Il Song and his entourage began to dismiss them from their offices again. The fate of the deputy chairman of the Pyongyang City Committee of the KWP, Hong Sun-hwan, who is mentioned in a few contemporary documents, is fairly typical of the period. Early in September 1956, Hong was relieved of his duties because he "had been in contact with Ch'oe Ch'ang-ik." At the end of September, Hong, in keeping with recent decisions, recovered his former post. But in November he was again dismissed and expelled from the party. The reason given this time was that "he did not break off his relations with Ch'oe Ch'ang-ik" (even though the latter had been officially rehabilitated by then).[6]

Significantly, soon after the crisis, the North Korean leadership decided to issue new party identification cards. On November 22, Pak Kŭm-ch'ŏl, while informing a Soviet diplomat of this decision, insisted: "These measures are not aimed at purging the party. On the contrary, [they] are necessary to improve the registration system of party members. The old identification cards have, in most cases, become unusable."[7] However, this declaration need not necessarily be taken at face value. It is more likely, as Suh Dae-sook has noted, that the entire campaign was a good pretext for a careful examination of virtually every party member's background and behavior.[8] This likelihood was indirectly acknowledged in an article published by *Nodong sinmun* in January 1957. The article explicitly stated that the issue of new identification cards provided cadres with a good opportunity to check the activities and reliability of all party members.[9]

In spite of being essentially an elite affair, the August crisis also reflected a more widespread dissatisfaction with the North Korean situation. The anxiety and uneasiness of top cadres to some degree mirrored the general mood of North Korean society—or at least an important strata of this society. As documents show, the August incident was merely the most visible part of a more profound crisis of Stalinism in North Korea. Because of North Korean peculiarities, this crisis did not, nor could it even remotely, assume the same proportions as it did in Hungary or Poland, but it was nevertheless quite real. The North Korean leadership was aware of a certain amount of discontent among the country's intellectuals and more educated party cadres. Soviet Embassy records show that in July 1956, just before the August confrontation, Kim Il Song, while analyzing the current crisis in Poland, stated that the Polish leaders had not paid enough attention to the "wrong ideological trends" among the intellectuals, and he went on to say that there were signs of intellectual unrest in the DPRK as well.[10]

These trends were encouraged by the developments outside North Korea. Indeed, the de-Stalinization campaign in the USSR, though halted somewhat after the Hungarian uprising, was not totally reversed, and information about changes in Moscow and other Communist countries continued to flow into Korea, encouraging those who dreamed of a more liberal society. For a brief while it even appeared as if the September decisions had granted them a modicum of protection. It is worth keeping in mind that North Korea in the mid-1950s, despite the strict political control, generally enjoyed a more open polity than was the case during the following decades. The number of Koreans studying or traveling abroad (albeit only to other Communist countries and only by official appointment) was very small, but still considerable in comparison with numbers in later periods. Foreign newspapers, including Soviet newspapers, were still sold freely in Pyongyang. Similarly, there was a greater access to information and increased opportunities for discussing political problems. Even the official press published much more than would be tolerated in later periods. For example, during the Hungarian uprising, from October 27 onward *Nodong sinmun* regularly published official Soviet reports of the "unrest" and "riots" in the Hungarian capital. With the important exception of the three most critical days (November 2–4, when the Soviet troops were fighting their way into revolutionary Budapest), reports on the state of affairs in Hungary appeared nearly every day until late November. The interpretation of the Hungarian revolt was extremely negative, but these reports still constituted a form of information.[11] The less dramatic "Polish October" got less publicity, but the North Korean press did mention the personnel changes in the leadership of the Eastern European Communist parties. In comparison with the later reluctance of the North Korean press to inform its readers of any kind of problem either within or between the "fraternal countries," this period would appear in hindsight to be rather open.

The Hungarian uprising found some resonance in Korean intellectual circles. For example, at Kim Il Song University, as its rector told a Soviet diplomat in February 1957, there had been some graffiti and handwritten leaflets supporting the Hungarian movement and demanding change in the North Korean industrial policy to provide a better standard of living (a theme that had been an opposition proposal during the August confrontation).[12] Of some fifty or so North Korean students who had been studying in Hungary during the uprising, three opted to escape to Austria,[13] while others were promptly recalled to Pyongyang to continue their studies in the "ideological safety" of their native country.[14] From Soviet Embassy materials, it is known that these students caused a lot of trouble for their supervisors. They asked lecturers "improper" questions and raised politically sensitive issues during "seminars" (tutorials of a kind, where discussion among the students was encouraged). Some of these questions, cited in one document, were indeed quite "improper" from the orthodox point of view. Among other things, these students repeatedly expressed their doubts about the professed superiority of the one-party system. They also argued that Janos Kadar's government, which had been recently installed by Soviet intervention, did not represent the Hungarian people, and so on. Both the university rector, Yu Sŏng-hun, and a professor of Marxism-Leninism complained to the Soviet diplomats about these students and their erratic behavior but promised "to place them under the control of reliable students" in order to fix their obvious ideological deviations.[15] The students who had studied in another center of ideological ferment, Poland, also caused similar problems, prompting Kim Il Song himself to complain to a Soviet chargé d'affaires.[16]

However, this discontent was not limited to troublesome students returning from Hungary and attending Kim Il Song University. It appears to have been shared by a substantial number of party cadres and intellectuals (the line between these two social groups in mid-1950s North Korea was often blurred). In May 1957, Chang Ik-hwan, a former Soviet Korean and the then deputy minister of education, told a Soviet diplomat: "A certain number of high school teachers, university professors, and [university] students demonstrated [their] political immaturity and ideological unreliability after the August incident and under the influence of the Hungarian events. In the middle and high schools of South P'yongan Province alone it has been necessary to replace three thousand teachers because of political considerations." If this figure was correct, taking into consideration the persistent shortage of educated personnel, the decision to replace some three thousand teachers would appear quite radical and probably indicated that Kim's entourage took the threat of dissent very seriously.[17]

As one might expect, Kim Il Song University acquired a reputation as a particularly unreliable and ideologically contaminated place.[18] This reputation arose partly because the university, by virtue of its position as by far the largest and best North Korean academic institution, was an obvious breeding ground for intellectual dissent and political free thinking. Academics tended to be better informed of, and more positive toward, concepts of intellectual freedom than either the general population or party functionaries. Potentially "dubious" elements from the Domestic, Yan'an, and Soviet factions (who were on average much better educated than the former guerrillas or newly promoted cadres) were also overrepresented at the university, the only grove of academe in the whole of North Korea. Consequently, when Kim decided to wipe out the seeds of dissent, the purges at Kim Il Song University were particularly thorough. So it is not surprising that in September 1957 the university rector told a Russian diplomat: "Some university teachers, without any knowledge of the existence of this group [the August opposition], criticized the policies of the KWP Central Committee and the [North Korean] government, in some cases extolled the 'democracy in Yugoslavia,' and expressed their critique of Kim Il Song's personality cult."[19] In this regard they were not much different from their counterparts in the Soviet Union and Eastern Europe or, for that matter, in China.

It was at Kim Il Song University that the campaign against the "factionalists"—real or alleged sympathizers of the August opposition— openly resumed late in the summer of 1957. Before this, the purges had a low profile. In early August a special party conference was held at the university. Kim Ch'ang-man, a rising ideological czar in the regime, personally took charge of the conference. On August 6, *Nodong sinmun* ran a lengthy article on the conference and the dangerous ideological tendencies that had been exposed during a three-month-long campaign against the "factionalists" and "enemies" at the university. This was the first official signal that the September decision had been in effect reversed, for the article mentioned only "decisions of the August Plenum," as if the September Plenum had not been held. In addition, the article, for the first time in almost a year, openly referred to Ch'oe Ch'ang-ik, Pak Ch'ang-ok, and others as "factionalists." Among the victims of the purges at the university (as the deputy minister of education and the university rector both later told Soviet diplomats) were Yi Ch'ŏng-won, a prominent historian and member of the DPRK Academy of Sciences and, indeed, one of the founding fathers of Korean Marxist historiography; many other scholars and teachers; and as many as a hundred students and postgraduates.[20] Hong Nak-ŭng, the university party secretary, was another prominent target of the campaign. As early as October 1956 he was accused of having connections with (the then formally acquitted) Ch'oe Ch'ang-ik. Since then Hong had been practically ousted from his position (in August 1957, *Nodong sinmun* called him "an ideological traitor").[21] However, Hong Nak-ŭng proved to be resilient, and when summoned to a meeting, instead of expressing the usual penitence, he stubbornly defended his "antiparty opinions." A North Korean participant of the meeting disdainfully recollected to a

Soviet diplomat sometime later: "[Hong] did not renounce his ideas about improving the people's living standards and developing intra-party democracy within the KWP and suchlike."[22] Such terrible ideas were indeed supposed to be renounced.

The typical pattern of purges is evident from the fate of Song Kun-ch'an, head of the university's Department of Marxism-Leninism. Though he was far from being a senior figure, his name (perhaps by sheer coincidence) is found in a few unrelated documents, enabling us to reconstruct what happened to him in 1956 and 1957. It was Song who in January 1957 complained to a Soviet diplomat about "ideologi-cally contaminated" Korean students from Hungary.[23] By May he had already been subjected to criticism at party meetings for his alleged sup-port of the opposition (here he saw himself betrayed by his students, who rushed to denounce him).[24] Later he was expelled from the party, was unfavorably mentioned in *Nodong sinmun* in August, and was ar-rested in early September as a "factionalist," that is, an opposition sup-porter (being a "factionalist" constituted sufficient grounds for arrest by late 1957).[25] This scenario seems to be fairly typical of the period.

The purges were not confined to the academy, and by the summer of 1957 the North Korean establishment was in the midst of the worst witch hunt it had ever experienced, far larger in scale than the campaign against the Domestic faction over the years 1953–1955. "Criticism meet-ings" and "ideological examinations" began to spread throughout the country. These two peculiar forms of public humiliation were developed in North Korea under a Maoist influence, but with a local touch. In both cases the victim—normally a party cadre or a similar sinner of some eminence—was subjected to lengthy public sessions in his or her "orga-nization" in which all participants were to "criticize" (that is, basically, insult) the victim. Sometimes, when the emotional temperature rose to a particularly high level, the accusers were allowed and even encouraged to use physical measures of persuasion, and severe beatings were not un-usual. These sessions, with the same victims, were normally repeated on a daily basis for many days and even, sometimes, weeks in a row. For ex-ample, in the Central Party Cadre School one member, Ha Kap, commit-ted suicide in early November 1957 after a month-long series of these "criticism meetings."[26] This type of extralegal "justice" gained a degree of notoriety during the Cultural Revolution in China, but in Korea it achieved its peak of popularity earlier, in the late 1950s. It is noteworthy that this style of persecution was much different from the Stalinist tradition: in Stalin's Russia a victim was not expected to deliver "self-criticism" and sit through days of public humiliation by his former coworkers. With few exceptions, the victims were taken promptly to the privacy of the prisons to meet their humiliations and tortures there.

It was during these purges that public executions became a customary practice in North Korea. There are no indications that at this stage "factionalists" were executed in public, although this is not impossible. However, the very reappearance of public executions was significant in itself, because it afforded another indication of the increasing distance between the Korean practice and its onetime Soviet prototype. Even under Stalin the Soviet legal practice, in spite of great real differences from Western jurisprudence, always followed and imitated, however superficially, external forms and traditions of Western law. Stalin's secret police killed people in droves, but there was usually a trial, however farcical or biased, by officially appointed judges, and the execution could be held in public only under the most exceptional circumstances (in the battlefield, for example, or sometimes in a prison camp). This probably reflected the respect that Soviet Stalinism had for Enlightenment traditions and legal formalities. The newly born "national Stalinisms," more populist and less rooted in European traditions, had few qualms about discarding those vestiges of early Marxism.

The main victims of purges were functionaries who were accused of real or imaginary connections with Ch'oe Ch'ang-ik and, at times, with Pak Ch'ang-ok. Often these victims were simply members of the Yan'an faction (at this early stage the Soviet Koreans were generally not targeted). As Yi Tae-p'il, vice-chairman of the Pyongyang City Committee of the KWP, told Titorenko, a young and investigative Soviet diplomat, in October 1957, "In certain party organizations in the city, party meetings are conducted. Their task is to unmask factionalists in a given organization, disclose their collusion with the main factionalists, find out each party member's attitude toward the factionalists, elevate class consciousness, and expose unreliable elements."[27]

Severe purges were also taking place in the Academy of Science, which was, like the university, another predictable source of ideological contamination. Party meetings aimed at revealing and punishing "factionalists" were launched at the academy in August and continued until November.[28] Sometimes the same victim was subjected to "criticism" for days or weeks on end. For example, on October 17 a scholar told Titorenko that in the academy during the previous twelve days they had been "discussing" the behavior of a fellow scholar named Kim So Ryon[?], a former member of the South Korean Communist Party who, "after the Twentieth Congress of the Soviet Communist Party, openly insisted we must not use the phrase 'our beloved leader Kim Il Song' and must increase the people's living standards."[29]

As has already been mentioned, on August 6, 1957, *Nodong sinmun* published the first article openly criticizing the "factionalists." After that, articles of that sort began to appear regularly in *Nodong sinmun*,[30] and the short-lived conciliatory decisions of the September Plenum of 1956 were no longer mentioned in the press. The media campaign against the "conspirators" was in full swing by early 1958 and continued, though with somewhat declining intensity, into the early 1960s. During these years hardly any major article on the party's internal problems failed to mention the devious schemes and treacherous plans of the factionalists. Occasionally, these indictments gave some insight into the opposition's actual demands. For example, party propaganda material in February 1958 stated: "Some factionalists who had managed to sneak into the law enforcement and judiciary bodies even used deceptively good-looking pretexts of 'human rights protection' to release [from prisons] not a small number of hostile elements."[31] The same collection of propaganda material also stated that the "antiparty counterrevolutionary factionalist elements . . . created unprincipled slogans of 'democracy' and 'freedom' in order to break the steel-like unity of our party."[32] By and large, however, such unwittingly revealing statements were few and far between, and most accusers insisted that the opposition leaders had always been traitors, immoral and unreliable types who somehow had managed to conceal their depraved nature for a brief period.

The number of people who were accused of secretly supporting the opposition continued to grow. It was a pattern well known also from Stalin's Soviet Union as well as from many other regimes of the same type: a group of actual opposition members was followed to exile, prison, or the execution chamber by those who presumably knew about their plans and whom the first victims denounced under pressure and torture. The latter in turn were followed by their friends and associates, who might have known something. It meant that the number of purge victims kept growing continuously and at times very rapidly. Such witch hunts always have a tendency to develop into a self-perpetuating process.

Apart from the dissenting intellectuals, the main victims of these purges were party cadres accused of real or imaginary connections with Ch'oe Ch'ang-ik and occasionally Pak Ch'ang-ok, often by virtue of simply being members of the Yan'an or the Soviet faction (though, as mentioned above, the Soviet Koreans were seldom targeted at this early stage). As Yi Tae-p'il, vice-chairman of the Pyongyang City Committee, had told Titorenko in October 1957, one of the tasks of party organizations was to "expose unreliable elements."[33] And there appeared to be an abundance of "unreliable elements." For example, in the Ministry of Justice, as the deputy minister related to a Soviet diplomat in October 1957, "it is possible to say that in the legal, judicial, and procuratorial systems no leading official has retained his previous post." Among those who lost their positions in the legal system were the minister of justice and the attorney general themselves, who were both purged for being "too soft" on the counterrevolutionaries. Other victims of the purge included a deputy minister, the deputy attorney general, and the head of the Supreme Court, as well as some heads of departments in the Ministry of Justice (some of them were proclaimed "factionalists" whereas others were accused of lacking "revolutionary vigilance").[34] Such a development is not surprising, if one takes into consideration the significance of this ministry during the purges. In late 1958 a high-level North Korean executive told a Soviet diplomat that 3,912 members had been expelled from the KWP during the year from July 1, 1957 to July 1, 1958. Most of them were accused of being supporters of Ch'oe Ch'ang-ik.[35] Also, 6,116 KWP members died during this period, so that the number of dead and purged members combined (10,028) precisely equaled the number of newcomers (10,029). This meant that the KWP membership did not increase during this period (the KWP had 1,181,095 members and 18,023 candidate members as of July 1, 1958). This stagnation is rather striking if one takes into consideration Kim Il Song's long-standing commitment to the rapid growth of party membership.

Under such circumstances those members of the Yan'an faction who had escaped to China after the August confrontation prudently decided not to return to Korea. They had no reason to believe that Kim Il Song would honor his word not to persecute them. And they were obviously correct in this assumption. The families of both Sŏ Hwi and Yun Kong-hŭm were eventually purged and probably executed.[36] However, the example of Sŏ Hwi, Yun Kong-hŭm, and their friends who managed to save their lives by defecting to China proved too tempting for some other victims of the purges. Since China was obviously not going to extradite defectors (as far as we know, every North Korean cadre who managed to cross the border to China was granted asylum there), and since the Chinese border was close and not very strictly controlled, the number of fugitives to take this route continued to mount. Several defections of prominent cadres to China took place in 1956 and 1957. The former party secretary of Kim Il Song University (not Hong Nak-ŭng, whose determined resistance was mentioned above, but his predecessor) and the former deputy chairman of the Pyongyang KWP City Committee both escaped to China in December.[37] On December 17, 1956, Pak Chŏng-ae told the provisional chargé d'affaires, Pelishenko, that some nine party and state officials of differing ranks (four belonging to Yun Kong-hŭm's group and five others) had escaped to China by that time.[38] In January 1957, Nam Il (then minister of foreign affairs) told Pelishenko that two other alleged members of the opposition who had visited Moscow with an official mission decided to remain in China while on their way home.[39] In July 1957 several other officials were said to have been arrested while preparing their escape to China (however, it is not possible to determine conclusively whether this assertion is true or not).[40] Thus the escapees could have numbered at least a dozen and possibly many more. It is noteworthy, however, that no North Korean politician of significance defected to South Korea, Pyongyang's archenemy. China and the Soviet Union were seen as natural asylums by the opposition members. We can surmise that these mostly lifelong Communists perceived a defection to the ultracapitalist and pro-Western

South Korea as an unforgivable act of treason; Communist China and the USSR were seen as ideologically far more acceptable places to seek political asylum.

Among these many escapes and defections, the refusal of Yi Sang-jo, a former ambassador to the USSR and a leading figure of the Yan'an faction, to return to Korea was of particular significance. Yi Sang-jo had been prominent in North Korean politics after the late 1940s, and in 1956 he was a Central Committee candidate member. From the spring of 1956 he had been increasingly critical of Kim Il Song and his politics and had evidently stayed in touch with the Ch'oe Ch'ang-ik group. On a number of occasions Yi had met with Soviet officials and told them about Kim Il Song's personality cult and the political and economic mistakes of the North Korean leaders. In early August he wrote an open letter to Kim Il Song. He showed the letter to Soviet and Chinese diplomats and officials in Moscow but did not send it at the time.[41] After the plenums, Yi Sang-jo again wrote a highly critical letter to Kim Il Song in October and, this time, sent it.[42] By the end of November, Yi had been ousted from his post and recalled to the DPRK, but he prudently decided to stay in Russia. Yi's example was imitated by a dozen Korean students who had been studying in the USSR and who opted to become "non-returnees." The defection of such a prominent figure as Yi annoyed the North Korean authorities, and they attempted to persuade the Soviets to extradite the runaway ambassador. The Soviets refused to do so. According to both rumors and documents, a special role was played by Yuri Andropov, the future KGB head and the party general secretary, who was then responsible for relations with socialist countries. Andropov took a firm stance on the question.[43] It is known from the embassy papers that the Soviet Central Committee even sent a special letter to Kim Il Song, explaining Moscow's position on the matter. The text of the letter is not available at the time of this writing, but its main message is basically clear from other documents: Moscow refused to deport the runaway ambassador back to Korea and instead granted him asylum.[44] The only compromise was that the Soviet authorities would not allow Yi to live permanently in Moscow or in any other city with a significant North Korean community (Yi Sang-jo later became a professor in Minsk, about a thousand kilometers from Moscow). The same policy was eventually applied to Kim Sŭng-hwa and other defectors: the Soviets granted these figures asylum on the conditions that they refrain from contacting North Korean citizens in Russia and from making public political statements on North Korean affairs in general. Usually these conditions were enforced by settling the defectors outside Moscow and Leningrad.[45] Being unable to get the defector Yi Sang-jo back, Pyongyang had to console itself with purging members of the North Korean Embassy in Moscow who were considered to be Yi Sang-jo's accomplices.[46]

We may deduce that the reasons for the Soviet willingness to accommodate these refugees were complex. The purely humanitarian consideration cannot be completely ignored; few Soviet officials would be prepared to send back to a certain death people who had applied to the USSR for help and protection, especially after Stalin's death, when ideals of the "socialist humanism" were resurgent in the Soviet collective psyche. The excesses of Stalinism were remembered with disgust, not only in the proverbial "Moscow kitchens" of increasingly restive intellectuals but also in the offices of the Kremlin. However, the Soviet decision likely had a less benign motivation as well: Moscow could count on the defectors as a potential subversive force that could be used against Kim Il Song should the need arise. We must remember the fate of the Yugoslav students and officials who refused to return to Titoist Yugoslavia after the split between Stalin and Tito; they were welcomed by the Soviet authorities and later widely used for propaganda purposes, both domestically and internationally. This analogy was likely not lost on Pyongyang.

All of these new developments underline a serious question that we must try to answer. Since early 1957 it had been increasingly obvious that Kim Il Song was not going to keep the promise he had been forced to give to the Soviets and the Chinese in September 1956. The Soviet Embassy was aware of a multitude of facts that left no room for doubt about the current political situation and the ongoing purge of the Yan'an group and local dissenters. However, it appears that the Soviet Union made no attempt to enforce the September decision, even though it was still in position to do so. In the available embassy documents there are no traces of any such attempts. Why was this so? So far, no known Soviet document gives a straightforward answer to the question. Sufficiently frank and revealing documents might exist, but if so, they remain classified. Therefore, in order to answer this question, we have to rely on our more or less learned guesswork.

It appears very likely that such passivity on the part of the Soviets might have been caused, above all, by the profound changes occurring on the international and domestic Soviet scenes in late 1956 and early 1957. First and foremost, in autumn of 1956 two crises struck the Communist camp almost simultaneously and with profound consequences. In Poland and Hungary, outbreaks of popular protests erupted on an unprecedented scale. A moderate critique of the local Stalinist bosses—initially permitted, encouraged, and even demanded by Moscow—triggered much more radical movements. We can assume that the crises in Hungary and Poland caused the Soviet government to be less tolerant of dissent of any kind and more inclined to suppress such dissent by any means necessary, including the classical Stalinist methods. Poland and especially Hungary vividly demonstrated that dangerous destabilization might be a likely outcome of democratic experiments, and this unpleasant discovery made Moscow a more reluctant player in the anti-Stalin crusade. As Hŏ Chin put it: "The small spark of the Hungarian uprising was possibly sufficient to burn the buds of the North Korean democracy."[47] Contrary to Khrushchev's earlier expectations, the removal of the Stalinist restraints did not result in a massive growth of Communist support in Eastern European countries; instead it merely provoked more dissent of an essentially anti-Communist and anti-Russian nature. As often happens, concessions did not solve the problems but simply encouraged the pressure for even greater concessions. These new trends constituted a grave danger to Soviet strategic interests and made Moscow lose some of its initial ardor for promoting de-Stalinization throughout the Communist camp. The Chinese leadership shared these concerns. Initially rather ambivalent about the reforms, Mao, citing Hungarian events, explicitly warned the Chinese Party in late 1956 against the dangers of uncontrolled reforms and insufficient class struggle against the counterrevolutionaries.[48] At the same time, the bloodshed and the international repercussions of the Hungarian revolt also demonstrated to Moscow that the use of force was becoming rather costly and had to be avoided whenever practical.

One must mention that a special and lasting impression on the North Korean leadership was produced by the so-called October Declaration of the Soviet government, issued on October 31, 1956, when the Hungarian crisis was at its peak and shortly before the decisive Soviet intervention. By now this declaration, once widely discussed, has been largely forgotten. It is indicative that students of the history of relations between the Soviet Union and the Communist countries of Eastern Europe seldom even bother to mention this document. Modern scholars, not incorrectly, tend to perceive the declaration as a kind of tactical maneuver that was necessary to appease the more restless elements in the "people's democracies" and to win some precious time in Hungary. However, as we know now from the original documents, there was also an element of sincerity involved.[49] At any rate, the subsequent events in Hungary obviously rendered the declaration meaningless. However, in North Korea the October Declaration was taken quite seriously. It was published on the front page of *Nodong sinmun* the next day, November 1, and since then has been regularly referred to by North Korean politicians and their press.

The declaration was a kind of mild repentance issued by the Soviet authorities. In the first paragraphs it was recognized that "serious mistakes" had taken place in the relations between fraternal countries: "There were errors and actions that violated principles of equality in the relations between the socialist countries." However, the declaration assured, the Soviet government had realized the mistakes of the past and was now serious about righting all these wrongs: "The Twentieth Congress of the CPSU emphasized the necessity to consider peculiarities and historic experiences of the countries that were now entering the way of the construction of new life." The declaration pledged that the sovereignty of all Communist countries would be solemnly respected henceforth. The Soviet government promised to discuss the possible withdrawal of Soviet military and technical advisers, whose presence was often annoying in some "people's democracies," and it even hinted that the very presence of Soviet military forces in these countries would be open to discussion.[50]

The declaration was obviously aimed, above all, at disaffected Soviet allies in Eastern Europe. For the North Koreans, the key words were "'the indestructible foundation of the respect of the total sovereignty of every socialist country' . . . , which were stated at the Twentieth Congress of the CPSU," for this was a general Soviet promise to avoid meddling in the domestic affairs of other Communist countries. Irrespective of the actual Soviet intentions, the North Korean leaders perceived (or at least pretended to perceive) the October Declaration as an assurance against all future attempts to interfere in the affairs of other Communist states and parties. Kim Il Song and his entourage might have harbored doubts about how sincere Moscow really was, but the highly publicized declaration gave them some kind of quasi-legal protection, some official text to appeal to. So it was widely mentioned in the press.

There might have been some other reasons why the Soviets did not interfere a second time when Kim Il Song purged the opposition and proceeded with his new policies. For example, it is not improbable that the increasing rift with China might also have made the Soviets less inclined to protect persons who were widely (and correctly) perceived to be agents of Chinese influence. The initial thrust of the purges in 1956–1957 was directed primarily against the leaders of the Yan'an faction. Their fall meant the decline of Chinese influence in Pyongyang, something Moscow would increasingly not mind. At the same time, Moscow's willingness to accommodate the defectors from North Korea and to grant them asylum and protection was, among other things, a clear warning sign directed at Pyongyang.

The coeval developments in China no doubt also encouraged the harsher treatment of the internal opposition in Korea. In China a short-lived outburst of liberalism under the Hundred Flowers slogan in June 1957 was suddenly replaced by an Anti-Rightists Campaign.[51] During this campaign, large numbers of intellectuals and other dissenting individuals, including party cadres who had been too sympathetic toward reformist ideas one or two years earlier, were subjected variously to public humiliation, exile, and imprisonment. After a short period of uncertainty and vacillation, Mao's China began steering away from the perils of de-Stalinization and toward the frenetic personal dictatorship of the Great Helmsman. Kim Il Song, himself fluent in Chinese and an ardent reader of the Chinese press, was careful to monitor the developments across the Yalu River and would hardly have failed to notice the ongoing policy changes. From his point of view it would have looked quite unlikely that under the new circumstances the Chinese authorities would insist on enforcing the conciliatory, pro-liberal, almost "revisionist" decisions of the September Plenum.

It also seems highly probable that the internal Soviet crisis of 1957 greatly influenced North Korean developments as well. In early July a group of moderate Stalinists led by Malenkov, Voroshilov, and Kaganovich challenged Khrushchev's anti-Stalinist line and tried to replace him with somebody less radical and more predictable. After complicated political intrigue and bureaucratic maneuvering, Khrushchev won majority support in the Central Committee and emerged victorious from the crisis. But it seems that despite the utter dissimilarity of the ideological goals of the Soviet and Korean oppositions, the situation in Moscow closely reminded Kim Il Song of the recent August incident in North Korea. Indeed, technically speaking, the two crises had much in common: in both countries a group of discontented top officials tried to win majority support to oust the current party leader and radically change the political line. However, the Soviet moderate Stalinists were much closer to victory than the Korean moderate anti-Stalinists. It is worth noting that in July and August 1957 the North Korean press carried lengthy articles describing the crisis in the USSR. This coverage was especially striking because normally the North Korean newspapers tried to conceal, or at least play down, clashes and disagreements in or between the allied countries and "fraternal parties."[52] Kim Il Song might have perceived the actions that Khrushchev took against the Soviet "factionalists" as an absolution for his own harsh measures.[53] In any case, the North Korean campaign against factionalists, which had been kept almost totally concealed to that point, was suddenly to receive publicity just weeks after the outbreak of the internal crisis in Moscow.

In November 1957 the representatives of forty-six Communist parties gathered to celebrate the fortieth anniversary of the Russian Revolution. This was the last such gathering before the Sino-Soviet split permanently changed the Communist movement. By this time both the international and the domestic situations in the DPRK had undergone extensive changes. Kim Il Song and his circle of trusted former guerrillas had greatly strengthened their grip over their country. The surviving members of the Yan'an and Soviet factions no longer dared to think of any kind of protest or resistance; their main concern was survival (more often than not, by means of emigration to the USSR or China). On the other hand, the position of the Soviet Union and its ability to control international Communism had been seriously damaged by a number of factors: the first signs of estrangement with China, the bloody suppression of the Hungarian uprising, severe clashes within the Soviet leadership, and, above all, the manifold impacts of the campaign against the personality cult. Much later a prominent historian remarked that all things in world Communism were different after 1956, when "the heart had gone out of the [Communist] movement."[54] Though by no means publicly clear in 1957 or 1958, the cracks in the traditional Communist solidarity were becoming more and more visible to insiders.

It was under these circumstances that Mao Zedong had a long personal conversation with Kim Il Song in Moscow. After Kim Il Song's return home, a meeting of about 150 top North Korean cadres was convened in Pyongyang. Kim Ch'ang-man, a member of the North Korean delegation in Moscow who was then a rising star within the North Korean hierarchy (a few years later he was to disappear during a new wave of purges), informed them of this unofficial but meaningful encounter between Mao, the soon-to-be-hailed Great Helmsman, and Kim Il Song, the Sun of the Nation in the making. Among those present at this briefing was Pak Kil-yŏng, at that time the head of the First Department of the Ministry of Foreign Affairs, a Soviet Korean who had always been quite eager to inform the Soviet Embassy of any recent news. He spoke to a Soviet diplomat just three days later, quoting Kim Ch'ang-man as having said: "During his conversation [in Moscow] with Kim Il Song, Comrade Mao Zedong repeatedly expressed his apologies for the unjustified interference of the Chinese Communist Party in the affairs of the KWP in September of last year. Kim Ch'ang-man said that the Chinese comrades had asked that a conversation between Mao Zedong and Kim Il Song be arranged prior to the meeting [of the Communist parties' leaders], [since] they were afraid we would raise the question of the interference at the Moscow meeting. However, we were above this and protected the authority of the fraternal parties. The decision of the September Plenum was imposed on us from outside, and life has demonstrated that we were correct at the August Plenum. This bitter experience shows that we must educate party members to be proud of their party, and [we must] fight cosmopolites who follow not their own but other parties."[55] Kim Ch'ang-man informed the gathering that Peng Dehuai, present at the Mao-Kim meeting in Moscow, also expressed to Kim Il Song his personal regret for the "September affair," as well as for other improper actions of the Chinese troops stationed in North Korea (Kim Ch'ang-man quoted Peng Dehuai as recognizing that the Chinese forces were engaged in illegal intelligence gathering activities and also in printing North Korean money).[56]

No doubt, Mao's self-effacement in Moscow was primarily a maneuver of a crafty politician. Plotting his own break with Moscow, he needed to ensure himself of Kim Il Song's support or, at the very least, Kim's neutrality. An apology for the September incident did not cost Mao much in real terms; after all, by then it had become obvious that the September decisions had been no more than a piece of paper from the very beginning. Hence, Mao did not lose much by recognizing the obvious; Kim Il Song completely controlled the situation in Korea and could discard his enemies at will. However, if for Mao the apology was a cheap means of achieving some of his own goals, for Kim Il Song it had a real, albeit symbolic, meaning. Whatever the real reason and calculations behind Mao's actions, from Kim Il Song's point of view Mao's statement was akin to the capitulation of a Great Power, and Kim was anxious to inform the North Korean elite about this new development and to boast about his significant diplomatic victory.

On December 3–5, 1957, a new extended plenum of the KWP Central Committee was convened in Pyongyang. Soon one participant (and again it was Pak Kil-yŏng) reported the plenum to a Soviet diplomat. It was an unusually large gathering with a remarkable number of "special guests," up to fifteen hundred functionaries. Kim Ch'ang-man spoke again at length about the Moscow meeting of Kim Il Song with Mao Zedong and about Mao's apology. Then Ko Pong-gi, an alleged Ch'oe Ch'ang-ik supporter who had been under house arrest and investigation for a few months, delivered a speech "unmasking" and "disclosing" the alleged plans of the August opposition. Before his disgrace, Ko had been the first secretary of the KWP Pyongyang City Committee, the Yan'an faction's traditional stronghold. There is no reason to doubt that his speech had been written by the authorities or, at least, under their guidance (as Pak Kil-yŏng himself explicitly told his Soviet inter-locutor), and therefore the speech is more interesting as a propaganda exercise than a real testimony to the opposition plan. Ko said the op-position had intended to appoint Pak Il-u as the new chairman of the party, while Ch'oe Ch'ang-ik, Pak Ch'ang-ok, and Kim Sŭng-hwa were to be his deputies. Pak Ŭi-wan, a prominent and outspoken member of the Soviet faction, was also cited for the first time as not just a passive sympathizer but an active participant in the opposition.

Pang Hak-se, the minister of the interior and the supreme supervisor of the North Korean security services, alleged that the opposition had planned to start an armed revolt. As far as I know, this was the first time such an accusation was mentioned in the embassy papers. Thereupon the opposition members began to deliver their customary penitence. An exception was the outspoken Pak Ŭi-wan, who, with his usual boldness and audacity, denied the accusations. When Kim Ch'ang-man began to yell at him "You are Ivan! Ivan!"—hinting at his Russian origins—Pak simply quit the tribunal. Another victim was Kim Tu-bong, who had been recently ousted from his position as the North Korean head of state. The aged intellectual and scholar was now for the first time pub-licly (or almost publicly, since it happened at a secretive meeting of influential party figures) accused of being a member of the opposition. Kim Tu-bong obediently "recognized his guilt before the party," even if he probably did so in vague terms. Prominent politicians targeted during the plenum also included Kim Ch'ang-hŭp, former minister of commu-nications, who was branded a "traitor of the workers' movement" by Kim Il Song himself.[57]

Speakers insisted that heavy punishments be inflicted on the oppo-sition. For example, "The party secretary from the Ponggung Chemical Factory said that his factory workers had suggested that they would throw all 'factionalists' into a tank of boiling carbide, where the tempera-ture is 2,000°C."[58] Various similar threats made by Kim's faithful are mentioned in North Korean publications. The authors of *Chosŏn chŏnsa* (General history of Korea), for example, wrote: "The workers from the Kangson Steel Works, as well as the entire working class of our country, asked that the factionalist bastards be given to them, so [they could] cut every one of them to pieces."[59] The newly appointed minister of justice, Ho Chŏng-suk, was less melodramatic and merely suggested that "the factionalists be judged by the People's Court." Her suggestion was soon to become a reality, although not in the classical Stalinist sense of a highly publicized show trial.

The December Plenum of 1957 officially reversed the short-lived September decisions. Henceforth the purges against the real or potential supporters of the opposition gained official recognition and unconditional approval of the supreme authority. Kim Ch'ang-man, in his speech at the plenum, argued: "It [the visit of the joint Sino-Soviet delegation] was an expression of chauvinism by big nations toward a small nation. We had, and still have here, some people who like to wait for [foreign] planes. We know these people. . . . They do not trust our party and blindly believe other parties. There is no reason for them to wait for planes. There will be no more planes!"[60] The phrase about planes was etched into the memories of many of the participants, and Lim Ŭn (Hŏ Chin) later quoted it (with a slightly different wording) in his book. This approach was in stark contradiction to the earlier doctrine, with its emphasis on internationalism and the special role reserved for "fraternal countries." However, this was indicative of a pending change in North Korean policy. Kim Ch'ang-man's phrase was also a deft piece of rhetoric, although perhaps not terribly accurate—in September 1956, Mikoyan and Peng had arrived in the North Korean capital by train. Nevertheless, Kim Ch'ang-man proved to be right about the "planes" with overseas supervisors. The times had changed, and Kim Il Song was now the unquestioned master of the situation in North Korea.

The December Plenum launched a new wave of purges. It also meant a further tightening of the ideological control over a society to be transformed into a Stalinist monolith as soon as possible. The late 1950s was the time when the above-mentioned mass relocation of the "unreliable elements" reached its peak. Tens of thousands of people whose main and only crime was having a landlord grandfather or a relative in the South were deported from urban centers to the countryside. The purges also moved deeper into Korean society, and an increasing number of low-level cadres and party rank and file were becoming their targets.

After the December Plenum the representation of the August incident in the North Korean press also underwent a considerable change. The conspirators were depicted not only as splittists but also as traitors who were planning a military coup in the North Korean capital. For example, on April 11, 1958, Kim Yŏng-ju, Kim Il Song's younger brother and a high-level apparatchik, told a Soviet diplomat:

> Taking advantage of the uneasy international situation and difficulties within the country, Ch'oe Ch'ang-ik's group had been planning to attack the Central Committee openly prior to the August Plenum in order to achieve a change of leadership and to establish their "hegemony" in the party. Back then we had not been aware of all their treacherous plans, which included a possible military coup and terrorist acts against the leaders of the party and government. . . . However, as the August [1956] Plenum demonstrated, Ch'oe Ch'ang-ik's group had the far-reaching goal of provoking in the DPRK a crisis similar to the Hungarian one. Currently . . . Ch'oe Ch'ang-ik and other factional elements who were devising a counterrevolutionary plot have been arrested, and the investigation is proceeding. The testimonies of these traitors demonstrates how low they fell, preparing the DPRK for bloody events like those that happened in Hungary. Each passing day of investigation brings fresh facts about the attempted treason. Although no direct evidence of connections between Ch'oe Chang-ik's group and the American and Yi Sung-man's agents have been uncovered, it is clear that the South Korean ruling circle counted on the factionalists' plans. In February–March 1956 they were preparing a provocation in the DPRK, disguised as "revolt of the North Korean population against the Communist regime."[61]

From then on, the accusations of a planned military mutiny became standard.

In March 1958 the First KWP Conference was convened in Pyongyang. According to the KWP Statute, which simply followed the Soviet mold, a party conference was to be a "minor party congress" of a sort. A conference could be convened between the regular congresses whenever the situation required, in order to discuss urgent matters of party and state. No timetable was established; it was completely up to the discretion of the Central Committee to decide whether and when a new conference was necessary. Actually, the conferences seldom took place in Communist countries, and they were much less common than congresses. The KWP has only ever held two of them.

In other Leninist countries a decision to convene a conference was an indication that the party and/or the state was experiencing some problems, and the same was true for the First KWP Conference. However, one of the KWP Conference's most striking features was the unusually low publicity it was accorded at that time. During any major party convention in a Leninist country one would expect a flurry of official publications reporting alleged nationwide outbursts of the "masses' enthusiasm" and related labor feats, as well as dutifully reproducing standard banal speeches delivered by the convention members. During such events the official press (the only press available) would publish special, usually very large issues to accommodate this voluminous material. This well-established Soviet tradition had also been followed for the KWP Third Congress in 1956. However, the First Conference was reported in a very different and rather unusual way. *Nodong sinmun*'s front page contained brief official reports about the conference and published some material, but 70 percent of the articles published by the official daily had no connection to the conference. In a remarkable break with tradition, *Nodong sinmun* did not even publish the speeches of the delegates. The only major texts published by the North Korean official daily were two large reports, delivered by Yi Chong-ok and Pak Kŭm-ch'ŏl.

The conference had two major topics on its agenda. First, to approve North Korea's First Five-Year Plan. According to a Soviet tradition followed by most "people's democracies," major economic plans had to be rubber-stamped by a party convention, normally by its congresses. Hence, Yi Chong-ok, a young technocrat who had just emerged as an economic czar of North Korea (a position he was to retain well into the 1980s), duly delivered a lengthy and rather boring speech full of economic data and forecasts.[62]

However, the major issue on the conference agenda was a "struggle against the factionalists," and this was the real reason why the conference had been convened. Certainly, the delegates were not expected to "discuss" the situation; rather, they were to be "educated" about the crimes of their erstwhile comrades and bosses and also, by denouncing fallen leaders, to prove their worth and reliability. The activity of factionalists was the topic of another published speech, delivered to the conference by Pak Kŭm-ch'ŏl. Entitled "Tang-ŭl t'ongil-gwa tangyŏl-ŭl tŏuk kanghwahaneun te taehayŏ" (In regard to further strengthening the party's unity and solidarity), this speech began with the still compulsory reference to the "unbreakable unity" and "enormous achievements" of the "great socialist camp led by the Soviet Union," as well as ritualistic eulogies to the wisdom of Kim Il Song, who was said to lead a "core force of the Korean Communists." Then Pak proceeded to the main issue, the hideous crimes of the wicked factionalists. In accordance with the new accusations, Pak said: "As it has been clearly exposed, Ch'oe Ch'ang-ik's clique not only committed antiparty factionalist actions but also trod the path of betraying the revolution." However, the accusations were rather imprecise and lacked hard evidence: the opposition members were "conspiring with enemies," "advocating freedom of the factionalist activity," and so on. Only a few remarks shed light on the opposition's demands. According to Pak, "Ch'oe and his factionalist supporters were breaking the laws of the people's democracy and used the excuses of 'human rights' and 'respect for the law' in order to release the counterrevolutionary elements who had received the well-deserved punishments from the people's court" (an obvious reference to the opposition's abortive attempt at limiting the scale of political repression). At the same time, Pak did not accuse the Ch'oe group of plotting a military takeover, although such an accusation was raised at the conference. The speeches delivered by the delegates did not appear in *Nodong sinmun* at that time, and even Kim Il Song's own speech was not published until much later.

This unusually moderate coverage and the attempt to present the conference as a primarily economy-related event could only be intentional. The likely aim of such an approach was not to draw too much attention to the "factionalist question." This approach was likely sanctioned by Kim Il Song himself. At least, shortly before the conference, Nam Il told a Soviet diplomat that "a question of factionalism will occupy a small place in the conference."[63] It is doubtful whether that was actually the case, given that the verbal attacks on the real and alleged opposition supporters constituted a major part of the conference activity, but the authorities indeed tried to persuade the general North Korean public (as distinct from party cadres) and foreign observers that the "question of factionalism" was not too high on the conference agenda. We can only speculate about the reasons behind such a restraint. Perhaps Kim Il Song was worried about the adverse impact that a high-profile attack would have on domestic political stability or on North Korea's important relations with the USSR and China.

Unpublished speeches were full of invective against the "traitors" and "conspirators." According to Kim Hak-jun's data, the main target was Kim Tu-bong, who was made to sit and listen to endless accusations delivered by his former comrades. Some of these accusations were of a very personal nature, such as a rumor that he illegally procured sexual stimulators after he had married a much younger woman.[64] All other "factionalists" (Ch'oe Ch'ang-ik, Pak Ch'ang-ok, and others) were stigmatized as well. The opposition was again accused of plotting a military takeover in Pyongyang, and these improbable accusations led to a considerable lengthening of the list of victims, who now came to include some prominent military personalities.

According to Soviet records, Pak Kŭm-ch'ŏl's lengthy speech on March 5 was followed by the harangues of Pang Hak-se (minister of the interior), Hŏ Chŏng-suk (minister of justice), Kim T'ae-gŭn (head of the army's Political Department), and others. Pang Hak-se briefed the delegates on "how the factionalists had been plotting against the party and government," and Kim T'ae-gŭn informed them about the allegedly planned coup.[65] Yang Kye—a prominent Yan'an cadre, the former head of the cabinet secretariat, and an alleged conspirator—was made to deliver a speech in which he described the opposition's alleged actions and plans in 1956. It appears that Kim and his cabal were using the same tactic as they had in December 1957. Back then, Ko Pong-gi, another alleged supporter of the opposition, was "unmasking" the opposition's plans before a gathering of the party's power brokers. Although these speeches were written by the authorities and by no means could be taken at face value, their delivery by former opposition members made the information look more convincing to the audience. On the next day, Kim Il Song in his speech vehemently criticized the "factionalists" and, above all, Kim Tu-bong and Han Pin (the latter politician, hitherto seldom even mentioned, featured prominently in Kim's speech.)

The purges among the top functionaries continued after the conference. In June 1959 a new plenum of the Central Committee dismissed ten Central Committee members, about one-seventh of its total 1956 membership. All ex-members were accused of being supporters of the antiparty functionaries. They included two former Soviet Koreans, three survivors of the Domestic faction, and five members of the Yan'an faction. The newcomers included four guerrillas, two Soviet Koreans, and two Domestic Communists, but it is noteworthy that of all these newcomers only the four guerrillas retained positions in the next Central Committee, "elected" by the Fourth KWP Congress two years later, in 1961.[66]

Meanwhile, the participants in the "August affair" and their alleged co-plotters disappeared from public view. The pre-August Soviet papers had directly mentioned only seven members of conspiracy: Ch'oe Ch'ang-ik, Pak Ch'ang-ok, Yun Kong-hŭm, Sŏ Hwi, Kim Sŭng-hwa, Yi P'il-gyu, and Yi Sang-jo. With some reservations, we can also include Kim Tu-bong as a sympathetic outsider, for, according to Kim Sŭng-hwa's remarks, Kim Tu-bong had been aware of at least some of the opposition plans. Of these eight "authentic" conspirators, whose direct involvement in the plot is beyond doubt, five managed to flee to China or the USSR in 1956. The others—Ch'oe Ch'ang-ik, Pak Ch'ang-ok, and Kim Tu-bong—remained in North Korea. Ch'oe Ch'ang-ik and Pak Ch'ang-ok had been arrested by September 1957, while Kim Tu-bong briefly appeared at the First KWP Conference and was subjected to public humiliation there. However, from early 1958 onward the August incident had been presented as a large-scale conspiracy, so the North Korean authorities needed many more "conspirators" to make the new version of the story look more plausible. The increase in the number of conspirators was also a convenient way to justify ongoing large-scale purges. If the conspiracy was indeed large and omnipresent, the only way to deal with it would be a purge of a hitherto unprecedented scale. Hence the number of alleged participants swelled to include many prominent members of the Soviet faction and particularly the Yan'an faction.

In late October 1959, Pang Hak-se, who was still the North Korean minister of the interior, briefed Pelishenko, a prominent Soviet diplomat, about developments. Pang said that the investigation of the "August conspiracy" had been completed by then. Indeed, there had been two separate investigations: one handled by the Ministry of the Interior and the other by military security agencies. Pang did not explain the difference between these two investigations, but we may presume that the latter was chiefly engaged in making up charges of a "military conspiracy" among the generals. Eighty defendants were investigated by the Ministry of the Interior, and "approximately the same number" of defendants were dealt with by the military investigators. This means that by late 1959 about 160 former party cadres and military officers had been declared active participants in the "August affair."[67] Considering the methods likely employed by the North Korean investigators in such a situation, we must not be surprised that most defendants pleaded guilty. During the conversation, Pang showed Pelishenko a copy of Pak Ch'ang-ok's statement. Pak Ch'ang-ok admitted all accusations, including the most improbable one—staging a military takeover.

Hence, a trial should be expected. Pang said that the KWP Standing Committee had not decided whether the trial would be open or secret. Pang reported: "Depending on their crimes, the defendants will be divided into three groups. The first group [will consist of] leaders of the factionalists who committed heavy crimes: Ch'oe Ch'ang-ik (former vice-premier), Pak Ch'ang-ok (former vice-premier), Kim Wŏn-sul (former deputy minister of defense), and others, including some from the military. The second group [will consist of] those defendants who completely exposed and condemned their criminal activity. The third group [will consist of] those defendants who did not completely expose and condemn their crimes against the party and state. Depending on this [division], the punishments will be different." Pang said that the first group would get death sentences. He also mentioned some additional information about the death sentences: "The minister of the interior believes that the death sentence must be applied to twenty to thirty defendants. However, comrade Kim Il Song expressed the opinion that the death sentence must be applied to the smallest possible number of the defendants, three or four persons."[68] This information about Kim's special opinion is interesting, although it is somewhat doubtful whether we can take it at face value. It is also remarkable that at least some defendants "did not completely expose and condemn their crimes against the party and state," that is, were not broken by their interrogation and did not plead guilty. This outcome represents a remarkable act of courage, although the names of these courageous people still remain unknown.

This conversation took place shortly before the actual trial, so we can surmise that Pang Hak-se deliberately briefed the Soviet Embassy in order to prepare Moscow for things to come. Somewhat surprisingly this time the North Korean leaders decided to break with the Stalinist tradition and did not stage a show trial. As Pang Hak-se briefed Pelishenko just a few months later, in February 1960, Ch'oe Ch'ang-ik and Pak Ch'ang-ok, along with other real and alleged participants of the August conspiracy, were tried secretly in January 1960. It is noteworthy that Kim Tu-bong was not mentioned among the defendants. Perhaps he was spared the trial or, much more likely, was dead by 1960. The secret trial was presided over by Kim Ik-sŏn, who was then the chairman of the KWP Central Control Commission and had also presided over the tribunal during a large show trial of the Domestic faction cadres in 1953.[69] Other members of the court included Yi Hyo-sun (former guerrilla, secretary of the Pyongyang KWP City Committee), Sŏ Ch'ŏl (former guerrilla, head of the KPA Chief Political Directorate), and Kim Kyŏng-sŏk (former guerrilla, head of the Administration Department of KWP Central Committee).[70]

According to Pang's briefing, twenty of the thirty-five defendants were shot, and the fifteen others received long prison sentences. Thus the sentence was as harsh as the Ministry of the Interior had suggested, and Kim Il Song must have withdrawn his initial recommendation for a somewhat milder approach (if it was indeed his opinion and not a fabrication of Pang Hak-se's or some kind of hypocritical public relations exercise).[71] Among the people who received the death sentence were both of the leaders of the August incident—Pak Ch'ang-ok and Ch'oe Ch'ang-ik. The list also included Ko Pong-gi, former secretary of the Pyongyang KWP City Committee, and the "Yan'an generals" Kim Wŏn-sul, Yang

Kye, and Kim Ung. Pang also said that the death sentence had been executed by the time of the conversation. If that is true, then all leaders of the revolt would have met their death in January or early February 1960. There is, however, a truly persuasive reason not to believe this statement. Kim Ung, allegedly shot in 1960, was very much alive in the 1970s. He was indeed one of the major "Yan'an generals" who became victims of the purge, and, like all other alleged "factionalists," he disappeared from public view after 1958. Nevertheless, he made a sudden political comeback in 1968 and subsequently began a diplomatic career.

There may be some explanations for this contradiction, but it is a reminder of how much work on North Korean history remains to be done.[72] At this stage, a few possible explanations for the contradiction between Pang Hak-se's statement and the hard fact of Kim Ung's survival can be suggested: (1) Pelishenko made a mistake while writing down his record of the conversation. Kim Ung was not actually mentioned by Pang Hak-se at all, or he was mentioned as one of the defendants who got prison terms. Taking into consideration Pelishenko's experience and qualification, such an explanation looks rather unlikely but still could be possible. (2) Pang Hak-se deliberately included Kim Ung on the list of executed generals in order to mislead Pelishenko (and the Soviets) for some unknown reason. (3) Pang Hak-se was lying when he said that the sentence had been carried out by the time of the conversation. At least some of the defendants were still alive and their lives were spared for at least a few more years. Kim Ung was one of them, and he was eventually rehabilitated—presumably by virtue of his "good" behavior in prison and perhaps also because of some change of Kim Il Song's mood. It is possible that Kim Ung's comeback in 1968 was somehow related to the split in the Guerrilla faction and the subsequent disgrace of the "Kapsan group" in 1967–1968. I tentatively prefer the third explanation.

It is also worth noting that in the early 1960s many people believed that Kim Ung had indeed been shot. For example, Plotnikov, a prominent Soviet military expert on Korea, mentioned to me in 1990 that Kim Ung had been executed in the "early 1960s" (obviously, he was unaware of Kim's eventual comeback).[73] In short, the riddle may not be solved without further research in North Korean archives if and when that becomes possible.

In this regard it is also possible to make a rather speculative suggestion. Pang Hak-se mentioned in October 1959 that Kim Il Song allegedly wanted to shoot "only" three or four of the "worst" offenders, whereas the Ministry of the Interior favored much harsher punishment. Perhaps the North Koreans managed to combine both options. Perhaps twenty people received the death sentence (as had been suggested by the Ministry of the Interior), but only three or four were actually shot (as had been proposed by Kim).

While talking to Pelishenko, Pang Hak-se also mentioned that new trials were in the making and that the total number of accused was "about one hundred and fifty" (which corresponds pretty well with the above-mentioned estimate of 150). However, Pang did not explain how the defendants had been divided into groups and who had to face the accusations first. Judging by the above-mentioned lists that include Pak Ch'ang-ok, Ch'oe Ch'ang-ik, and other key opposition figures, we may presume that the defendants of the January trial were those seen as more serious criminals, and lesser sinners were to stand trial at some later date. No information about any subsequent trials is available at the time of writing. However, this is understandable, given that the relations between the USSR and North Korea spiraled downward around 1961, so in the later periods the Soviet Embassy would hardly have gained access to information that was seen as politically sensitive. At least it is known that no information about these trials appeared in the official North Korean press.

Nevertheless, the fierce attacks on the "August group" in the Korean press continued for another few years. These publications occasionally contained even harsher accusations. For example, a 1962 pamphlet on party unity stated: "The Ch'oe Ch'ang-ik clique . . . mostly consisted of elements who [in the colonial period] had already capitulated and transformed themselves into the lackeys of Japanese imperialism or elements who served the imperialist aggressive forces as spies of Chiang Kai-shek and lackeys of U.S. imperialism. After liberation, with the support of American imperialism, they instigated the factionalist splittist policy. They undertook a two-faced treacherous position of ostensibly behaving as if they followed the party, while secretly opposing the party."[74] This was followed by the remark that the opposition had acted under the "direct guidance" of "American imperialism."[75] Thus, North Korean propaganda came very close to defining the "August opposition" as spies. However, unlike the official approach to Pak Hŏn-yŏng and his Domestic Communist followers, this accusation, though sporadically raised, did not become standard. The "August conspirators" remained in the North Korean historical mythology as, first of all, "splittists" and "traitors" but only occasionally as "spies."

9 North Korea Changes Course

BY THE SUMMER OF 1957 it was clear that the decisions of the September Plenum of 1956 were dead, and their death had come with the tacit approval of the very forces that had once imposed them. While many "little Stalins" of Eastern Europe were wiped out by popular protests and/or schemes of their fellow leaders, Kim Il Song was emerging from the crisis with nothing to be afraid of, either within or outside the party.

His victory had profound consequences for the general situation in the country and greatly influenced the everyday lives of all North Koreans. The late 1950s marked important changes in North Korean society. The North Korea of 1945–1956 was a rather typical Soviet-sponsored "people's democracy," and its domestic policies followed the prescribed universal set with only minor variations. The situation changed in the late 1950s, after North Korean leaders refused to follow the de-Stalinization trend. They chose to keep restrictive Stalinist policies (then abandoned by most other Communist countries) and indeed began to modify these policies. To some extent, these modifications reflected the increasing impact of Mao's China on Korea. Many new policies were obviously influenced by the concurrent Chinese developments, but Mao's ideas could not have taken root in North Korea without a fertile soil in which to thrive.

The general trend was clear: a trend toward greater governmental control over both society and the economy; toward a harsher persecution of real, potential, and imagined dissent; toward a greater restriction of the already limited international exchanges (now deemed potentially subversive); toward a tightening of control over the arts and culture; and, last but not least, toward the deification of the godlike Great Leader. In short the trend was toward preserving and strengthening the Stalinist institutions, in an increasingly nationalized form. The mid-1950s had been a period of relative ideological relaxation in North Korea. Even *Nodong sinmun* could publish cartoons (albeit normally depicting "the U.S. imperialists and their South Korean puppets"), articles on foreign culture, and even verse in such an outrageously "feudal" and "reactionary" language as classical Chinese. But the time for such frivolities was fast running out.[1] At the same time, the "new" North Korean Stalinism was acquiring a distinct nationalist flavor. In this regard it was not so different from other Stalinisms, including the Soviet prototype. To be sure, until the early 1960s the Soviets had kept the nationalist tendencies of the dependent regimes at bay, for local nationalisms would unavoidably contradict and undermine the "major" (Soviet/Russian) one. Only certain elements of the nationalist heritages were allowed—namely, those that would not create problems for Moscow. They included things like stories of the great victories over foreign invaders if the invaders' descendants happened to belong to the "imperialist" camp in the 1950s (Bulgarian campaigns against Turks, Polish conflicts with Germans, and so on). North Korea was not an exception to this; such "controlled" nationalism had existed there since the late 1940s, and it had a strong anti-Japanese flavor. However, from the early 1960s the situation in North Korea changed and the local nationalism began to liberate itself from its former restraints. In culture and politics the emphasis was to be on the indigenous traditions, often radically reinterpreted or simply invented, while all outside connections and influences on the Korean culture began to be played down or denied. The regime—whose initial inception by a foreign power was still recent history, vividly remembered by a majority of its population—strove to "nationalize" itself.

No doubt, these trends primarily served the interests of Kim Il Song and his close entourage and were often initiated and always encouraged by them. However, these policies could not have been successful without at least some support from below. We might assume that the new line reflected the ideals and values of a large number of middle- and low-level cadres and, perhaps, of the wider North Korean population. These people, mostly with a traditional peasant background, supported the regime because it was seen as an essentially national Korean system. Given that the Soviets were foreigners, and culturally very alien foreigners, the appeal of the Korean patriotism was very powerful. We can presume that many Koreans welcomed the new policy, which was perceived as an attempt to get rid of the tiresome Soviet omnipresence while keeping intact both the truly Korean essence of the regime and its egalitarian spirit.

Among the major contributors to the new sense of national identity was the generally successful educational policy of the DPRK. The contribution of modern schooling in a national language to the formation of national identity and nationalism has been noted by scholars.[2] In the DPRK the post-1945 Koreans were the first generation to receive an education in the national language that centered around the question of national identity. Although only 23 percent of males and a mere 5 percent of females had any formal education in 1944,[3] by the mid-1950s virtually all children of school age attended at least primary school. The new school curriculum was unavoidably influenced by the ideas of nationalism. The recurrent topic of "heroic struggle for independence against foreigners" can be found throughout the North Korean textbooks on history, language, and other humanities subjects. We can assume that in Korea the Soviet supervisors were more comfortable with these ideas than they were in, say, Eastern Europe, where in many cases the memory of the struggle against the past Russian invasions was an essential component of the nationalist myth. In Korea the role of the "vile other" was conveniently played by the Japanese and, in the North Korean interpretation of national history, by the Americans as well.[4] Nevertheless, this approach, although far from being specifically anti-Russian, for the first time in Korean history educated numbers of ordinary Koreans in the spirit of nationalism. The ideals of the new, true, and authentic Korean society, free from foreign oppression and control (and, if practicable, even foreign influences), could not but resonate with these former peasants who had recently become city dwellers, minor cadres, or military officers.

These developments were not unique to North Korea. If we take a look at other regimes of "national Stalinism"—Romania, Albania, and, in some respects, North Vietnam—we cannot fail to notice that they had many features in common. These countries had the highest percentages of rural population among the Communist states. With the conditional exception of Romania, none of them had experienced any kind of democracy before the Communist takeover, and their education levels were very low, even by the moderate standards of the Communist camp.

The growing nationalism was accompanied by increasing radicalization of North Korean policy in general. In late 1958 the Soviet diplomats noticed a general change in the wording of North Korean documents. In December of that year Kim Il Song suddenly declared that North Korea would complete the construction of socialism within four to five years. The remark was ostensibly influenced by the recent Chinese experiments, since Mao also drastically changed his forecast on the time needed for the construction of socialism in China. These new statements by Kim brought a veiled disapproval from the Soviets. To Moscow, such a statement was a minor heresy, because the Soviet orthodoxy of the time held that the transitional period of a "people's democracy" must last decades, not years, especially in such a backward country as North Korea. However, these new declarations expressed Pyongyang's determination to speed up the tempo of reform and to crush any resistance in the process.[5] For North Korean leaders who were educated in the classical Stalinist traditions, these frantic efforts had special meaning. As mentioned above, the "people's democracy" theory discriminated against allegedly "immature" socialist societies of the new Communist states and, in doing so, implicitly reinforced the notion of Soviet supremacy. Such a notion was not welcome anymore. North Korean leaders sought to be on equal footing with the "elder brothers," in both real and symbolic terms.

Perhaps the most important indication of these new trends was a headlong rush to reconstruct society along the lines of orthodox Leninism or, rather, Stalinism, by speeding up its transformation from a somewhat immature "people's democracy" into a full-scale "socialist society." These developments were likely influenced by the concurrent changes in China, where Mao's radicalism was carrying the day. The best example of this new policy was probably the collectivization of

agriculture. Orthodoxy insisted that in a fully socialist country all farmers were expected to be members of the state-controlled agricultural cooperatives (of course, when joining the cooperatives, the farmers were
required to give up a major part of their land, livestock, and tools). Collectivization began in the DPRK in 1954–1955, and by the end of 1956
about 80.9 percent of all households had been forced to join the cooperatives. By the end of the next year, 95.6 percent of all North Korean
peasants were members of agricultural cooperatives.[6] The ongoing political crisis obviously failed to slow this process. Indeed, it even looked
as if the Pyongyang leaders had decided to increase the tempo of collectivization after the August crisis in 1957. As late as April 1956 a final resolution of the Third KWP Congress explicitly stated that there was no
need to rush to collectivization, which must be "gradual" and "voluntary."[7] However, 1956 became the year of intense collectivization. This
escalation was presumably another manifestation of the Chinese
influence, for in September 1955 Mao repudiated the earlier cautious
approach and demanded the speeding up of the collectivization movement. As a result of this "high tide" of collectivization, by the end of
1956 about 83 percent of all Chinese peasant households had enrolled
in the "advanced producers'" cooperatives (comparable to the North
Korean figure of 80.9 percent reached at the same time).[8]

Small private commerce and the handicraft industry suffered the
same fate. Heretofore severely restricted but tolerated, they were put
under increasing pressure from late 1956 onward, and by 1958, within
a mere two years, they ceased to exist.[9] Perhaps the turning point came
in November 1957 when the North Korean cabinet passed Resolution
102. The resolution prohibited all private trade of cereals from December 1, 1957, on; henceforth, agricultural cooperatives would be allowed
to sell their surplus grain only to the state. The former vendors had to
join cooperatives or get other official employment; otherwise they
would not be eligible for rationing coupons.[10] The complete liquidation
of private commerce was a rather harsh measure, especially since orthodoxy held that private commerce would have to be gradually incorporated into the socialist economy as a result of a long process of
transformation. According to a Hungarian document, when Pyongyang
moved to abolish private trade and small-scale industry in the late

1950s, some Eastern European diplomats worried about the possible negative consequences of such hasty nationalization.[11] This attempt to speed up again was probably the result of Chinese influence; in October 1955, Mao had suggested spreading the "high tide" of socialist reconstruction to private enterprise as well, and by 1956–1957, private businesses in China ceased to exist.[12]

Stalinist orthodoxy would hold that these changes in agriculture and handicraft meant the complete destruction of the residual non-socialist elements within Korean economy, and hence there would be a rapid development in North Korean society toward the maturity of "complete socialism." These changes undoubtedly put additional pressure on the struggling North Korean population, but as far as we know, this pressure did not lead to any significant outbreaks of mass defiance.

There are many explanations for the political passivity of the masses. The most obvious (but perhaps not the most important) one was harsh and efficient political control, enforced by the vigorous activity of an omnipresent secret police and assisted by the party and state structures. Indeed, from 1957 the regime began to tighten its already strong grip over the populace. The period of 1957–1958 was marked by show trials of alleged South Korean agents and saboteurs, as well as of "traitors" who had collaborated with the South Korean and American armies during a short occupation of the North by United Nations forces (mostly from the United States) in October–December 1950. The punishments were harsh, with death sentences being common.[13] We will probably never know how many of the victims were really agents of the South Korean and/or American intelligence, but judging by the experience of Stalin's Russia and Mao's China, we might assume that probably only a tiny fraction of the accused were actually guilty of any collusion with the South Korean government. The show trials, public executions, and constant lectures about "revolutionary vigilance" influenced the general atmosphere in the country. The press made it clear that the halfhearted relaxation of the previous years had inflicted much harm on the Korean revolution: "[Some cadres] do not understand correctly and distorted the . . . party policies directed at furthering the revolution. The hostile elements, those who have committed serious counterrevolutionary crimes or clearly attempted counterrevolutionary actions, are nevertheless dealt with lightly if they just denied this [counterrevolutionary involvement] or submitted their penitence. Such a lack of vigilance is not a small danger to our revolution."[14] The same article stated that "revolutionary vigilance" was to be applied to the "factionalists" as well: "We'll have to increase our vigilance in regard to the remaining factionalists [who] could survive within our party, and block all their activity."[15]

The new wave of terror did not target only party cadres; commoners were not spared either. Because of the paucity of available sources, we are better informed about purges among the party leaders than about the mass terror, but there are indications that the latter had also increased and reached unprecedented proportions by the late 1950s. On May 30, 1957, the KWP Standing Committee (the North Korean term for the KWP Politburo) issued a special decision entitled "On Transforming the Struggle against Counterrevolutionary Elements into an All-Party, All-People's Movement." This document was of singular importance, for it laid the foundations for the eventual classification of the entire North Korean population into a few dozen sociopolitical categories—the birth of the notorious *sŏngbun* system. Every North Korean was to be designated as belonging to one of these groups, depending on his or her family origin, previous political behavior, and perceived political loyalty. These categorical classifications eventually became a hallmark of the North Korean social structure. The mammoth task of classifying the entire population into fifty-one categories was not completed until the early 1970s, but the work began in 1957.

Another major policy decision was establishment of the "five households responsibility system" *(o ho tamdang che)*. This system, which was first introduced in July 1958, eventually developed into the current *inminban* (people's group) structure, another hallmark of North Korean society.[16] Under this new system, every North Korean had to belong to a neighborhood unit. These units were responsible for the ideological education and "politically reliable" behavior of their members and also served as a conduit for various mobilization campaigns. These units had numerous prototypes in East Asian history (but not in the Soviet tradition) and were to grow into a powerful tool for social control over the entire population. Around the same time, the North Korean government began the forced relocation of "unreliable elements" to remote mountainous parts of the country (the infamous Resolution 149 of the Cabinet of Ministers).[17] The period of 1958–1959 was a time of large-scale purges among the common people, an epoch of the greatest witch hunt in North Korean history.

The campaign was impressive indeed. Yŏ Chŏng, a Yan'an faction cadre who eventually managed to flee to China, recalled these days: "1958 and 1959 were an unending nightmare both for me and for all people in this country. People were spending day after day as if in the midst of a nightmare."[18] This recollection, incidentally, would describe pretty well the feelings of a great many Soviet party cadres in the midst of Stalin's Great Purge (or the Chinese elite during Mao's Cultural Revolution), and it does not appear to be much exaggerated. Even if the remark about "all people" is a generalization, both the KWP cadres and the commoners with "wrong connections" had good reasons to perceive the political developments in such a way.

Newly discovered material gives us for the first time some reliable quantitative data on the terror, and these data are gruesome indeed. In February 1960, Pang Hak-se, the DPRK minister of the interior, told a Soviet diplomat that during the campaign from October 1958 to May 1959 the North Korean secret police "exposed" approximately 100,000 "hostile and reactionary elements." To fully appreciate the frightening scale of this statistic, one must remember that, according to Pang Hak-se's testimony, the number of "enemies" exposed by the North Korean security services during 1945–1958 was also 100,000.[19] In other words, within just nine months of 1958–1959 as many people were persecuted on political grounds as during the entire first thirteen years of North Korean history. These figures appear even more frightful if one takes into consideration that the North Korea of 1945–1958 was not a democratic society. The years 1945–1958 for Korea were years of "dependent Stalinism." The period was also marked by three years of bloody civil and international war, when one could reasonably expect harsher-than-usual security measures. Nevertheless, during the entire turbulent period of 1945–1958 fewer people were formally persecuted for political crimes than in a single year in the late 1950s. Pang Hak-se told his Soviet interlocutor that only a minority of the cases led to formal persecution, while most "reactionary elements" were subjected to "reeducation." However, such "reeducation" most likely meant a relocation to recently established exile camps. It should be mentioned that this campaign was to a large extent influenced by the contemporary campaign in China, where Mao's regime launched a large-scale persecution of the "rightists."

Against this background, on August 27, 1957, the first postwar elections to North Korea's Supreme People's Assembly took place. The elections themselves hardly had much practical meaning, since they followed the well-known Stalinist tradition of "one candidate per seat" elections. The predictable result was 99.92 percent support for the party, while the participation rate also achieved a suspiciously similar 99.92 percent (beginning with the subsequent elections of 1962, Kim Il Song established a unique North Korean tradition: Pyongyang began to claim 100 percent participation and 100 percent support for the government candidates). Though the elections were an obvious hoax, and the "elected" legislature was a politically impotent rubber-stamp gathering, the very fact that elections were held at all had some special symbolic meaning. After all, they were the first elections since 1948, and by holding them the North Korean leadership tried to demonstrate both the popular support and the stability it allegedly enjoyed. As Kim Il Song himself proudly declared in his speech delivered on November 27, 1957: "Recently, foreign visitors to our country, amazed at the elections to government bodies in our country, said that we were doing it in Korea when a certain country [Hungary] is in a state of chaos because of an antigovernment revolt."[20]

The elections had other important and noteworthy peculiarities as well. First of all, only 75 of the First Assembly's 527 members in 1948 were reelected to the Second Assembly. This high replacement rate indicates the scale of the personnel changes among the North Korean elite (most of these changes were probably due to the purges).[21] Second, the Second Assembly was much smaller, having only 215 members. This time the North Korean leaders gave up their pretensions of nationwide representation, so the Second Assembly, unlike its predecessor, did not include the "representatives" allegedly elected in South Korea—hence its smaller size. Another ominous sign was the replacement of Kim Tu-bong, who from 1948 had been the head of the Supreme People's Assembly and, technically, head of the North Korean state. The election occurred just a few months before the downfall of Kim Tu-bong. In 1957 his position as chairman of the Supreme People's Assembly was taken by none other than Ch'oe Yong-gŏn. Ch'oe remained in this symbolically important but politically impotent position until his death in 1976.

The year 1957 was also marked by the emergence of the first and perhaps most famous of the endless mass mobilization campaigns, which later became so typical of North Korean society. In 1957, Kim Il Song launched the much trumpeted Ch'ŏnlima (Flying Horse) movement, which was initially an imitation of some contemporary Soviet schemes but soon came to be influenced by and modeled on the Chinese "Great Leap Forward." The people were encouraged to work more and more, to do their utmost to achieve high (and often completely unrealistic) production targets. The unusually intense propaganda barrage deliberately created in workplaces an atmosphere of extreme fervor, somewhat akin to a battlefield mentality. The Ch'ŏnlima movement, with its distinctly Maoist flavor, indicated an ongoing shift toward ideological, rather than material, incentives. Such a shift might have made some sense in postwar North Korea, when resources were very scarce and the authorities had to rely on the relatively inexpensive option of ideological mobilization to encourage the people to work harder and better. The concept of the mobilization campaign initially originated in Stalin's Soviet Union (the Stakhanovite movement of the mid-1930s), but it was China under Mao that made the greatest use of this political and social device. In spite of all the contemporary fanfare, in China it was a disaster, whereas in Korea the actual results proved to be moderate at best. Nevertheless, the imprint of the Chinese "Great Leap" on the North Korean Ch'ŏnlima movement is obvious. The launch of the Ch'ŏnlima movement also reflected the general move away from the "revisionist" ideas of Khrushchev's Soviet Union, where the authorities were (albeit reluctantly and inconsistently) giving up their original inflated hopes concerning ideological incentives and were gradually coming to the conclusion that people would not work well unless they were paid adequately.

The new trends were also seen in literature and the arts. The brief period of 1956–1958 was arguably the most liberal in the entire history of North Korean arts—despite the persecution of gifted writers with

South Korean backgrounds. The officially approved demand to get rid of "schematism" was interpreted by writers and art managers as permission to be more free aesthetically, to feel less bound by the harsh ideological prescriptions of mature Stalinism. However, this period of relative relaxation did not last long. From late 1958 onward, the main catchphrases in literary politics were "educating the Ch'ŏnlima riders" and "struggling against revisionism" (the latter term was increasingly used to hint at the Soviet Union and "decadent" Soviet influence). In practice this meant that harsh political restrictions were reimposed on writers and artists, so that ideological liberties would no longer be tolerated. The artists were expected to compose odes to the party and the Great Leader, as well as invectives directed against the "class enemies" and their "revisionist henchmen."[22]

The picture of the DPRK in the late 1950s would be incomplete without mentioning the impressive performance of the North Korean economy. The official reports about "successes" and "labor victories" must be taken somewhat critically, but the tempo of the economic development was indeed impressive. The First Five-Year Plan was claimed to be completed by 1960, two years ahead of schedule. According to the official declarations, by mid-1959 industrial output had increased 2.6 times, a degree envisioned by the plan for the end of 1961. The official statistics showed that industrial output in 1960 was 3.5 times higher than it was in 1956.[23] All these assertions are disputable and almost certainly exaggerated to some degree, but even most skeptical observers have to agree that the North Korean economic performance in the late 1950s was remarkably sound, especially if compared with the near disastrous state of the South Korean economy. The most recent independent estimation is that the North Korean gross national product nearly doubled from 1956 to 1960, going from $1.007 to 1.848 billion (in current U.S. dollars).[24] This was a very impressive growth measured by standards of any country.

We can only guess to what degree this performance was stimulated by very generous Soviet and Chinese aid, but there is no doubt that the results did not fail to please the North Korean leadership and party cadres, as well as the general population. The high-speed economic growth did not bring much improvement to the everyday lives of the North Korean populace (and was not intended to do so), but the feeling of rapid and successful development was likely shared by many Koreans. The North Korean press and, more broadly, the Communist press have always been known for their penchant for reporting real or imaginary economic achievements and record-breaking labor feats. Nevertheless, even against such a background, the number of economy-related articles in the North Korean press of 1957 and 1958 is striking. The newspaper pages were full of cheerful reports from the construction sites and factories; large tables and graphs illustrated the recent economic triumphs, as well as expectations for the triumphs to come; and the moderate but still impressive technological achievements, like the production of the first Korean tractors and trucks, were widely publicized.[25] Undoubtedly, the populace at large, and especially the party cadres, associated the apparent economic successes with new policies, and these policies were in turn credited to Kim Il Song. This situation was conducive to further strengthening Kim's hold on power, just as the similar situation in the 1930s Soviet Union had strengthened Stalin's influence. At the same time, the role of generous foreign aid in the economic developments was probably not fully credited by the authorities and was increasingly underreported by the press. Eventually, this economic hubris led to a series of rather careless policy decisions in the early 1960s, when the North Korean leadership provoked a near termination of Soviet aid without seriously looking for an adequate substitute for it.

Another feature of the 1957–1960 period was a steady decline of the Soviet influence and Soviet presence. In early 1957, in the wake of the October Declaration of 1956, the number of Soviet advisers was reduced considerably. This reduction was made on Soviet initiative, in line with a new policy of abolishing or reducing the network of the Soviet advisers in the "people's democracies," where the Soviet omnipresence was seen as an annoying and unnecessary reminder of the local regimes' dependency. In early 1957 seventeen Korean ministers and central government agencies had Soviet advisers who directed and, to some extent, controlled the agencies' activity (this figure does not include lower-level advisers and advisers in the military and secret services). In January–February 1957, after some consultations with the Korean authorities, nine of these seventeen ministerial-level advisers were recalled by

Moscow.[26] Others followed soon, although some technical staff and military advisers remained in North Korea until the early 1960s.

In a symbolically important gesture, in 1957 the North Korean authorities ordered that all classes in the Sixth High School be taught in Korean. This school *(che yuk kodŭng hakkyo)* was a place where a majority of the second-generation Soviet Koreans (and children of some other Soviet residents of Pyongyang) were receiving their education. Russian had been the language of instruction in this privileged educational institution, which trained the younger Soviet Koreans for entry into Soviet universities. The curriculum of the school was also basically Soviet, albeit with some minor "Koreanization" (like classes on Korean history and introductory lessons on the Korean language). The school was a quite specific institution, surprisingly isolated from the Korean environment, and the interaction between its students and their "purely Korean" peers was kept at a minimum. We may assume that the very existence of the school could be seen by the local Koreans as a symbol of the special privileges enjoyed by the Soviets, as well as of the special role of the USSR in North Korean culture and education. The language switch to Korean in late 1957 led to another predictable and perhaps not entirely undesirable result. Soviet Koreans—who, like most Koreans everywhere, wanted only the best available education for their children—were not happy about sending them to Korean colleges, which were much inferior to their Soviet counterparts. The closure of the Russian-language school in Pyongyang induced some Soviet Koreans to move their families or at least their older children back to the USSR, where they could better prepare themselves for their future studies at Soviet universities.[27]

Because the Soviet Union was increasingly seen as a source of ideological contamination, the unofficial contacts with this onetime patron had to be limited. In 1950s North Korea the most obvious channel of Soviet influence (apart from the former Soviet Koreans) was students who studied in Soviet colleges. This was the only group of North Koreans to remain in this ideologically dangerous environment for any length of time and to be able to communicate freely with the ideologically contaminated Soviet population. In addition, students' contacts could not be efficiently traced, let alone controlled. In 1957 and 1958 the number of North Korean students overseas was greatly reduced. In May 1957 the deputy minister of education informed a Soviet diplomat that the DPRK would not send undergraduates to other "people's democracies," with the exception of the USSR. Many students were to be recalled home from these other countries. In early 1958 the North Korean government took the next logical step: it decided to send only postgraduates to the USSR.[28] Presumably, student defections in Moscow and the Soviets' apparent unwillingness to extradite such defectors also contributed to this decision.

On December 16, 1957, the Soviet Union and North Korea signed a new agreement on citizenship. It explicitly and unconditionally forbade dual citizenship and required everybody who had been a citizen of both the USSR and the DPRK to make a choice. This agreement was a logical development of earlier trends, given that both Moscow and Pyongyang had been encouraging the former Soviet Koreans to officially denounce their USSR citizenship since the early 1950s. However, in the political atmosphere of the late 1950s, this agreement was an additional blow inflicted on the already depleted and demoralized Soviet Koreans, many of whom had technically kept their Soviet citizenship (although they did not normally bother to extend or replace their expired Soviet passports). They were now facing a tough choice. They could either relinquish their Soviet citizenship, thus losing even the remote hope of gaining some protection from the still influential Soviet Embassy, or they could become Soviet citizens, thus losing their high positions and good jobs within the North Korean bureaucracy (soon it became clear that the latter decision also meant almost automatic repatriation to the USSR). Most of them eventually made a wise choice and decided that staying alive took precedence over having a career. However, the new agreement undermined the very existence of the Soviet faction and further restricted the Soviet influence on North Korean domestic politics.

In general, the Soviet Embassy did not act on behalf of the Soviet Koreans. When a Soviet Korean applied for permission to return to the USSR, such permission was given. But there was no active interference by the embassy; no attempts to rescue Soviet Koreans took place (or, at least, nothing is known about such actions). In fact the Soviet Embassy was a passive witness to the purge. Such an approach was not unusual. Perhaps, after 1958 or 1959, the Soviets could hardly influence the course of events anyway.[29]

Shortly afterward, Pyongyang scored another diplomatic victory, this time in its relations with China. In 1958, China and North Korea signed an agreement about the withdrawal of Chinese troops (euphemistically called the Chinese People's Volunteers) from Korean territory. The relevant papers were signed in February 1958, during Chou En-lai's visit to Pyongyang, and by October of the same year the last Chinese soldier had left the DPRK (though some Chinese military advisers remained).[30] Their withdrawal did not considerably change the strategic situation: after all, in case of a new war or another emergency the Chinese forces could be sent across the border in a matter of days, so in real terms the DPRK's security was not jeopardized in any meaningful way.[31] At the same time, this withdrawal provided the still united Communist camp with an important propaganda asset: the U.S. troops were still stationed in South Korea, whereas the North was ostensibly free of foreign military presence. However, like the agreement on the citizenship questions with the USSR, the Chinese withdrawal also had important implications for the North Korean domestic situation: it greatly restricted the Chinese ability to influence North Korean internal politics directly. The direct intervention of the Chinese forces on behalf of some political force had never been a particularly likely possibility, but after the withdrawal of the Chinese troops this possibility was eliminated.

At about the same time, the Soviet Koreans also began to feel the impact of the ongoing purges. As was mentioned above, initially the major attack was directed against the Yan'an faction. That tactic was reasonable: in August 1956 the former "Chinese Koreans" had formed a majority of the opposition speakers and supporters, so they had to be dealt with first. Once the Yan'an faction was annihilated, Kim Il Song could turn his attention to the Soviet faction. By then it was clear that any Soviet intervention, direct or indirect, would be highly unlikely. Pak Ch'ang-ok, a leader of the Soviet Koreans and an active participant in the August incident, had been arrested in 1957. In the autumn of 1958, new arrests of Soviet Koreans took place. Among the first victims were Kim Ch'il-sŏng, a former chief of staff in the North Korean Navy;

Kim Wŏn-gil, another high-level officer; and Pak Ŭi-wan, the out-spoken deputy prime minister who had so stubbornly refused to deliver a "self-criticism."[32] In 1959, arrests and the "ideological examination" of Soviet Koreans became common. People were disappearing one after the other. Some of them were arrested, while others lost their privileged positions and were either exiled to remote villages or demoted to low-ranking posts. According to the estimates of their former comrades, at least forty-five prominent Soviet Koreans (roughly a quarter of their initial total) were purged and later perished in the North in the late 1950s and early 1960s.[33] A majority of them were arrested in 1959 and 1960. Although the Soviet Embassy in general seldom intervened in support of the Soviet Koreans, for minor figures their Soviet citizenship could afford some protection.[34]

The steady deterioration of the Soviet-Korean relationship and intensifying purges meant that connections with the Soviet Union ceased to be a basis for the Soviet Koreans' privileged status. On the contrary, these connections were viewed with increasing suspicion: interaction with the Soviets was gradually acquiring a patina of danger. Yu Sŏng-hun, the rector of Kim Il Song University, lost his job in the middle of 1959 and was subjected to a humiliating "criticism." The main accusation was that he was deliberately implanting the Soviet tradition in Korea.[35] In the Ministry of the Interior around the same time, top officials with a Soviet Korean background also became targets of the well-orchestrated criticism. One of them was even asked which party's interest he protected—the CPSU's or the KWP's—a question that would have been outrageously unthinkable before 1957.[36]

Some Soviet Koreans (especially in the military and the police) were included in the ever-expanding list of alleged conspirators who were said to have been planning a military coup in 1956. As already noted, these accusations were probably groundless, but after the December Plenum of 1957 they featured more and more prominently in the North Korean press. Most of the accused were "Yan'an generals." This was understandable, because the "Yan'an group" had been a major force behind the entire August incident, and the group's members had traditionally been well represented in the army. However, some Soviet Koreans also found themselves accused not just of befriending Pak

Ch'ang-ok and occasionally saying something nasty about Kim Il Song's policies but also of something more sinister—secretly preparing a military takeover. In September 1959, Pak Il-mu, the head of the KPA Armor Department, was suddenly arrested by the military security service and spent eighteen days in prison. He was ordered to provide evidence of his innocence of any alleged connections with Pak Ch'ang-ok and other "factionalists."[37] Around the same time (probably the same day), Pak Kil-nam, the head of the KPA's engineers, was also arrested and subjected to forty days of interrogation.[38] This, however, was one of the rare—indeed, exceptional—cases in which the Soviet Embassy intervened. Pak found shelter in the Soviet Embassy, where he lived in the apartments of General Malchevski, a Soviet military attaché. After a few weeks of negotiations and paperwork, Pak Kil-nam was promptly sent back to the USSR. In case North Korean agents tried to intercept him, the Soviet officers escorted Pak to the Soviet train, and the train crew was instructed to raise alarms if something unexpected happened on the way to the Soviet border. (Nothing happened, and Pak died in comfortable retirement in the USSR in the 1970s.)[39] An official statement, soon relayed to the Soviet Embassy by the North Korean authorities, accused both Pak Il-mu and Pak Kil-nam of "factionalist activity" and conspiracy. For example, Pak Il-mu allegedly expressed his support for the Hungarian revolt and discussed plans of the military takeover with General Ch'oe In, a prominent member of the Yan'an faction. These particular accusations sound fantastic, but some others may have a more plausible foundation. For example, documents citing Pak Il-mu and Pak Kil-nam's earlier sympathetic remarks on the difficult life of common North Koreans (no doubt sincere and well-intended remarks) were considered to be proof of their alleged counterrevolutionary activity.[40]

Even Kang Chin, a Soviet Korean who was once prominent in the pre-1945 Communist underground but had been purged from politics and seemingly forgotten in the late 1940s, faced serious trouble. Born in 1905, he had lost all political connections but kept his Soviet citizenship. Even though he worked as a humble translator, he was accused of terrorism.[41] Under these circumstances, we can appreciate the prudence of Pak Pyŏng-yul, deputy minister of the interior, who, after applying for permission to go back to the USSR, ceased to attend his office under the pretext of high blood pressure; he stayed in hiding for six months, until the necessary paperwork was completed.[42]

Purges continued in 1960. The main victims were those Soviet and Yan'an Koreans who in 1956 had unwittingly expressed some kind of public sympathy toward the decisions of the September Plenum. Now former open support of that decision, once officially endorsed and ostensibly supported by Kim Il Song himself, was tantamount to subversion. These accusations led to dismissals of Yi Mun-il (a KWP Central Committee official), Sŏ Ch'un-sik (a secretary of the KWP North P'yongan Committee), and other prominent Soviet Koreans.[43] They were not arrested but sent to various manual jobs in the countryside. In such punishments the obvious influence of Mao's approach can be seen, since the Great Helmsman also liked to expose disgraced officials to the redeeming power of hard manual labor (Stalin's preferences were rather different and, one must add, less liberal).

Some Soviet Koreans tried to adapt to the new situation. A few of them even took an active part in the purges, in the hope of securing Kim Il Song's trust. Such was the case for Pang Hak-se, Nam Il, and Pak Chŏng-ae, for example. However, the vast majority of former Soviet citizens made a realistic appraisal of the new situation and did their best to leave Korea and return to the USSR. The exodus of Soviet Koreans from the DPRK to the USSR began in early 1958 after the initial arrests and lasted until late 1961. It is unknown if a similar "voluntary repatriation" of Yan'an Koreans was allowed. In any case, even if some Yan'an Koreans obtained the authorities' permission to return to China, the scale of their exodus would have been moderate in comparison with the large-scale return of Soviet Koreans. The precise data are not available at the moment, but it appears that more than half of some 150 Soviet Korean cadres, present in the DPRK in the 1950s, managed to return to the USSR.

This exodus saved many a life, but it was beneficial to Kim and his entourage as well. The main goal of Kim Il Song was not so much the physical as the political elimination of the Soviet faction, and the best way to accomplish this was by pushing these potentially troublesome people out of politics and, preferably, out of the country. "Ideological inspections," "criticism meetings," and the arrests of some well-known

Soviet Koreans were all integral parts of this intimidation campaign. Intimidated Soviet Koreans were more likely to remain silent or, better still, to start packing their bags. In the late 1950s, Soviet Koreans were not usually prevented from leaving the country if they wished to do so. Indeed, in many cases the Korean authorities explicitly encouraged Soviet Koreans to leave. In 1959, for instance, the chief of the North Korean General Staff called a special meeting of all Soviet Korean senior officers and openly stated that all who wished to return to the USSR could do so.[44] Around the same time, Nam Il, then still a foreign minister, told a Soviet diplomat that Pyongyang "would not mind" if those Soviet Koreans who had chosen Soviet citizenship were to apply for repatriation to the USSR.[45] In early 1960 the staff of the North Korean Foreign Ministry was told that all officials with a Soviet background were free to leave North Korea for the USSR.[46] This coherent pattern makes it likely that in all these cases the North Korean officials followed instructions from the very top, from Kim Il Song himself. Sometimes offers to leave were made individually. For example, Yu Sŏng-hun, the former rector of Kim Il Song University, was first fired from his job and then advised by his superiors to go to the USSR "to have a rest and to improve his health." It was also made clear that he had better postpone his return indefinitely.[47]

The North Korean security service even tried to hunt down enemies outside the country's borders. The defection of Yi Sang-jo in late 1957 triggered a chain of new defections, mostly among the North Korean students in Moscow. The impact of de-Stalinization ideas on these idealistic and well-educated young Koreans was considerable. They had spent a few years in the post-Stalinist Soviet environment, spoke fluent Russian, and could not help but see the ugly features of the emerging Kim Il Song dictatorship. The ideas and ideals of the thaw, so powerful in the Moscow of 1957, came to influence their worldview. When a dozen North Korean students from the prestigious State Institute of Cinematography (VGIK) refused to go back and asked for Soviet asylum, a major scandal ensued. Their asylum was eventually granted by Moscow, to the great resentment of the North Korean government. This decision of the Soviet authorities was both a humanitarian step and a clear warning sign to Pyongyang, indicating Soviet disapproval of Kim's new

policies of harsh treatment of opposition figures and his stubborn refusal to follow the Soviet example and soften his regime. For Kim Il
Song, this new Soviet position meant that Moscow (and to a lesser extent Beijing) was becoming not only a source of dangerous or, at the
very least, disturbing ideological trends but also an important base for
potential oppositions. We know now that the potential was never actually realized—the defectors were never used by Moscow for influencing
North Korean domestic politics—but back in 1959 and 1960 this outcome was far from certain.

As mentioned above, from 1957 onward Pyongyang officials were
taking measures to reduce the number of North Korean students in the
USSR. They also took more drastic steps to limit the danger and give lessons to the "unreliable elements" among the students. In 1958 the North
Korean special services undertook a near successful attempt to kidnap a
particularly troublesome student from Moscow. The student was none
other than Hŏ Chin (Hŏ Un-bae), a close associate of Yi Sang-jo and a remarkably vocal critic of Kim Il Song's dictatorship who, as noted above,
eventually wrote a well-known pioneering study of North Korean history
under the pen name "Lim Ŭn." In Moscow, Hŏ Chin was a leader of the
VGIK students who refused to go back to the DPRK, so the anger of the
North Korean authorities is easy to understand.[48] The attempted kidnapping of Hŏ Chin ended in a rather spectacular failure, when he managed
to flee from a guarded compound of the North Korean Embassy. Shortly
thereafter, however, a successful abduction of a North Korean citizen
inflicted new damage on the already strained Soviet-Korean relations. In
the autumn of 1959, Yi Sang-gu, a postgraduate student at the Moscow
School of Music, applied for Soviet asylum and sent a letter very critical
of Kim's regime to the Korean Supreme People's Assembly. His applica-
tion was being considered, and on October 16, Yi met a Soviet official
who tried to persuade him (obviously without much enthusiasm) to return home.[49] On November 24, Yi Sang-gu (in some Soviet documents he
is also called Yi Sang-un) was abducted by North Korean agents. This incident happened in the center of Moscow in broad daylight. Yi was
forced into a car and promptly (on November 25, the day following his
kidnapping) shipped to Pyongyang. His further fate is unknown, but
there is little doubt that his chance of survival was close to zero.

This incident triggered a tough response from the Soviet authorities, and even the personal intervention of Khrushchev himself was deemed necessary. On December 7, 1959, Andrey Gromyko, the then Soviet minister of foreign affairs, delivered a memorandum to the North Korean ambassador and required an explanation of the "Yi Sang-gu incident." In a few days Yi San-p'al, then the DPRK ambassador to Moscow, was recalled to Pyongyang, and the DPRK government had to make a formal explanation. As one might guess, the entire affair was blamed on overzealous officials, but the formal explanations did not help Yi Sang-gu: the hapless musician disappeared into the Pyongyang prisons forever.[50] The decision to demand a recall of an ambassador was, however, unprecedented in the entire history of the relations between the Communist countries. Yi San-p'al was replaced by Yi Song-un, the ex-guerrilla and former Pyongyang KWP secretary who had been so prominent in purges of the Domestic faction before 1956, as well as in the elimination of the Soviet and Yan'an factions afterward. We can surmise that the appointment of this zealous and trusted fighter against the opposition menace had some political meaning: in the early 1960s, Moscow indeed could be seen by Pyongyang as a likely base for anti-Kim forces.

The authorities also took some measures against those North Koreans who had been exposed to Soviet influences inside the country. For example, in the late 1950s a Soviet military attaché informed Moscow that all Korean interpreters who had worked with the Soviet military advisers were beginning to disappear. It was learned that they were being sent to the countryside. The official explanation was that among the interpreters there could be some spies, but this odd justification hardly misled anybody.[51] The same complaints were made by Czechoslovak ambassador Kohousek, and Hungarian ambassador Prath in December 1960. During talks with their Soviet counterparts, the ambassadors said that their most talented and enthusiastic Korean employees had been dismissed from their embassy jobs on the flimsy charge of "political unreliability." Another topic often discussed during the ambassadors' meeting was the increasing isolation of the embassies of "fraternal countries" in North Korea, since the North Korean guards of the supposedly friendly foreign missions did their best to harass Korean visitors and scare them away.[52] This was a further development of the trend that had begun in 1956, when the North Koreans began to limit the interactions between foreigners and North Korean officials. Very soon the Soviet Embassy was to become a sort of besieged fortress in the center of Pyongyang, completely off-limits for all North Koreans, with the exception of a handful of trusted government agents who were all carefully chosen and screened.

Among the many changes in North Korean society that were directly or indirectly connected with the general move toward "national Stalinism," I must mention an offensive against the "nonproletarian" parties. Apart from the Leninist KWP in North Korea, there were two other "nonproletarian" parties: the Democratic Party and Ch'ŏndogyo-ch'ŏngwudang (which may be translated into English as the Party of Young Friends of the Celestial Way). The former was normally perceived, or at least officially portrayed, as a party of the Christians and/or the petite bourgeoisie, while the latter included supporters of the indigenous religious cult of Ch'ŏndogyo, largely peasants from remote parts of the country. Both parties featured rather prominently in the North Korean politics of 1945–1948, when they had considerable support. However, by the mid-1950s both parties had long been puppets of the official regime, and their membership was very small (in 1956, Ch'ŏndogyo-ch'ŏngwudang had 1,742 members, and the Democratic Party was hardly any bigger).[53] These parties were kept alive largely for purposes of public relations and overseas propaganda. Nevertheless, the existence of "nonproletarian" parties in the transitional society was allowed and indeed even encouraged by the theory of the "people's democracy." The parties were seen as an indication of North Korean society's transitional nature: it was presumed to be steadily moving toward socialism but still immature.

In their rush to reach "complete socialism" in the shortest possible time, to redesign the North Korean social structure in full accordance with the prescriptions of Leninism (as understood and interpreted by Stalinist orthodoxy), the North Korean leaders could not overlook the "nonproletarian parties." These parties had been subjected to various restrictions since 1955–1956, but the real attack began in earnest in 1958. In the summer of 1958, Kim To-man, the head of the Agitation and Propaganda Department of the KWP Central Committee, bluntly explained to a Soviet diplomat the intentions of the KWP leaders. According to Kim To-man, there were some "unreliable elements" among the leaders of both non-Communist parties; hence it was necessary to purge them. Kim To-man said, "We intend to arrest about twenty persons whose views are of the most reactionary character, while the rest will be subjected to [ideological] reeducation only. We think that numerous nonproletarian parties and groups, which are of no political importance, will disappear. This process is natural, and we do not think it is necessary to support these parties artificially."[54] This commentary perhaps indicated that the Pyongyang leaders at that time intended to get rid of the superfluous "nonproletarian" parties altogether. Significantly, the Soviet diplomat did not agree with Kim To-man's remark and said that "nonproletarian" parties were essential, among other reasons, for conducting a "correct policy" toward the South.

On November 7, 1958, Kim To-man, while attending a reception at the Soviet Embassy, said that a "reactionary conspiracy" had just been revealed in the Democratic and Ch'ŏngwudang parties. On November 10 the Soviet Embassy received official documents outlining this alleged conspiracy. The main accusation was brought against the chairmen of both parties, Kim Tal-hyŏn (Ch'ŏngwudang Party) and Hong Ki-hwang (Democratic Party). According to the charges, both politicians were highly opportunistic "fellow travelers" who at a very early stage had subordinated themselves and "their" parties to the interests of the Communists in exchange for a measure of security and privileges. Nevertheless, Kim Tal-hyŏn, who had obediently served the regime for more than a decade, was declared to be a "hireling of Japanese imperialism." The authorities alleged that he had been a secret collaborator of Yi Sŭng-yŏp and Pak Hŏn-yŏng and, of course, had connections with Ch'oe Ch'ang-ik and other disgraced "factionalists." According to the official tale, Kim Tal-hyŏn and "his clique" had even planned "assassinations of members of the [Korean] Workers' Party and their relatives," as well as attempted to plan riots. It was officially asserted that Kim Tal-hyŏn and his associates, "pretending to be democratic leaders, actually contemplated the overthrow of our system of people's democracy and tried to establish a regime of landowners and capitalists, thus committing anti-Soviet and anti-Communist acts." In the Democratic Party the main defendant was also the party chairman, Hong Ki-hwang. Like Kim Tal-hyŏn, Hong Ki-hwang was charged with spying and with having had "contacts with American imperialism" and with Ch'oe Ch'ang-ik's group.[55]

The attack on the non-Communist parties was part of a more general purge of institutions that had all played a similar role; they had provided the regime with a more liberal-looking facade so that the largely notional United Front coalition could be maintained. Given the new situation, these vestiges of the domestic United Front could be easily discarded, and this was done in the most Stalinist manner. In late 1958 the Pyongyang authorities announced that they had uncovered a conspiracy in the so-called Committee for the Promotion of a Peaceful Unification (P'yŏnghwa t'ongil ch'okjin hyŏpŭihoe) as well. This committee consisted mainly of South Korean politicians who had been captured by the North Korean forces during the war and eventually had agreed to collaborate with Pyongyang, in most cases simply by signing propaganda declarations of various kinds, in exchange for life and some privileges. This committee was officially inaugurated in early 1956 but did not last long. In 1958 many of its prominent members (Cho So-ang, Om Hang-sŏp, Kim Yak-su, and others) were accused of spying and subversive activity. The official accusations stated that, "following instructions from the Americans," they, together with some leaders of the Democratic and Ch'ŏngwudang parties, "attempted to set up a reactionary group directed against the [Korean] Workers' Party."[56]

After such accusations Kim Tal-hyŏn, Hong Ki-hwang, and other leaders of the non-Communist parties were doomed. In February 1959 their cases were still under investigation, but they had already pleaded guilty.[57] On February 16, fifteen deputies of the Supreme People's Assembly who had been charged with participating in the alleged plot were deprived of their immunity by a special decree of the assembly's Standing Committee.[58] Naturally, the number of arrests was much higher, given that not all victims were members of the North Korean "parliament." Available sources do not provide us with information about the further fate of the prisoners. No show trial was staged, and the victims simply disappeared without much publicity.

In February 1959, Kim To-man admitted to a Soviet diplomat that the Democratic and Ch'ŏngwudang parties had by that time actually ceased to exist, their local organizations had been destroyed, and nothing but small central bodies remained (these bodies exist to the present day, serving largely the interests of overseas propaganda and the "United Front policy" toward South Korea).[59] At the same time, these Central Committees of both parties were preserved at least on paper, essentially functioning as propaganda decoys. In August 1959 the head of the Organization Department of the KWP Central Committee explained to a Soviet diplomat with a remarkable frankness: "The Central Committees of these parties in Pyongyang are preserved to attract some social groups in the South to the democratic [pro-Communist] forces. These parties' Central Committees now consist of people loyal to the KWP and DPRK government, and their activity is chiefly targeting certain groups of the South Korean population."[60] The name of the official was Kim Yŏng-ju, and being Kim Il Song's younger brother, he doubtless had some insight into the current plans of the North Korean leaders.

Another series of changes that attracted much Soviet attention (largely unfavorable) was connected with resurgence of Kim Il Song's personality cult. The personality cult per se was not something new for North Korea. Indeed, it has been an integral part of the North Korean political landscape since 1945. Classical Stalinism, apart from promoting one grand cult of the omnipresent and sagacious worldwide leader (that is, of Stalin), also created minor localized cults, albeit clearly subordinated to the main one. The Soviet Union itself was not an exception: the leaders of the Soviet republics or even major industries got their share of mandatory praise. Hence, Kim's name—with the appropriate title of *"suryŏng"* (leader)—had been frequently mentioned in the North Korean press since the late 1940s. In 1956–1957, however, the glorification of the leader was considerably muted. Among other things, Kim was seldom if ever referred to as *"suryŏng"* in that period (the less emotionally charged title of *"susang,"* or prime minister, was normally used instead). In 1958, Kim's cult resurfaced. It soon reached the pre-1956 levels and kept increasing steadily, achieving unprecedented and quite farcical heights by the early 1970s. As early as the summer of 1957, Hwang Chang-yŏp, a recent graduate of Moscow University and a distant relative of Kim Il Song's by marriage who eventually became a Pyongyang chief ideologist in the 1960s, wrote in a pamphlet: "Everybody knows that the factionalists have demagogically applied the name of 'personality cult' to the masses' love and respect for leaders of their party and, in doing so, attempted to separate the masses and leaders and to destroy the masses' respect for and trust in our party and its leaders."[61]

Judging by *Nodong sinmun* articles, a resurgence of Kim's cult became visible in the last months of 1958. From November or December that year, Kim's name began to appear in the newspaper with increasing frequency, sometimes accompanied by ecstatic eulogies addressed to the "leader of the Korean people." It appears that Kim's official visit to China and North Vietnam (from November 21 to December 10, 1958) also contributed to the resurgence of his personality cult. During the overseas trip the North Korean press was lavishly flooded with panegyrics to Kim's greatness and wisdom. A majority of these tributes to Kim were translations from the Chinese media, which applied to Kim the epithets normally reserved for Chairman Mao. These translated eulogies were soon followed by the original ones. It was one of the first manifestations of a pattern, noticed by Kim Sŏk-hyang: throughout the history of North Korea, changes in the propaganda representation of the country's leaders were often associated with some alleged declarations by the foreign media or Kim's overseas admirers. Only after the foreigners had been reported as making some statements in favor of a new "line" did the North Korean agencies join the chorus.[62] Kim's trip to China and Vietnam may have influenced the development of the North Korean personality cult in a different way as well. It is probable that Kim and his entourage were impressed by their firsthand observations of Mao's personality cult and tried to emulate it on their own turf.

Apart from the frequent referrals to Kim's name in the press, there were other signs of the cult's steady resurgence. Kim's portraits began to appear at public events, and his activities were reported in greater detail than before.[63] Toward the end of 1958 the first "rooms for study of the Great Leader Marshal Kim Il Song's revolutionary activity" *(Kim Il Sŏng wŏnsu hyŏkmyŏng hwaldong yŏngusil)* were established throughout North Korea. An official history later proudly stated: "Within the short period of late 1958 and first half of 1959 the 'rooms for study of the Great Leader Marshal Kim Il Song's revolutionary activity' were established at almost all government agencies, factories, agricultural cooperatives, and schools in our country."[64] The scale and coordination of this movement makes very unlikely that it was started by a spontaneous action of zealous local officials—almost certainly it was a centrally organized and orchestrated campaign. In December 1958 in the Northern P'yongan Province alone there were 863 of these rooms.[65]

These new changes in the official North Korean ideology attracted some unfavorable attention from Soviet diplomats, who were particularly displeased with and disapproving of the resurgence of Kim Il Song's personality cult. In the USSR after Stalin's death the personal deification of the leader decisively went out of fashion, and when Brezhnev's entourage in the late 1970s undertook halfhearted attempts to revive the tradition, it was seen by the entire population as a joke and had no serious impact whatsoever. Hence the revival and further development of Kim's personality cult was perceived by the Soviet observers as yet another indication of the wrong direction that the North Korean policy was obviously taking. In January 1959 the Soviet ambassador A. M. Puzanov wrote at some length in his official diary about the increasingly visible signs of the new cult. But being a rather cautious politician, he attempted to sound neutral; nonetheless his disapproval is not too difficult to detect.[66]

10 The Inception of the "Guerrilla State"

IN THE LATE 1950S the interpretations of North Korea's recent past underwent drastic changes. The new versions of the country's history, widely promoted from late 1957, began to give special prominence to the guerrilla exploits of Kim Il Song and his Manchurian fighters. In earlier periods, Kim had been portrayed as a major Korean Communist leader of the pre-1945 period, but from the late 1950s he was presented as the only true Communist leader of the 1930s. All other Korean Communists were depicted as either Kim's loyal followers or outright traitors. At that stage the North Korean propaganda machine had not yet made absurd claims of a crucial role that the Great Leader (then fifteen to eighteen years old) had allegedly played in Korean politics during the late 1920s, but that was not far ahead. The new myth was promulgated through a torrent of publications on the Manchurian guerrillas and their alleged victories. In 1958 *Kŭnloja,* the KWP official monthly, published eleven articles on history-related topics, and in 1959 it published ten. However, in 1958 only two of the articles dealt with the guerrillas, whereas in 1959 seven articles were dedicated to the (largely invented or at least grossly exaggerated) exploits of Kim's Manchurian fighters.

This new approach to history was designed to fit two important requirements: first, to stress a special role allegedly played by Kim Il Song, who was to be represented as the only true leader of the Korean Communist movement from its beginning; and second, to depict the history of Korean Communism in a more "nationalized" way, in order to stretch out the embarrassingly short history of the Korean Workers' Party. As Yi Song-un noted in his *Kŭnloja* article: "Although the history of our party is short, its roots are deep."[1] One of the first articles on the subject, published in the May 1957 issue of *Kŭnloja,* stated much the same, but with an added emphasis on Kim Il Song's personal role: "In Korea under the Japanese imperial rule the united Marxist-Leninist party was not reestablished, but the organizational and ideological base for the [eventual] founding of the Marxist-Leninist party was created by the true Communists, loyal to Comrade Kim Il Song."[2] For us, familiar with the almost unbelievable deification of Kim in the 1970s and 1980s, this remark about "loyalty to Kim Il Song" seems somewhat innocuous, but in 1957 it was yet another important indication of the special role that official mythmakers began to ascribe to the future Great Leader. The official publications arrived at a predictable conclusion: "Major historic roots of all these [achievements by the DPRK] lay in the anti-Japanese revolutionary struggle conducted from the 1930s under the leadership of true Communists led by Comrade Kim Il Song."[3]

In December 1957, Hwang Chang-yŏp published in *Kŭnloja* a highly critical review of Yi Ch'ŏng-won's recently published monograph *Struggle for the Proletariat Hegemony in Korea.*[4] This publication was remarkable in several ways. First, it contained a harsh political critique of Yi Ch'ŏng-won, the founding father of North Korean Marxist historiography. Unlike a majority of his colleagues, Yi never collaborated with the colonial administration. He was disgraced in the summer of 1957; the main accusation leveled against him by Hwang was that in his book on the history of North Korean Communism, Yi mentioned the Domestic Communists favorably. In the new mythology they were depicted as unreliable factionalists, if not traitors. In addition, Yi had ignored the role of Kim's guerrillas, who had come to be portrayed as the only real Korean Communists of the 1930s. It would be a mistake to believe that Yi Ch'ŏng-won's much criticized book was an act of hidden dissent. Despite his remarkable integrity in the pre-1945 period, Yi himself was not above praising Kim Il Song, and his book, like many books of his rivals and future accusers, faithfully reflected the pre-1957 official vision of Korean contemporary history. However, because of his lifelong connections with older Communists, Yi unluckily became a victim of the purges. He and his writings became an easy target for denunciation, once the official vision suddenly changed.

Around the same time, Kim Il Song's younger brother Kim Yŏng-ju began his accelerated ascent in the party bureaucracy. Lack of any provable pre-1945 revolutionary credentials did not prevent Kim's younger brother from becoming a top functionary at the Central Committee bureaucracy in the late 1950s and a Central Committee member from 1961. The emergence of Kim Il Song's distant relative Hwang Chang-yŏp in ideological politics was another confirmation of this new trend. It was Hwang who eventually redefined the initially vague *chuch'e* concept and transformed it into something resembling a coherent ideology (and the same Hwang who toward the end of his life, in 1997, became the highest-ranking North Korean defector to the South).

From early 1958 on, the North Korean press and publishing houses began to turn out a growing amount of printed material on the heroic feats of the guerrillas. In the July 4 issue of *Nodong sinmun* an entire page was dedicated to the "revolutionary traditions" of the guerrillas and especially to the Poch'ŏnbo battle, a guerrilla raid on a small border town in 1937 that eventually became a cornerstone of Kim's myth.[5] Soon afterward the daily began to use the new catchphrase—"shining revolutionary tradition" *(pich'nanŭn hyŏkmyŏngjŏk chŏnt'ong)*—with respect to the guerrilla movement in 1930s Manchuria.[6] As was customary, the catchphrase came into use suddenly and instantly spread throughout the press—a development that clearly indicates that the term was first coined and then deliberately introduced to the press by the authorities.

The new ideological campaign was openly endorsed by Kim Il Song himself, who began to mention the anti-Japanese guerrillas and their exploits with increasing frequency and demanded that the party and the entire population learn from the "guerrillas' experience." In February 1958, while visiting a military unit, Kim Il Song delivered a lengthy speech in which he explicitly stated that the true history of the North Korean Army began not in 1948 but in 1932. He made that clear from the first paragraph: "The Korean People's Army is heir to the glorious traditions of the anti-Japanese armed struggle. The KPA was founded as a regular army on February 8, 1948. However, it was not only after the Liberation that our people got its own army. The KPA was founded ten years ago, but since 1932, Korean people have already had anti-Japanese, anti-feudal armed forces that truly belonged to the people."[7] In this passage one can easily see the same recurrent theme of the DPRK propaganda in the late 1950s: the formal history of North Korean political institutions might be short, but it has deep historical and essentially indigenous roots that can be traced back to the guerrilla campaigns in 1930s Manchuria.

A major contribution to the rapidly developing cult of the guerrillas and Kim Il Song was made in the 1959 publication of the first volume of *Memoirs of the Anti-Japanese Guerrillas (Hang-il ppalch'isan ch'amgajadŭl-ŭi hoesanggi),* which was eventually followed by three more volumes. This book, which had a large circulation, was instantly promoted as fundamental material for ideological indoctrination. Every adult North Korean was pressed to read the book and then "discuss" it at numerous indoctrination sessions. The country was virtually flooded with copies of the book. According to official North Korean data, the total circulation of *Memoirs* and other books on the guerrilla movement, published in 1957–1960, reached the astonishing number of 95.8 million copies.[8] If that figure is true, then for every North Korean man, woman, and child, roughly nine books on this topic were published during these three years.[9] This is even more extraordinary if one takes into account that throughout the same period the North Korean publishers turned out "only" 12.1 million copies of the books on the current KWP policy.[10] The entire campaign was made official in December 1958 when the KWP Standing Committee passed a special decision, demanding the study of the "shining revolutionary tradition."[11]

In a new myth of the Communist movement history, only those who had supported Kim right from the beginning deserved the name of a "true Communist" (*kyŏnsilhan kongsanjuŭija*—a widely used standard idiom of the period). Consequently, the guerrilla movement in Manchuria began to be presented as the only proper form of Korean Communism in the 1930s and as an embodiment of the party spirit that had existed well before the KWP was formally established. It is important and indicative of changes in North Korea that the guerrilla movement was depicted as both Communist and nationalist. The official propaganda never mentioned that the Korean guerrilla detachments had been fighting as an integral part of the Chinese Communist forces in China's northeast.[12] Contrary to the historical facts, Kim Il Song's guerrilla forces were presented as an essentially independent Korean national army that was fighting the Japanese on its own, with only some limited interactions with the Chinese units. All nonguerrilla trends of pre-1945 Korean Communism came to be depicted as suspicious and unreliable, as breeding grounds of "factionalism," if not dens of malicious traitors and paid agents of imperialism. Special scorn was reserved for the units of the "Righteous Army" *(Ŭiyŏnggun)*—Korean Communist forces in China that had been controlled by Kim Tu-bong, Ch'oe Ch'ang-ik, and other Korean exiles in Yan'an. In his above-mentioned speech in February 1958, Kim Il Song himself said: "Can we continue the traditions of Kim Tu-bong's 'Independence League' and his 'Righteous Army,' who did not fight the Japs even once and ran away as soon as they learned that the Japs were coming? We cannot continue this anti-Marxist tradition."[13] From the purely military point of view, the achievements of the "Righteous Army" were rather trivial, but exactly the same thing can be said about Kim's own pre-1945 exploits.

Another tendency was a diminishing number of references to the role of the Soviet Army in the liberation of Korea (although the news from the USSR and exaltations of the Soviet achievements were still abundant in the North Korean press, these items began to disappear gradually from its pages from 1959 onward). This new approach to the history of Korean Communism had to become a foundation for the political indoctrination work throughout the country, and many Koreans began to learn their "new" history.[14] The main goal of the entire campaign was easy to see—Communism had been "nationalized" and, to some extent, "appropriated" by Kim Il Song. It was depicted as an essentially indigenous movement that had developed in Korea (or at least among the Koreans) independently, with few if any foreign contributions and support, and had achieved remarkable prominence prior to 1945—all largely thanks to Kim's brilliant leadership. The role of foreign influences and foreign connections in the Korean Communist movement was deliberately downplayed or erased from the official history. Consequently, one of the accusations against the August conspirators was their alleged plans to corrupt the indigenous "shining revolutionary tradition," embodied by the guerrillas, by doubting Kim's supremacy and kowtowing to foreign ideological fashions.[15]

The great ideological turn of the late 1950s had an immense impact on North Korean society. In the 1950s, Kim Il Song managed to use the differences that deeply divided the North Korean ruling elite to eliminate his enemies one by one by pitting them against each other. His victory was celebrated in 1961 at the Fourth Congress of the KWP, which was marked by unprecedented praising of the Great Leader. The new situation was reflected in the composition of the party's highest organ—its Central Committee, which was "elected" by the Fourth Congress. The composition of this Central Committee is directly indicative of changes that the DPRK and KWP had undergone in 1956–1961.

The 1961 Central Committee consisted of 85 members and 50 candidate members. This was an increase from the 71 members and 45 candidate members of the 1956 Central Committee. It has been customary in the KWP, as in most other ruling Communist parties, that every subsequent Central Committee is larger than its predecessor (yet another confirmation of Parkinson's Law?). Of 85 full members who were "elected" in 1961, only a third (28) had been members of the 1956 Central Committee. It is remarkable that of 11 ex-guerrilla members of the 1956 Committee, all but Yu Kyŏng-su, who died in 1958, were re-elected. These 10 ex-guerrillas from the 1956 Central Committee were also joined in 1961 by 27 additional newcomers from the same faction. It was the largest gain any of the KWP factions ever had in the party's history. Six of the newly elected guerrillas had been candidate members before (some of them had been promoted to full members between the congresses), but the vast majority appeared on the 1961 Central Committee roster for the first time. The 37-member strong representation of the Guerrilla faction by far exceeded that of any other. Given that the guerrillas likely numbered approximately 130–140 when they arrived in North Korea with Kim Il Song in 1945 and some of them had died by 1961, approximately a third of all former guerrilla fighters had become full members of the Central Committee. Such an overrepresentation was to last until the late 1970s, and it gave Wada Haruki a good reason to label the DPRK a "guerrilla state."[16]

This increase in the guerrillas' representation was done at the expense of all other factions. Perhaps it was the Soviet Koreans who suffered the greatest setback: only 2 of them (Nam Il and Pak Chŏng-ae) remained on the 1961 Central Committee. Even the notorious Pang Hak-se, the head of the secret police, was not reelected at that stage. He had been ousted from his security job in November 1960, and for a while it looked like he would be another victim of the purges. However, he regained his Central Committee membership at the next congress in 1970. The Yan'an faction hardly fared better, with only 3 survivors on the 1961 roster: Kim Ch'ang-man, Ha Ang-ch'ŏn, and Kim Ch'ang-dŏk. Of the original South Korean Domestic faction, only 1 person was reelected, Paek Nam-un, but he had rather apolitical occupations and a weak connection with the Domestic faction's initial core. Paek was a well-known historian of pre-1945 fame who had moved to the North in 1948 to become a prominent academic administrator there. Several other Communists with pre-1945 experience remained in the 1961 Central Committee, but they had been active in the North from 1945 and never had close connections with the South Korean Communist Party. After the guerrillas, the second-largest group in the 1961 Central Committee were young officials and technocrats who were the product of the fifteen years of Kim's rule. Roughly 30 to 35 members of the committee could be classified as such.

The 1961 Political Council (a new name for the KWP Politburo) consisted of 11 members. Six of them, a secure majority, were ex-guerrillas; 2, Kim's trusted lieutenants Nam Il and Pak Chŏng-ae, were remnants of the Soviet faction; and the former Yan'an faction was represented by Kim Ch'ang-man, who had proven his reliability through zealous participation in the purges. Two other members, Chŏng Il-ryong and Yi Chong-ok, were local North Koreans who had made their careers entirely after the Liberation. For most of their life, these 2 had worked in industrial management. They did not belong to any faction in a strict sense and were the first technocrats ever appointed to the KWP Politburo.

In short, Kim Il Song's victory was complete. The party's supreme bodies had been purged of all unreliable elements. The unconditionally loyal, if somewhat undereducated and inexperienced, guerrillas formed an upper strata of the KWP hierarchy. From the early 1960s on, the DPRK was run by former guerrillas who were often aided by young technocrats.

The latter were also "Kim's men" in their values and worldview. All possible channels of dangerously liberal Soviet influences had been safely blocked, and the North Koreans were mobilized to build endless monuments of the Great Leader, Sun of the Nation, and Ever-victorious General.

This narrative is almost over, and the reader might be interested in the subsequent fate of some of the main protagonists. Many of them fell in the unceasing purges, and after the mid-1950s, Kim decisively abandoned the Stalinist tradition of show trials, so the end of most of them is shrouded in mystery. After that time Kim's victims began to disappear without any official explanations. It will be impossible to learn more about the final years and months of these initial creators and eventual victims of the regime, until the regime either collapses or substantially changes.

Some former members of the opposition found asylum overseas. Kim Sŭng-hwa and Yi Sang-jo spent the rest of their lives in the Soviet Union, while Yun Kong-hŭm and Sŏ Hwi remained in China. According to Kim Hak-jun's account, the wives of both Sŏ Hwi and Yun Kong-hŭm were eventually executed in North Korea. Sŏ Hwi, who in the early 1960s was afraid that Beijing would sacrifice him as an unnecessary pawn in attempts to woo the Pyongyang leadership into an anti-Soviet alliance, attempted to escape to Russia but was caught and imprisoned for a while. He died in China in 1993. Yun Kong-hŭm also died in China, in 1978. Kang Sang-ho, a deputy minister of the interior who tried to stop Yun Kong-hŭm, and Pak Kil-yŏng, a deputy minister of foreign affairs, also made it to Russia in the late 1950s and lived the term of their natural lives (Kang Sang-ho died in 2000).

It might be somewhat surprising to a reader who is not very familiar with the inner mechanics of a Stalinist state, but those politicians who decisively sided with Kim during the August crisis hardly fared better than their onetime adversaries. Nam Il and Pak Chŏng-ae, two Soviet Koreans who joined Kim's inner circle in the late 1940s, survived until the late 1960s, though they gradually lost much of their original prominence. In 1976, however, Nam Il died in a suspicious car incident, and Pak Chŏng-ae disappeared from the public scene in the late 1960s. She was commonly thought to be imprisoned or killed, but, much to everyone's surprise, she resurfaced in the mid-1980s, though she did not regain any of her earlier influence. Han Sŏl-ya, the "literary genius" and Kim's most zealous adulator, shared the same fate: he was purged in the early 1960s, but his life was spared and he was pardoned in 1969, shortly before his death. Kim Ch'ang-man, another architect of Kim's personality cult who was so eager during the purges of 1957 and 1958, later enjoyed a short spell of prominence as a chief ideologue of the regime (in 1961 he ranked fifth in the party roster) but was purged in 1966 and, according to the rumors, soon afterward died while working on a farm somewhere in the countryside. The same end also befell Pak Kŭm-ch'ŏl, another nemesis of the Soviet and Yan'an factions and "party man number 4" in 1961. He was purged in 1967 when internal cracks within the Guerrilla faction led to the elimination of those members who, prior to 1945, had not been fighting in the guerrilla units but were engaged in the underground supporting networks. Perhaps, of all major actors, only Ch'oe Yong-gŏn, whose role in summer 1956 was so ambiguous, avoided eventual disgrace. He died in 1976 at the height of his power and fame, as the third-highest-ranked official in the North Korean party hierarchy.[17]

Conclusion
Why the "August Group" Failed

THE ATTEMPT TO DISMISS Kim Il Song ultimately failed. The North Korean government survived the crisis, although similar attacks by opposition groups led to profound changes in Bulgaria, Poland, and Hungary. Kim Il Song did not become another Chervenkov, Bierut, or Rakosi. Unlike those "little Stalins"—the now forgotten Communist strongmen of Eastern Europe—Kim, for better or worse, was to lead North Korea for four more decades and eventually became the world's longest ruling Communist autocrat. Why was this so? And why did the opposition attempt fail that fateful year of 1956?

To a great extent, the August challenge in Korea came about from outside influences and perhaps partly from the scheming of Great Powers. However, it also had domestic roots; it reflected a longing for change that was shared by some party cadres and many intellectuals within North Korea. They were not dissenters in the later Soviet sense, for their goals were definitely within the established framework of Leninist socialism. The "August group" sought to construct a more human-oriented, less constrictive kind of state socialism. They wanted a society that would give more material and cultural benefits to the common people but would still leave most political and social fundamentals unchanged and most control firmly in the party's hands. Like all politicians, they did not forget to further their own personal agendas while fighting for the cause, but it is difficult to blame them for this.

Undoubtedly, Kim Il Song's own personal qualities—his prudence,

211

his remarkable capacity for tactical maneuvering and Machiavellian intrigue, and his undeniable charisma—greatly contributed to his eventual political victory. He succeeded in isolating the opposition and then engineered the course of the August Plenum. Occasionally he was simply lucky. However, the eventual success of Kim was not simply a victory of his ruthlessness (or wisdom) over the naïveté (or stupidity) of his opponents. The general situation in the country at the time must also be considered; the North Korea of 1956 was very different from, say, Poland or Hungary in many important respects.

The reformist ideas, so strong in Eastern Europe, did not enjoy comparable popular support in North Korea. There were few, if any, serious signs of public discontent outside academic circles, students, and party functionaries. Thus the opposition in Korea could hardly have relied on mass support, something that proved to be so important and even decisive in Poland and Hungary.

Aside from the efficient work of the secret police, there were numerous reasons for the relative political tranquillity, and I will mention just a few of the more important ones. Unlike the countries of Eastern Europe, North Korea was not subjected to the "demonstration effect" of nearby capitalist affluence and democratic freedoms. While Eastern Europeans could easily see, just across the border, a multitude of societies with much greater freedom and with increasingly greater prosperity, North Korea had no examples of such prosperous and free capitalist neighbors. South Korea of the mid-1950s may have had marginally higher living standards than the North, but even this is far from certain, and the gap, if it existed at all and if it was in the favor of the South, was quite small.[1] Syngman Rhee's South Korea could by no means be seen as a model of democracy; until the late 1950s it could easily rival or even surpass the DPRK in harsh treatment of both the regime's political opponents and the general populace. The hardships in the North were also more easily accepted because they took place a mere three or four years after a devastating war, in which the heavy destruction inflicted on North Korean cities and industry by the savage bombing raids was still very visible. The peasantry had to carry a heavy burden of taxation, but it was not yet alienated by the mandatory introduction of the notorious Stalinist collective agriculture. Hence many peasants had reason to hope that their hardships might be only temporary, while, after all, they still were owners of the land they toiled (alas, this was to change all too soon).

In addition, Korea was different from the East European countries in its lack of meaningful democratic traditions. North Korea had never experienced any type of democracy, and the very idea was probably quite alien to the majority of its population, most of whom were traditional peasants or former peasants. A vast majority of the Koreans not only had never been involved in elections or democratic politics of any sort but also had hardly even been citizens in the strict sense of the word. If anything, civil liberties in the DPRK were no worse than in pre-Communist times when, as second-rate colonial subjects of a foreign monarch, the North Koreans lived under a particularly harsh and oppressive type of colonialism. Unlike the peoples of most Baltic or Eastern European states, the North Koreans did not share memories of a democratic past or civil liberties of which they had been deprived.

Nevertheless, contrary to the popular beliefs, the mass discontent in the Communist countries did not necessarily arise from calls for democracy. Neither Hungary nor Poland had been bona fide democracies before the Communist takeover in the mid-1940s (indeed, both used to be authoritarian regimes). In these countries, the main inspirations for an anti-Communist mass movement were nationalism and, to a lesser extent, religious beliefs, rather than "pure" democratic ideals. In this regard too the North Korean situation was different. Religion was not an important factor in the North Korean politics of the 1950s. Politically active, nationalist, pro-Western (and eventually anti-Communist) Protestantism had managed to become a significant part of North Korean spiritual life before 1945. However, by the early 1950s its strength had been severely undermined by aggressive antireligious propaganda, constant police harassment, and an exodus of religious activists, as well as by its obvious connections with the Americans (U.S. bombing raids on Pyongyang and other North Korean cities were also not exactly helpful in endearing the United States to North Koreans). Most former right-wing nationalist intellectuals or religious activists (they often were the same persons), who otherwise could have led a ferment of unrest, had fled from the North in the turbulent period of 1945–1951, when such an escape was feasible and even at times technically easy.

It was also much more difficult to arouse nationalist feelings in North Korea than in Eastern Europe. Although the Kim Il Song regime was conceived as a product of Soviet political engineering, it nevertheless had replaced a colonial administration as a legitimate national regime. This was a major difference from the situation in Poland, Hungary, and most other Eastern European countries. Furthermore, Kim Il Song probably had more reason to appeal to Korean nationalism than his opponents, whose overseas connections were only too obvious and who were advocating "imported" concepts. If nationalism could have been mobilized in the North Korea of the late 1950s, it would have probably been in support of the local Stalinist regime rather than against it. A similar paradox was shrewdly exploited by other proponents of "national Stalinism," for example, the leaders of Romania and Albania. Obviously Kim Il Song himself read this popular feeling quite well. From 1955 on, Kim was putting increasing emphasis on "Korean-ness" and skillfully portrayed himself as an embodiment of the "truly Korean" qualities and as a defender of the genuine Korean traditions against polluting foreign influences. It is probable that the nationalist overtones of Kim's new ideas found positive resonance among many Koreans, including intellectuals and midlevel party cadres, who had had enough of the obligatory Russo-mania and would have been ready to hail a more independent and national-oriented policy as personified by Kim Il Song (though had they fully appreciated the future effects of such a policy, a great many of them would undoubtedly have had second thoughts).

In addition, a social base for the opposition was undermined by an exodus of refugees from North Korea in 1945–1951. A bulk of the refugees who then fled to the South consisted of privileged social groups: former landlords, small businessmen and merchants, petty officials in the colonial institutions, Christian activists, and the former gentry. According to the most reliable estimations available, some 580,000 people left North Korea in 1946–1949.[2] A large number of later wartime refugees (between 400,000 and 650,000, according to one recent estimate) also left North Korea in 1950–1953.[3] These figures mean that between 10 and 14 percent of the entire North Korean population migrated to the capitalist South between 1945 and 1953, an exodus unparalleled in most other Communist countries. North Korea was partly compensated by a significant inflow of the internal migrants from the South, mostly leftists, but that is irrelevant to this part of our story. Another important but often underreported event must also be considered: a forceful relocation of the ethnic Japanese population from both South and North Korea. Before 1945 this population was considerable, some 650,000 by the end of colonial rule.[4] The ethnic Japanese constituted a major part of the administrative, cultural, and economic elite, which in a non-colonial society would consist of the "locals."[5] In 1945–1946 all of these ethnic Japanese were forcefully deported from the entire Korean Peninsula, a rare instance when the South and North Korean policies were near identical. This low-profile but large-scale "ethnic cleansing" never attracted much publicity overseas, even in Japan itself, but its impact on the Korean social structure was substantial: a majority of top- and medium-level bureaucrats and many of the businessmen and professionals were moved away virtually overnight, leaving their jobs for the native Koreans to fill.

These mass departures of the privileged groups, both ethnic Korean and Japanese, left North Korea more socially homogenous than most other Communist countries. The DPRK had fewer people who were longing for lost prosperity and privileges and hence ready to welcome any opposition to the system or any softening of the regime. People who had remained in the North had mostly been peasants or unskilled manual workers under the Japanese rule. Thus the new regime did not deprive them of any meaningful wealth or social importance but rather gave them new social aspirations and opened new horizons—not least through mass education, a common device of the Communist forced-modernization policy. The regime also gave many new hope through a large-scale recruitment of "workers and peasants" into service in the new bureaucracy and the new armed forces. Indeed, the KWP government was perhaps the first regime in Korean history to remove restrictions on upward social mobility for a majority of the country's population. The discriminated groups, the people of "bad class origin," however numerous they were, did not form a majority of the population of the 1950s DPRK, whereas the peasants and *nobi* (serfs) during the Chosŏn period did. Eventually a new set of restrictions on upward mobility was imposed in the DPRK as well, and the new North Korean elite gradually developed into a closed hereditary caste in which commoners had few if any chances to make a successful career. However, these changes took place much later, in the 1970s and 1980s. In the 1950s the new opposition could have appeared only as it actually did—among the party intellectuals and industrial workers—and its slogans could not be anti-Communist.

Another important factor made mass protest on the Hungarian or Polish scale unlikely to happen in 1950s North Korea. The DPRK and KWP elite did not allow the general populace any major indication of internal disagreements; conflicts began to unfold quite rapidly and were invariably unknown to the vast majority of the population. In Eastern European countries the open quarrels among *nomenklatura* (mid- and high-level officials) or at least widely circulated rumors about such quarrels, contributed to the rise of mass protest. Such information encouraged the moderate opposition, whose members at the grassroots level could count on eventual support from above. It also demonstrated to the radicals that the once monolithic enemy was experiencing internal troubles and was demoralized and dispirited; hence an open attack against these Stalinist regimes did not look hopelessly suicidal anymore. The policies of Nagy and Ochab softened the soil before the real breakdown of the Stalinist systems in Hungary and Poland. No comparable softening happened in Korea.

Thus Kim Il Song's opposition might not have had many chances to win the mass support of the general population. However, a mass movement (whether democratic, nationalist, or other) was by no means a necessary precondition to the opposition's success. After all, in Bulgaria the change from the orthodox Stalinist Chervenkov to the marginally more open-minded Zhivkov in 1956 was achieved in almost exactly the same manner that Ch'oe Ch'ang-ik and Pak Ch'ang-ok once envisaged for North Korea—through intricate and secretive political dealing at the top levels of the party hierarchy and secret consultations with Moscow, but without any explicit mass support or indeed any mass involvement. The Bulgarian success demonstrated not that it was necessarily impossible for the Korean conspirators to achieve their goals but merely that the lack of popular support somewhat reduced their chances. The absence of a mass protest movement did create obstacles to their plans, but these obstacles were not insurmountable, and Kim Il Song could still have been replaced by successful and well-designed bureaucratic intrigue. The opposition members, however, lost this intrigue, and the main reason, apart from their own tactical mistakes and the shrewdness of their enemy, obviously was the lack of support from middle- and top-level party cadres, whose attitude toward the opposition was decisive in the absence of any mass movement.

The majority of these cadres indeed proved to be unsympathetic to the opposition's cause, especially given that this cause was pursued by people who were widely perceived as "strangers" and even "half-foreigners." The middle- and top-level cadres chose to support Kim, not his challengers, as is proven by the unfolding of events. The attack on Kim Il Song in August 1956 was wrecked by the actions (or, rather, by the inaction) of the majority of the Central Committee members, who failed to support the opposition and, to a greater or lesser degree, actively helped to shout it down. As was mentioned, none of the Central Committee members sided with the opposition on the fateful morning of August 30. As Kovyzhenko recollected, "Kim Il Song was known to be backed by the majority of both rank-and-file Korean Communists and party cadres, including Central Committee members. Under the circumstances, how could he have been dismissed?"[6] Here Kovyzhenko is referring to the September events, but this remark is equally applicable to the August crisis.

The reason for this support of Kim is probably connected with the new composition of the North Korean ruling elite, which had undergone considerable changes since 1945–1946. By 1956 the bulk of the middle- and low-level *nomenklatura* consisted of native North Koreans who had entered the party after 1945 and whose worldview had been shaped by the Korean War and the intense glorification of Kim Il Song. These people had on average a much lower education than their predecessors from the earlier generations of the Korean Communists. In 1958, of 40,028 secretaries of the party cells nationwide, 55.6 percent had only primary education, and a mere 23.6 percent had secondary education.[7] We can assume that a majority of the remaining 20.8 percent likely had no formal education at all (although this was not explicitly stated in the source of these figures). This situation was not surprising, given that 77 percent of Korean males lacked any formal education in 1944.[8] Therefore the ideas of democracy were not familiar to those who yesterday had been peasants and unskilled or, at best, semiskilled workers. At the same time, the appeal of nationalism was quite strong and was well received among them. These new recruits were also markedly more nationalistic than the Communists of the older generation, who had spent much time overseas, were fluent in foreign languages, and had been exposed to a significant amount of foreign culture. The attitude of these younger officials toward rather arrogant "foreigners" from both the Yan'an and the Soviet factions was not exactly positive. This fact is even mentioned in the Soviet Embassy documents, although the Soviet diplomats usually tried to circumnavigate such perilous subjects. For example, Filatov acknowledged the existence of a degree of friction and noted that many Soviet Koreans "treated local cadres rather arrogantly."[9] In 1956, First Secretary Biakov met Song Chin-p'a, a Soviet Korean, who just returned from a stint of "labor reeducation" (he had worked as a laborer on a building project for a month as punishment for his "irresponsible remarks about the personality cult"). Song, as his interlocutor wrote, "began to speak of the unhealthy attitude of the [local] people toward Soviet Koreans." However, he was not given an opportunity to express his concerns at any length; as soon as the conversation began to get a little too sensitive, the cautious diplomat abruptly decided to change the subject.[10]

During the interviews I conducted, some informants mentioned controversies between "local" and "foreign" Koreans on the everyday level as well. For example, Dr. Kim Mil-ya, Kim Chae-uk's daughter and a keen observer, was in high school in the mid-1950s and, like other children of former Soviet-Korean politicians, not only remembered the situation in the 1950s very well but also was now free of her parents' ideological taboos. She recollected: "Needless to say, at the time we did not think of those things, but now in retrospect, when I think over and analyze everything, I realize that we were not popular. We occupied a peculiar position: we were both strangers and privileged. The local people could not have liked it."[11] Dr. Valentina Dmitrieva, a well-known Soviet expert on Korea, shared the same opinion. She recalled her first visit to Pyongyang in 1948–1949 and answered my questions about the locals' attitude toward the Soviet Koreans: "[The perception of the Soviet Koreans by the locals] was bad or, better said, reserved. They came—educated, self-assured, well fed—and instantly got high positions. Not everybody liked it."[12] There is no reason to believe that this attitude was reserved only for the Soviet Koreans. It is most likely that the Yan'an group was perceived in much the same way. To the local functionaries of middle and low rank, both the Chinese and the Soviet Koreans remained arrogant and incomprehensible aliens, while Kim Il Song had succeeded in winning their recognition as "one of them." It is not incidental that the Korean propaganda always emphasized the indigenous roots of Kim Il Song and "his" movements, consistently playing down or hiding all his foreign connections (such as his sojourn in the USSR in the early 1940s).

In addition, it seems that the Korean tradition of personal power politics was deeply rooted in the minds of contemporaries. The conflict between the opposition and Kim Il Song was perceived largely in terms of a personal struggle for influence and power in which few people were willing to intervene. For many of them it was all about personal power, no matter what the participants said, and they did not see any reason to mingle with the personal quarrels of the leaders and their rivals.

Thanks to the recently available materials, we now have some telling insights into the minds of the Korean bureaucrats during that fateful year of 1956. In November of that year Titorenko met Ch'oe Chŏng-hyŏn, his former classmate at Kim Il Song University and a postgraduate in the "ideological" Department of Marxism-Leninism at the same school. Ch'oe, with some reservations, could be considered a young member of the *nomenklatura,* for he, in all probability, was well on his way to becoming a full-time party functionary. He would soon prove that he was already sufficiently ruthless and would renounce his own teacher and head of the Department of Marxism-Leninism, the aforementioned Song Kun-ch'an, during a great purge at the university in the summer of 1957. From the conversation between Kim Il Song and Ch'oe, it became clear that Ch'oe, who obviously learned from rumors that had circulated among university intellectuals and local party functionaries, already had generally correct information regarding the August Plenum, though he was patently ignorant of the visit of the Mikoyan-Peng delegation.

While talking with his Soviet interlocutor about the perception of the August and September Plenums at his university, Ch'oe Chŏng-hyŏn said: "There were different factions in the KWP, and many members of the KWP were aware of this. There were such factions as the group led by Pak Hŏn-yŏng, which was composed of the former members of South Korean Communist Party; the group of Soviet Koreans headed by Pak Ch'ang-ok; and the group of Chinese Koreans headed by Pak Il-u and Ch'oe Ch'ang-ik. All of these courted Kim Il Song and Ch'oe Yong-gŏn, trying to gain high posts within the government and the party. They were office seekers. [Among them], Ch'oe Ch'ang-ik had more influence and was smarter than the others."[13] This is a reasonable assessment of the situation, remarkably free of any sympathy toward the opposition or any concern about its slogans of "the struggle against the personality cult" and "collective leadership." The opposition is seen as merely another bunch of power-hungry politicos, of unprincipled opportunists, and not as people fighting for a cause, even a "reactionary" and "counterrevolutionary" one. The opposition leaders (or some of them) may have been sincere in their slogans, but the middle- and low-level cadres did not understand them and did not believe them. Nevertheless, Ch'oe Chŏng-hyŏn's assumption was free of the influence of the official propaganda campaigns against the opposition and its supporters. It is noteworthy that Ch'oe did not mention even Pak Hŏn-yŏng as an "American spy" but simply referred to him as one of the "office seekers."

The prevalence of such an attitude is confirmed by another interesting insight into the mood of the North Korean bureaucracy. This testimony was obtained by two Soviet news correspondents during their conversation with the deputy minister of communications Sin Ch'ong-t'aek.[14] It is by no means accidental that this material was obtained by journalists rather than diplomats, given that the latter usually avoided discussing contentious topics and generally did their best to steer clear of anything risky. With few exceptions (such as Titorenko's reports), the Soviet Embassy materials are remarkably dull, devoid of any independent assessment and critical appraisal of the situation. If any assessment is done, it is usually well within the established framework of official reasoning and officially approved formulas. The Soviet journalists, although supervised by the state and party agencies, tended to be more flexible than the diplomats; the journalists were more likely to ask sensitive questions and to arrive, when necessary, at uncomfortable conclusions.

While Sin Ch'ong-t'aek met the Soviet journalists and had a long and frank conversation with them (lubricated, I dare imagine, with a certain amount of vodka), he, among other things, expressed his opinion of the August incident: "The group that had spoken out at the August Plenum of the Central Committee and was led by Ch'oe Ch'ang-ik, it had no program based on [any] principle. They were not against building socialism and Communism. Their single aim was to fight for power and for the prospect of placing their people in high posts and in the [KWP] Central Committee in the first instance."[15] Again, as in the case of Ch'oe Chŏng-hyŏn, the assessment of the situation is rather cynical. Both accounts are quite similar, and it is likely that the majority of the *nomenklatura* appraised the situation in much the same way. They did not want to participate in a dangerous affair, which they saw as nothing more than a power struggle and an attempt by people, whom they did not much like or trust, to satisfy their own personal ambitions. The demands of democratization and liberalization failed to produce any impact on the newly recruited members of the party bureaucracy, whose lifelong experience and education made them rather immune to these ideas. The opposition remained isolated within the party, as well as within the society at large, and it did not win any significant support outside relatively small groups of the intellectuals, academics, and better-educated cadres, who more often than not had overseas connections and experiences.

The crisis of 1956 basically was a conflict of two trends: the more indigenous, more independent, more nationalist, but also more repressive, reckless, and eventually harsh political line personified by Kim Il Song versus the more open-minded, more liberal, but also pro-foreign political line personified by the opposition leaders. Kim Il Song—or, rather, his camp—was on the (ostensibly preemptive) offensive in late 1955, maneuvering in early 1956, repelling sudden and forceful assaults in August and September, and eventually winning the struggle from late 1956 onward.

The confrontation of 1956 and its aftermath were a link in a long chain of events, both domestic and international. The confrontation was caused by major international upheavals and by the gradual spread of reformist ideas through the Communist world. North Korea, where Stalinist ideas had already found fertile soil, was not, however, a reserve of the unabashed Stalinism—or, rather, Stalinism there was not left unchallenged. As in many other Communist countries, some members of the ruling elite were ready to change the old ways, and as in many other countries, they were supported by some intellectuals. The resistance to Stalinism in North Korea was weaker than in most other Communist states because it had a rather limited social base.

However, the anti-Stalinist, moderately reformist forces could not change the political course of the DPRK. The crisis of 1956 concluded with the complete victory of Kim Il Song over his reformist rivals and led to a great strengthening of his personal power, though even he may not have fully appreciated this fact at the time. In 1956, Kim Il Song had taken a second and most decisive step in his passage to absolute power (the first step was in 1945–1946 when—with the Soviet backing—he became the head of the nascent North Korean administration).

Three main consequences of the crisis of 1956 and the following purges were to be of enduring importance for Korean (and not only Korean) history. First, a mortal blow had been inflicted on the factional system, a system that had considerably restricted Kim Il Song's personal power during the first decade of North Korean history. Though some former members of different non-Guerrilla factions survived the incident, they were deprived of their leaders, frightened, and isolated. A majority of them were doomed, in due time becoming victims of subsequent purges. The system of factions ceased to function. With that system vanished the original checks and balances that initially existed in the North Korean political system. The leader now could (and unavoidably would) become an autocrat, a dictator in the full sense.

Second, the direct and unequivocal Sino-Soviet interference in September 1956 had little effect whatsoever, although this fact did not become clear immediately. Neither Moscow nor Beijing could force Kim Il Song to keep promises that he had made at their insistence. This demonstrated to Kim Il Song (as well as to his foes and allies in the DPRK leadership) that, under the appropriate circumstances and with a necessary degree of care and cunning, he would be able to ignore pressure from Moscow and Beijing and act as he saw fit. This marked the first step toward a future independent North Korean stance within the Communist camp. North Korea eventually became one of a handful of Communist countries that managed to leave the orbits of Soviet satellites—for better or worse.

Third, North Korea was isolated from the ideas of a more democratic and reformed state socialism. The independent stance of some Communist countries after the 1956–1960 period does not necessarily mean that their peoples gained much from greater autonomy from the Soviet control. On the contrary, as the examples of Ceausescu's Romania, Hoxha's Albania, and Mao's China (but not of Tito's Yugoslavia) testify, the countries that shook off Soviet tutelage generally enjoyed a lesser degree of material prosperity and intellectual freedom than did their Moscow-controlled counterparts. The moderate and incomplete but still beneficent Khrushchev-type reforms that swept through a majority of the Communist countries in 1955–1960 were ruled out by the new political environment in North Korea. After the events of 1956 even the most discreet discussion of the personality cult in the DPRK was tantamount to treason. These conditions were ideal for an unprecedented development of Kim Il Song's personality cult and unlimited strengthening of his absolute power or, to borrow a term from Scalapino and Lee Chong-sik, his "monocracy."[16] The movement toward a less oppressive, more liberal society—perhaps not necessarily inconceivable in the 1950s—was halted. North Korean state socialism was to became one of the harshest, most inflexible, most oppressive, and, ultimately, most economically devastating of its kind.

The period of 1956–1960 must be considered a major turning point in North Korean history, the years of the definitive establishment of the Kim Il Song regime as we know it. In 1945–1956, North Korea had merely represented a second-rate "people's democracy," indistinguishable in many ways from the various Communist states of Eastern Europe. During 1956–1960, however, North Korea formed some of its own unique features.

Notes

1. NORTH KOREA AND ITS LEADERSHIP IN THE MID-1950S

1. *Chosŏn chŏnsa* (Complete history of Korea), vol. 28, 187.

2. Official data from *Nongŏp hyŏpdonghwa undong-ŭi sŭngli* (The success of the agricultural cooperative movement), vol. 1, 34.

3. Comintern, or Communist International, was the headquarters of the worldwide Communist movement in 1919–1943.

4. According to Wada Haruki, a leading expert in the history of the Korean guerrilla movement in Manchuria, thirty of thirty-six guerrillas whose social origin is known were farmers or urban poor. Only one guerrilla is known to have had a college education, and only a handful of them had studied at a secondary level. According to Wada, "The majority of the guerrillas were people who prior to entering the guerrilla units had not had an opportunity to receive any education." Wada, *Kim Il Sŏng-gwa manju hang'il chŏnjaeng* (Anti-Japanese War in Manchuria and Kim Il Song), 302–303.

5. Strictly speaking, the "Guerrilla faction" consisted of two subfactions: the Guerrillas proper (that is, former fighters in Manchuria) and the so-called Kapsan group, which included underground activists who ran intelligence-gathering, propaganda, and logistics operations for the guerrillas but did not fight themselves. The divide between these two groups became quite visible in the late 1960s, when the Kapsanites were subjected to severe purges by their onetime comrades. Nevertheless, this divide appeared only after the Guerrilla faction had been firmly in control for a considerable length of time and internal feuds had begun to develop among them. For the 1950s this division between the "actual Guerrillas" and the "underground supporters of the Guerrillas" is irrelevant and anachronistic. To the best of my knowledge, it is not mentioned in any document predating 1960.

225

6. Hŏ Ka-i (1908–1953) was born Alexei Ivanovich Hegai in Khabarovsk. In the early 1920s, he became an active member of the Soviet Komsomol (a Communist Party youth organization) and, eventually, a party cadre. He was active in the Soviet Far East and, after 1937, in Central Asia. In 1945 he was dispatched to Korea by the Soviet military authorities and soon became one of the top KWP leaders.

7. The DPRK official propaganda never recognized that it was the North that started the war. According to the official Pyongyang line, the South Korean forces invaded the North, but the glorious (North) Korean People's Army repelled the aggressors and launched a successful counteroffensive that made possible the crossing of the border just a few hours later. This remains an official position of the DPRK, despite its publishing of numerous Soviet and Chinese papers that have made these statements appear grotesquely unfounded.

8. The general history of factional conflicts in the KWP has been studied by many scholars. For more information, two standard, already classic works on North Korean history are recommended: Suh, *Kim Il Sung,* esp. 55–175; and Scalapino and Lee, *Korean Communism,* vol . 1.

9. Sim Su-ch'ŏl, interview with the author in Tashkent, January 23, 1991. In the late 1950s, Sim Su-ch'ŏl was a head of the personnel department in the North Korean army headquarters.

10. As just one of many examples of this kind of required approval, on February 3, 1948, the Soviet Politburo made a decision "to *allow* the People's Committee of North Korea to create the Department of National Defense and on the final day of the session of the People's Assembly to organize in Pyongyang a meeting and a parade of the Korean national military force" (copy of document in private collection; italics mine). Only after this decision from Moscow was the creation of a separate North Korean army (called Korean People's Army, KPA) duly declared by Pyongyang on February 8, 1948.

11. It appears as if the late 1950s was actually the worst time for the Soviet Embassy. Prior to 1953, Moscow had viewed Korea as a strategically important point where direct conflict with a major Soviet adversary was taking place. At that time the embassy and other Soviet agencies in Pyongyang were often run by bureaucrats in Stalin's mold: efficient, ruthless, hardworking, and prepared to take responsibility and to make decisions (Shtykov, Ignatiev, Shabshin, and Tunkin are the best-known examples of such bureaucrats). Most of them left Korea during the Korean War or shortly afterward, to be replaced by mediocre personalities. In the early 1960s the situation began to improve again, not the least due to the influx of professional experts. These people had a good command of the Korean language and were deeply interested in their work, because Korea was "their" professional subject—indeed, an important part of their identity. This went a long way toward compensating for the boredom of everyday life in North Korea. In addition, their connections in the academic circles

provided them with some job security: the loss of a diplomatic job often led to a respectable job, albeit probably not as well paid, in some research center back in the USSR. In the 1970s and 1980s, North Korea was rather unusual in having a very high proportion of country specialists among the embassy staff.

2. THE SOVIET FACTION UNDER ATTACK

1. S. N. Filatov (counselor of the Soviet Embassy), record of conversation with Pak Ch'ang-ok (vice-premier and member of the presidium of the KWP Central Committee), March 12, 1956. Hereafter, positions of Korean officials are shown as indicated in the records of relevant meetings. Additional data for archival documents, if not supplied in the notes, may be found in the bibliography. The Archive of Russian Federation Foreign Policy, Moscow, is abbreviated hereafter as AVPRF.

2. Okonogi, "North Korean Communism."

3. For a detailed description of the economic controversy and some of the ideological trends of 1954–1955, see ibid. and Koon, *North Korean Communist Leadership,* 103–104.

4. The official affiliation of Pak Chŏng-ae—the only woman in North Korean history who ever achieved a senior political position—is not certain. She was sometimes considered a member of the Domestic faction, but she still maintained very close relations with some former guerrillas, and as a fluent Russian speaker and former Soviet resident, she was often thought to be a member of the Soviet Koreans. However, she was one of the people who showed unconditional support for Kim Il Song and was incorporated into his inner circle because of this loyalty.

5. S. N. Filatov (counselor of the Soviet Embassy), record of conversation with Pak Yŏng-bin, February 25, 1956; S. N. Filatov, record of conversation with Pak Ch'ang-ok, March 12, 1956. These two documents express contradictory views in relation to the position of Pak Kŭm-ch'ŏl, a prominent member of the Yan'an faction. On February 25, 1956, Pak Yŏng-bin insisted that Pak Kŭmch'ŏl had also opposed the promotion of Ch'oe Yong-gŏn one year earlier, but just two weeks later Pak Ch'ang-ok recounted that Pak Kŭm-ch'ŏl had been the only supporter of this measure in the Political Council. This is probably somehow connected with the fact that Pak Yŏng-bin seemed to have been on good terms with Pak Kŭm-ch'ŏl (who even visited Pak Yŏng-bin in the hospital), whereas Pak Ch'ang-ok did not conceal his animosity toward Pak Kŭm-ch'ŏl.

6. V. K. Lisikov (third secretary of the Soviet Embassy), record of conversation with Kim Sŏng-yul (chairman of the Pyongyang City Committee of the Democratic Party of North Korea), May 8, 1956. In an endnote, Lisikov states: "The embassy is aware that, while being the Democratic Party chairman, Ch'oe Yong-gŏn is [also] a member of the Workers' Party."

7. Filatov, record of conversation with Pak Yŏng-bin, February 25, 1956.

8. Filatov, record of conversation with Pak Ch'ang-ok, March 12, 1956.

9. Pak Yŏng-bin himself told this to a Soviet diplomat a year later. S. N. Filatov, record of conversation with Pak Yŏng-bin, February 25, 1956.

10. A. M. Petrov (counselor of the Soviet Embassy), record of conversation with Song Chin-p'a (former editor of *New Korea* magazine), December 15, 1955.

11. I. S. Biakov (first secretary of the Soviet Embassy), record of conversation with Song Chin-p'a (former editor of *New Korea* magazine), February 15, 1955.

12. A thorough and informative study of Han Sŏl-ya's literature and political role has been made in Myers, *Han Sŏl-ya*.

13. Ibid.

14. Paek, "Chŏngjŏn hu 1950 nyŏndae Pukhan-ui chŏngch'i pyŏndong-gwa kwonlyŏk chaep'an" (North Korean political changes and power realignment in the 1950s), 32.

15. Ibid., 36–37n. Incidentally, the institution of house arrest seems to have been very common in North Korea, but it was virtually unknown in the Soviet Union under Stalin.

16. Filatov, record of conversation with Pak Ch'ang-ok, March 12, 1956.

17. S. N. Filatov (counselor of the Soviet Embassy), record of conversation with Pak Ŭi-wan (vice-premier), January 24, 1956.

18. Okonogi, "North Korean Communism."

19. Filatov, record of conversation with Pak Ch'ang-ok, March 12, 1956.

20. *Nodong sinmun,* January 6, 7, and 23, 1956.

21. Filatov, record of conversation with Pak Yŏng-bin, February 25, 1956.

22. Paek, "Chŏngjŏn hu 1950 nyŏndae Pukhan-ui chŏngch'i pyŏndong-gwa kwonlyŏk chaep'an," 36–37.

23. Filatov, record of conversation with Pak Ch'ang-ok, March 12, 1956.

24. S. N. Filatov (counselor of the Soviet Embassy), record of conversation with Pak Ŭi-wan (vice-premier), February 21, 1956.

25. Detailed information and analyses of these and other clashes between rival factions concerning literary policy may be found in Myers, *Han Sŏl-ya,* 79–82.

26. Filatov, record of conversation with Pak Ŭi-wan, February 21, 1956.

27. Filatov, record of conversation with Pak Ch'ang-ok, March 12, 1956.

28. Filatov, record of conversation with Pak Yŏng-bin, February 25, 1956. In March 1956, Pak Ch'ang-ok also estimated the number of participants at "about 400." See S. N. Filatov, record of conversation with Pak Ch'ang-ok, March 12, 1956.

29. The term *"chuch'e"* (subject) was not Kim Il Song's invention; it had existed long before his famous speech. In the writings of Korean nationalists, *"chuch'e"* and the closely related *"chuch'esŏng"* normally refer to Korean peculiarities or uniqueness. Kim Il Song did, however, introduce a new meaning to the word, with a new set of connotations; in employing the term, he was referring to

a certain ideology or, rather (since this ideology was never entirely coherent), a new political line.

30. The ruling Communist parties had a sophisticated system of information exchange. Its main task was to provide the cadres and, to some extent, all party members with information that was seen as unsuitable for release to the common populace. The simplest form was "letters" of the Central Committee, which had to be read aloud at all party cell meetings and, hence, were addressed to all party members. The information needs of the cadres were served by an array of daily, weekly, and monthly classified publications. The classification was strictly hierarchical, so depending on his or her position in the hierarchy, a party cadre had access only to a certain type of material. The higher the cadre's level was, the more highly classified (and, presumably, franker) was the literature he or she was allowed to read.

31. For example, on January 29, 1956, *Nodong sinmun* published on page 2 an article about a meeting held "recently" by the Pyongyang KWP City Committee. The meeting had been dedicated to the struggle against formalism *(hyŏngsikjuŭi)* and dogmatism *(kyojojuŭi)*—the same key words used in the now famous speech of Kim Il Song (the term *"chuch'e"* had not yet been mentioned). The article even mentioned recent *(ch'oegŭn)* remarks of Kim Il Song concerning the necessity of fighting against these two evils, but where and how Kim Il Song made these remarks was not clarified. The phrasing, however, indicates that the author knew the speech well, for some parts of the article amount to quotations. For example, the article declared that it was necessary "to eliminate formalistic and dogmatic mistakes" *(hyongsikjŏk'i'myŏ kyojojuŭi kyŏrham-ŭl t'oech'ihago),* basically paraphrasing from the speech's title ("Kyŏjojuŭi—wa hyŏngsikjuŭi-rŭl t'oech'ihago . . .").

32. It is not necessary to dwell on the speech itself in much detail, because it has been not only published numerous times but also analyzed in many well-known works—for example, in Suh Dae-sook's classic political biography, *Kim Il Sung,* 143–144.

33. Kim Il Sung, *Kim Il Sŏng chŏjak sŏnjip* (The selected works of Kim Il Song), vol. 1, 567. Because Kim Il Song's works were often reedited to conform with the latest changes in political line, I have attempted to use the earliest edition available, which is presumably most authentic. However, the edition cited here was published after Han Sŏl-ya's purge in 1962, so the positive remarks about Han Sŏl-ya are omitted.

34. Ibid., 567–568, 572. It is necessary to mention that, according to his son Pak Il-san, Pak Ch'ang-ok received some classical Confucian education and was proud of his knowledge of *hanja* (Chinese characters) (Pak Il-san, interview with the author in Petersburg, February 4, 2001). Such knowledge was indeed quite unusual among the Soviet Koreans of Pak Ch'ang-ok's generation and background. Hence we can speculate that Kim Il Song might have accused Pak of an

insufficient command of the *hanja* and *hanmun* specifically to humiliate him, to show that, in spite of all Pak's claims to the contrary, Pak did not actually understand the real Korean culture. Indeed, Pak, who had once studied *hanja* from his father, could hardly compete with the sophisticated local intellectuals, who were graduates of the best Korean and Japanese schools.

35. Official information about Pak Hŏn-yŏng's trial was published on December 18, 1955, in *Nodong sinmun,* but the date of his execution was not specified.

36. Paek Chun-gi noted: "The discussion could be superficially perceived as an argument about literary politics, but the core question went far beyond the field of art and literature. It meant that disagreements within the party leadership, which appeared due to mistakes in policy and economic failures, developed into ideological confrontation." Paek, "Chŏngjŏn hu 1950 nyŏndae Pukhan-ui chŏngch'i pyŏndong-gwa kwonlyŏk chaep'an," 39.

37. Filatov, record of conversation with Pak Yŏng-bin, February 25, 1956.

38. Filatov, record of conversation with Pak Ch'ang-ok, March 12, 1956.

39. Ibid.

40. Filatov, record of conversation with Pak Yŏng-bin, February 25, 1956.

41. *Chosŏn chŏnsa* (The general history of Korea), vol. 29, 295.

42. Filatov, record of conversation with Pak Ŭi-wan, January 24, 1956.

43. There is a certain contradiction here. According to Pak Ch'ang-ok, his retirement took place just after the January 18 meeting of the Political Council (when the above-mentioned resolution was adopted). Pak Ch'ang-ok recalled the circumstances of his retirement in vivid detail on March 12, 1956, just three months later, so any fading of his memory by this date is highly unlikely. It is also unlikely that he deliberately provided his Soviet interlocutor with false information—after all, this information was all easily verifiable (Filatov, record of conversation with Pak Ch'ang-ok, March 12, 1956). Masao Okonogi also quotes a contemporary executive order, published March 3, 1956, that dates Pak Ch'ang-ok's retirement to January 4 (Okonogi, "North Korean Communism," 187, 204n30). It is possible that the official executive order of January 4 was actually written at a later date.

44. Following the Soviet example, all ruling Communist parties had a sophisticated hierarchical system of information distribution. There were classified newsletters and bulletins with various levels of access and circulation. The number of people who had access to a certain classified document or party decision could be anything from dozens to many tens of thousands. Unfortunately, we have no means of knowing how any particular piece of information was distributed, and thus it remains a subject of guesswork.

45. A. M. Petrov (provisional chargé d'affaires), diary, February 9–15, 1956.

46. Biakov, record of conversation with Song Chin-p'a, February 15, 1955.

47. It is worth remembering that Yim Hwa, an outstanding poet and high-level functionary of the South Korean Workers' Party, was in 1953 the subject

of a mock trial and was subsequently sentenced to death as a "Japanese agent" and an "American spy."

48. *Nodong sinmun,* February 15, 1956.

49. Another article with a similar style and wording, by Kim Ch'ŏl-su, was published in *Nodong sinmun* on February 19, 1956.

50. According to Hong, the "protectors of the reactionary writers" were Ki Sŏk-pok, Chŏng Tong-hyŏk, and Chŏng Yul.

51. *Nodong sinmun,* March 7, 1956.

52. Ibid., March 19, 1956.

53. Chang Kil-jun, "Strengthening of the [Party] Cadres' Unity," *Nodong sinmun,* March 22, 1956; information from a meeting in Pyongyang of the City Committee of the KWP, *Nodong sinmun,* April 4, 1956.

54. Filatov, record of conversation with Pak Ŭi-wan, January 24, 1956.

55. Filatov, record of conversation with Pak Ŭi-wan, February 21, 1956.

56. S. N. Filatov (counselor of the Soviet Embassy), record of conversation with Pak Ŭi-wan (vice-premier), February 29, 1956.

57. Filatov, record of conversation with Pak Ch'ang-ok, March 12, 1956.

58. Filatov, record of conversation with Pak Ŭi-wan, January 24, 1956. Kim Il Song's trip to East Germany was to became part of a much more ambitious journey, which included not only the Soviet Union but also most other Communist countries. However, it is unknown when the original plan to visit only East Germany developed into the idea of such a prolonged trip.

59. *Nodong sinmun,* March 14, 1956.

60. Filatov, record of conversation with Pak Ch'ang-ok, March 12, 1956.

61. Filatov, record of conversation with Pak Ŭi-wan, February 21, 1956. "Mass" = Russ. *"massy";* "individual" = Russ. *"lichnost',"* also translated as "personality," as in "personality cult" *(kul't lichnosti).*

62. Regarding Bulgarian developments, see Bell, *The Bulgarian Communist Party,* 112–118.

63. *Nodong sinmun,* April 5 and 8, 1956. The April 5 article was a translation from the Soviet newspaper *Pravda;* the April 8 article, from the Chinese *People's Daily.*

64. For an example of such a deliberately misleading usage, see *Nodong sinmun,* February 16, 1956. On this day the official North Korean newspaper carried an article by Pak Kŭm-ch'ŏl, describing various "deviations" and "mistakes" within the party. Among these "mistakes," Pak mentions a "personality cult"; however, he explains this explosively sensitive phenomenon in such vague terms that to the uninformed reader it could almost certainly pass for "individual heroism." The article curiously combined attacks against the "personality cult" with quotations from Stalin, which were at that time still commonplace in the North Korean press.

65. Filatov, record of conversation with Pak Ŭi-wan, February 29, 1956.

66. V. I. Ivanenko (first secretary of the Soviet Ministry of Foreign Affairs), record of conversation with Pak Kil-yŏng (deputy minister of foreign affairs), May 17, 1956.

67. *Nodong sinmun,* March 19, 1956.

68. Petrov, diary, February 17–March 2, 1956.

69. Ibid; I. S. Biakov (first secretary of the Soviet Embassy), record of conversation with Yi Ho-gu (deputy chairman of the central office of the Korean Society for International Cultural Exchange), February 18, 1956.

70. Petrov, diary, June 19–July 10, 1956.

71. S. N. Filatov (counselor of the Soviet Embassy), record of conversation with Kim Sŭng-hwa (minister of construction), May 24, 1956.

3. THE THIRD KWP CONGRESS

1. There have been rare exceptions to this rule. For example, Khrushchev delivered his anti-Stalin speech to a secret closed session of the CPSU Twentieth Congress; some congresses of the Chinese Communist Party under Mao were convened in secret; and so on. Perhaps the ritual and highly symbolic nature of the congresses made publicity and openness generally unavoidable, except in rare cases.

2. As Kim Hak-jun remarks in *Pukhan 50 nyŏn sa* (Fifty years of North Korean history), Kim Il Song's speech at the Third Congress was to be the least publicized of all his KWP Congress speeches, although it has been published quite a few times. The text used here is that which appeared the next day in *Nodong sinmun,* for it is presumably the most authentic.

3. *Nodong sinmun,* April 25, 1956. It is interesting that in this editorial the term "collective leadership" is translated as *"chipch'e chido,"* not as *"chiptan chido."* The latter translation eventually became the norm.

4. Ivanenko, record of conversation with Pak Kil-yŏng, May 17, 1956.

5. Translated from the Russian text, published in *Otnosheniia Sovetskogo Sojuza s Narodnoj Korejej* (Relations of the Soviet Union and People's Korea). The Korean text, which differs only slightly, was published in *Nodong sinmun* on April 25, 1956.

6. G. Ye. Samsonov (first secretary of the Soviet Ministry of Foreign Affairs), record of conversation with Ki Sŏk-pok (a referent in the Ministry of Culture), May 31, 1956.

7. B. K. Pimenov (first secretary of the Soviet Embassy), record of conversation with Won Hyŏng-gu (deputy head of the Organization Department, KWP Central Committee), June 21, 1958.

8. A good example of this problem is the factional affiliation of Yim Hae. Obviously, Wada Haruki was not sure about this individual, since in Wada's

book Yim Hae is identified as a member of the Yan'an faction on page 307 and as one of the "others" on page 310; Wada, *Kim Il Sŏng-gwa manju hang'il chŏnjaeng* (Anti-Japanese War in Manchuria and Kim Il Song). In *Pukhan inmyŏng sajŏn* (Biographical dictionary of North Korea), 323, he is considered to be a member of the Soviet faction. The latter possibility seems unlikely, because the Soviet Koreans themselves, in their conversations with diplomats, often mentioned him among their staunch enemies and never referred to any connections between him and the Soviets. For example, see Filatov, record of conversation with Pak Ŭi-wan, January 24, 1956; in the embassy papers there are at least three additional remarks to this effect made by other Soviet Koreans. Meanwhile, Yim Hae, far from being an insignificant figure, had been a full Central Committee member since the party's first Congress. For some time after 1956 he was responsible for the intelligence and subversion operations in the South, and in 1956 he ranked twenty-sixth in the Central Committee roster. Still, even the most basic data about his background are unknown. This is indicative of the difficulties that students of North Korean history must deal with.

9. It is necessary to note that Suh Dae-sook's estimations are slightly different from my own. According to his calculations, of the 71 full members, only 28 were old-timers and 43 were newly elected; Suh, *Kim Il Sung*, 148. Kim Hak-jun, *Pukhan 50 nyŏn sa*, 188, repeats this same estimation. However, it is likely that Kim Hak-jun simply took his data from a well-known monograph by Suh Dae-sook (as I myself also have done several times in my earlier articles). Earlier, however, Suh Dae-sook published lists of the 1948 and 1956 Central Committees in *Korean Communism, 1945-1980*, 320–321. There he lists 29 members of the 1948 Central Committee who were reelected in 1956. These results are similar to my own, and the single difference (one person) is easily explainable: Suh Dae-sook accidentally failed to include Kim Sŭng-hwa in his calculations.

For a list of the 1948 Central Committee members, see also *Pukhan inmyŏng sajŏn*, 457. For an identical list, see *Pukhan ch'onglam* (North Korean review), 200–201. This list is slightly different from the one in Suh Dae-sook's *Korean Communism*. The minor differences between these lists are as follows: (1) Kim Hwang-il is not mentioned in the *Pukhan inmyŏng sajŏn* roster as a full Central Committee member, though the text of the same publication confirms he held this position (p. 136); (2) *Pukhan inmyŏng sajŏn* mentions another full member, Kim Kŭn-il, instead, but this name does not appear in Suh Dae-sook's register; (3) there are some differences in the ranking of some persons, including Pak Ch'ang-ok (number 11 in Suh's list, but number 67 in the *Pukhan inmyŏng sajŏn* list). I have not been able to check the roster in a contemporary official North Korean publication, but given that 1948 is beyond the scope of this book, and the differences are minor, this is not my main concern here. However, as we shall see, Suh Dae-sook's list for 1956 is authentic, and I have reason to believe that his list for 1948 is likely to be more reliable as well.

The lists of the 1956 Central Committee in Suh Dae-sook's book are identical to the first original list, published in *Nodong sinmun* on April 30. Lists in *Pukhan inmyŏng sajŏn* (p. 457) and *Pukhan ch'onglam* (p. 201) are indistinguishable, but they are quite different from the authentic roster: members mentioned are the same, but their order (a very important thing in Communist political culture) bears almost no resemblance to the original. I have not been able to determine where the South Korean authors obtained their list. In any event, the original document is available in *Nodong sinmun* and is accurately reproduced in Suh Dae-sook's book.

10. For the list of the (South) KWP Central Committee, see Kim Nam-sik, *Namnodang yŏngu*, 256. For the list of the South Korean delegates to the Supreme People's Assembly, see ibid., 530–531.

4. THE CONSPIRACY

1. Rothschild, *Return to Diversity*, 145.

2. It seems that, unlike the situation in many Eastern European countries, the approval indeed was tacit and the Soviet police experts did not take a direct part in preparing the only show trial in North Korean history. At least the embassy papers do not hint at any such participation, and Kang Sang-ho, who was to become a deputy minister of foreign affairs soon after the trial, explicitly denied Soviet participation; Kang Sang-ho, interview with the author in Leningrad, October 31, 1989. In this regard it is worth mentioning that Pak Hŏn-yŏng's daughter Viva, who then lived in the USSR and held Soviet citizenship, was not harassed by the Soviet authorities and later built a remarkable artistic career in Moscow.

3. Fairbank and Goldman, *China: A New History*, 364.

4. For a summary of the attempts to limit Mao's personal power and restructure the Chinese Communist leadership in the 1950s, see Sullivan, "Leadership and Authority in the Chinese Communist Party."

5. For the delegation list, see *Nodong sinmun,* June 2, 1956 (departure), and July 20, 1956 (return).

6. I. F. Kurdiukov (head of the first Far Eastern Department of the Soviet Foreign Ministry), record of conversation with Yi Sang-jo (DPRK ambassador to the USSR), June 16, 1956.

7. Pak Chŏng-ae's comment about Moscow's remarks was delivered to a meeting of high-level executives in late July and soon reported to the embassy by a participant at that meeting. S. N. Filatov (counselor of the Soviet Embassy), record of conversation with Yun Kong-hŭm (minister of commerce), August 2, 1956.

Yi Sang-jo mentioned this several times in the autumn of 1956. See, for example, I. F. Kurdiukov (head of the first Far Eastern Department of the Soviet Foreign Ministry), record of conversation with Yi Sang-jo (DPRK ambassador to the USSR), August 11, 1956.

Hŏ Chin (under the pen name "Lim Ŭn") in his early study, which is based mostly on data obtained via interviews with North Korean defectors to the USSR, also mentions the meetings and counts both Nam Il and Pak Chŏng-ae among its participants. "Lim Ŭn" also says that it was B. N. Ponomarev (at that time the head of the International Department of the Soviet Central Committee) and Khrushchev himself who made these remarks. Unfortunately, both statements cannot be verified yet, but they certainly appear plausible. See Lim, *Founding of a Dynasty*, 225.

8. A. M. Petrov (provisional chargé d'affaires), record of conversation with Nam Il (minister of foreign affairs), July 24, 1956.

9. Petrov, diary, June 19–July 10, 1956.

10. Note the date of the conversation—July 14. Later Petrov in his official report deliberately postdated the conversation to July 20.

11. A. M. Petrov (provisional chargé d'affaires), record of conversation with Yi P'il-gyu (head of the Department of Construction Materials), July 14 [July 20], 1956. In an excellent book on the origins of the Korean War, Pak Myŏng-lim mentions that, during the very first weeks after the Liberation, Yi P'il-gyu was active in South Hamgyŏng Province as an official in the security service; Pak Myŏng-lim, *Hanguk chŏnjaeng-ŭi palbal-gwa kiwŏn* (Sources and origins of the Korean War), vol. 2, 61. Another reference to Yi can be found in a Soviet document of 1948: list of candidates for study in the Soviet Union, RTsHIDNI, fond 17, opis 128, delo 618. In October that year, Yi P'il-gyu was among the Korean officials to be sent to the USSR for ideological training. According to this document, at that time Yi was deputy head of the Ministry of the Interior, that is, deputy minister of the interior.

12. The typed copy: A. M. Petrov (provisional chargé d'affaires), record of conversation with Yi P'il-gyu (head of the Department of Construction Materials), July 20, 1956. The handwritten copy: Petrov, record of conversation with Yi P'il-gyu, July 14 [July 20]), 1956.

13. In the typed text, Yi's reply is relayed in the following manner: "There are two ways of achieving this. . . . The first is a sharp and decisive [campaign of] criticism and self-criticism within the party. However, Kim Il Song will not agree to this course of action. . . . The second is forcible upheaval. This path is difficult and will probably call for some sacrifice. There are people in the DPRK who are ready to embark on such a course and are currently making appropriate preparations"; A. M. Petrov, record of conversation with Yi P'il-gyu, July 20, 1956. As can be seen, Yi's remarks about "the crimes committed by Kim" had disappeared from the edited copy, and in general Yi's emphasis on the underground resistance was softened. At the same time, the remarks about an existing organized

opposition group (which are absent from the handwritten original) were introduced into the text.

14. Petrov, handwritten memo to Ambassador V. I. Ivanov.

15. Petrov, record of conversation with Yi P'il-gyu, July 14 [July 20], 1956.

16. Ibid.

17. Ibid.

18. Ibid. It is worth asking why Yi P'il-gyu considered it proper to be so critical of Pak Ch'ang-ok, who was already his coconspirator (Pak Ch'ang-ok himself was soon to appear at the Soviet Embassy as another spokesman for the opposition group). One possible explanation is that such a critical attitude would indicate that the rivalry between members of the various factions did not stop even when they all had to work together toward a common goal.

19. Ibid.

20. S. N. Filatov (counselor of the Soviet Embassy), record of conversation with Pak Ch'ang-ok (deputy premier of the DPRK cabinet and member of the presidium of the KWP Central Committee), July 21, 1956.

21. S. N. Filatov (counselor of the Soviet Embassy), record of conversation with Ch'oe Ch'ang-ik (vice-premier and member of the KWP Standing Committee), July 23, 1956.

22. Ibid.

23. S. N. Filatov (counselor of the Soviet Embassy), record of conversation with Kim Sŭng-hwa (minister of construction and member of the KWP Central Committee), July 24, 1956.

24. Filatov, record of conversation with Yun Kong-hŭm, August 2, 1956.

25. Petrov, record of conversation with Nam Il, July 24, 1956.

26. Ibid.

27. Petrov, diary, July 20–August 3, 1956. This is but one reference to important documents that still remain beyond the reach of scholars.

28. G. Ye. Samsonov (first secretary of the Soviet Embassy), record of conversation with Ko Hŭi-man (head of department in the KWP Central Committee), August 31, 1956.

29. Memoirs of Kang Sang-ho, manuscript, copy in the author's archive. According to *Pukhan inmyŏng sajŏn,* 201, Sŏk San was the head of the Political Department of the North Korean Ministry of National Defense in 1956 (basically, a political commissar), but Kang Sang-ho mentions him as the person who was then responsible for the security apparatus in the military.

30. S. P. Lazarev (first secretary of the Soviet Foreign Ministry), record of conversation with Ko Hŭi-man (head of department in the KWP Central Committee), September 18, 1956.

31. Petrov, diary, July 20–August 3, 1956.

32. Filatov, record of conversation with Ch'oe Ch'ang-ik, July 23, 1956.

33. Ibid.

34. This "self-criticism" was delivered by Kim Il Song, perhaps for the first time, on February 18 to a group of high-level government and party officials. The embassy learned about the incident shortly afterward, from a participant at the meeting. See S. N. Filatov, record of conversation with Pak Ŭi-wan, February 21, 1956.

35. Filatov, record of conversation with Yun Kong-hŭm, August 2, 1956.

36. Ibid.

37. Ibid.

5. THE "AUGUST GROUP" BEFORE AUGUST

1. Kurdiukov, record of conversation with Yi Sang-jo, June 16, 1956.

2. Filatov, record of conversation with Kim Sŭng-hwa, July 24, 1956.

3. Many accounts of the August Plenum have already been published. These accounts sometimes differ significantly. On the evening of August 31, just after the plenum ended, one of the participants, Ko Hŭi-man, rushed to the Moranbong Theater. There he met a Soviet diplomat and, obviously excited, related to him what had just happened. Apart from the minutes of the plenum itself, which are still inaccessible, Ko Hŭi-man's recollection is probably the most contemporary authentic account of the plenum. Ko Hŭi-man revealed that Yun Kong-hŭm, Sŏ Hwi, Ch'oe Ch'ang-ik, Pak Ch'ang-ok, and Yi P'il-gyu had made or tried to make speeches critical of Kim Il Song. See G. Ye. Samsonov, record of conversation with Ko Hŭi-man, August 31, 1956.

4. See, for example, Lim, *Founding of a Dynasty;* and Kim Hak-jun, *Pukhan 50 nyŏn sa,* 190.

5. Filatov, record of conversation with Kim Sŭng-hwa, July 24, 1956.

6. Ibid.

7. Ivanenko, record of conversation with Pak Kil-yŏng, May 17, 1956.

8. Filatov, record of conversation with Pak Ch'ang-ok, March 12, 1956. As late as May 24, Kim Sŭng-hwa expressed the same negative attitude toward the "nationalist" Ch'oe Ch'ang-ik and obviously did not see any difference between him and Kim Il Song's staunch lieutenant Pak Kŭm-ch'ŏl. Therefore this date (May 24 or the day following) may be the earliest possible date of his (and Pak Ch'ang-ok's) joining the opposition cabal. See Filatov, record of conversation with Kim Sŭng-hwa, May 24, 1956.

9. Kim Ch'an, a onetime director of North Korean National Bank and a Central Committee member in 1948–1956, noted: "Ch'oe Ch'ang-ik visited the Soviet Union often but still disliked it strongly." Kim Ch'an, interview with the author in Tashkent, January 15, 1991.

10. Filatov, record of conversation with Pak Ch'ang-ok, July 21, 1956.

11. R. G. Okulov (*Pravda* correspondent) and S. V. Vasilijev (TASS correspon-

dent), record of conversation with Sin Ch'ong-t'aek (deputy minister of communications), February 3, 1957.

12. Petrov, record of conversation with Yi P'il-gyu, July 14 [July 20], 1956.

13. Kurdiukov, record of conversation with Yi Sang-jo, June 16, 1956; I. F. Kurdiukov (head of the first Far Eastern Department of the Soviet Foreign Ministry), record of conversation with Yi Sang-jo (DPRK ambassador to the USSR), August 9, 1956.

14. Filatov, record of conversation with Ch'oe Ch'ang-ik, July 23, 1956.

15. In 1956 these people held the following positions: Han Sŏl-ya—Central Committee member (ranked 18th in April 1956), Writers' Union chairman, the leading North Korean literary bureaucrat; Kim Ch'ang-man—Central Committee member (ranked 27th in April 1956), KWP vice-chairman, Standing Committee candidate member, minister of education (till May 1956), a party propaganda and ideological czar; Kim Il—Central Committee member (ranked 5th in April 1956), Standing Committee member, vice-premier; Yim Hae—Central Committee member (ranked 20th in April 1956); Pak Kŭm-ch'ŏl—Central Committee member (ranked 6th in April 1956), KWP vice-chairman, Standing Committee member; Han Sang-du—Central Committee member (ranked 11th in April 1956); Yi Chong-ok—Central Committee member (ranked 22nd in April 1956), Standing Committee candidate member, chairman of the State Planning Commission; Chŏng Chun-t'aek—Central Committee member (ranked 24th in April 1956), vice-premier (from May 1956). Biographical data are from Suh, *Korean Communism, 1945-1980;* and *Pukhan inmyŏng sajŏn.*

16. Both Ch'oe Ch'ang-ik and Yi P'il-gyu in their above-mentioned meetings with the Soviet diplomats explicitly included Ch'oe Yong-gŏn among the officials who were recently dissatisfied with Kim Il Song's policies. This was corroborated by Pak Ch'ang-ok, who revealed that he had some unspecified "suspicions" about Ch'oe's behavior.

17. Petrov, record of conversation with Yi P'il-gyu, July 14 [July 20], 1956.

18. Ivanenko, record of conversation with Pak Kil-yŏng, May 17, 1956.

19. Okonogi, *North Korean Communism.*

20. Filatov, record of conversation with Pak Ch'ang-ok, July 21, 1956.

21. One must suspect that in the future, after the unavoidable collapse or radical transformation of the Kims' regime in North Korea, there will be some politically motivated attempts to present the "August opposition" as real dissenters in the latter sense, that is, as secret anti-Communists who dreamed of the development of a liberal democracy in Korea. Of course, this was not the case and could not be the case. Not only did their lifelong experience as underground Communist activists, functionaries of the secret services, and guerrilla fighters make them quite insensitive to the lures of the "bourgeois ideas," but also the historical experience of East Asia in the mid-twentieth century did not provide them with any examples of working prosperous democracies. Both Chiang Kai-shek's

dictatorship in China and Syngman Rhee's regime in South Korea, the only self-proclaimed "democratic" regimes in the region, did much to undermine any positive connotations of the term "democracy" in the East Asian context.

22. Suh, *Kim Il Sung,* 152.

23. Lim, *Founding of a Dynasty,* 229.

24. Suh Dae-sook cites these rumors, which were based on information obtained from defectors; ibid., 151.

25. Kurdiukov, record of conversation with Yi Sang-jo, August 9, 1956.

26. B. K. Pimenov (first secretary of the Soviet Embassy), record of conversation with Pak Kil-yŏng (head of the first Department in the DPRK Ministry of Foreign Affairs), December 8, 1957.

27. V. I. Pelishenko (counselor of the Soviet Embassy), record of conversation with Pang Hak-se (minister of the interior), October 24, 1959.

28. Filatov, record of conversation with Pak Ch'ang-ok, July 21, 1956.

29. Petrov, record of conversation with Nam Il, July 24, 1956.

30. Lim, *Founding of a Dynasty,* 225.

31. See Suh, *Kim Il Sung,* 150. Suh is quite conclusive: "It is not true . . . that Kim had to cut short his trip to Moscow." It is rather strange that South Korean scholars have ignored such a remark by a leading specialist in the field and continue to write about a Kim Il Song who hurried back home to fight the conspirators.

32. Lazarev, record of conversation with Ko Hŭi-man, September 18, 1956.

33. Petrov, record of conversation with Nam Il, July 24, 1956.

34. As quoted by Pak Kil-yŏng during the latter's meeting with a Soviet diplomat. See Pimenov, record of conversation with Pak Kil-yŏng, December 8, 1957.

35. V. Ivanov (Soviet ambassador to the DPRK), memo to N. T. Fedorenko (deputy minister of foreign affairs), September 28, 1956.

36. Petrov recognized the omission in his handwritten memo to Ambassador V. I. Ivanov.

37. This document was found and provided to the author by Balazs Szalontai. Archives of the Hungarian Ministry of Foreign Affairs, XIX-J-1-j Korea 1945–1964, box 4, 5/a, 003133/1956. Translation of all cited Hungarian documents is by Balazs Szalontai.

38. Kang Sang-ho, interview with the author in Leningrad, October 31, 1989.

39. Kurdiukov, record of conversation with Yi Sang-jo, August 9, 1956.

40. The Chinese approach to the Hungarian and Polish crises is described (according to the recently discovered original documents) in Chen and Yang, "Chinese Politics," 263–265. Recently discovered original documents about the Sino-Soviet argument over possible intervention in Poland are abundant and make for interesting reading. See, for example, Kramer, "The 'Malin Notes,'" 392; and Gluchowski, "Khrushchev, Gomulka, and the 'Polish October.'"

41. Chen and Yang, "Chinese Politics," 264.

6. THE AUGUST PLENUM

1. A good specimen of the genre is an extensive article by Yi Song-un, himself a prominent participant in the purges of the 1950s: Yi Song-un, "P'alwol chŏwonhŭi-wa tang taeryŏl-ŭi t'ongil tangyŏl (The August Plenum and the unity of the party ranks)."

2. Koon Woo Nam, *North Korean Leadership;* Suh, *Kim Il Sung,* 149–152; Kim Hak-jun, *Pukhan 50 nyŏn sa,* 189–192; Ch'oe Sŏng, *Pukhan chŏngch'i sa.*

3. Suh, *Kim Il Sung,* 368n36.

4. Lim, *Founding of a Dynasty.*

5. According to *Nodong sinmun* (September 2, 1956), a performance by a Hungarian folk music group took place on August 31 in the Moranbong Theater. All his very possibly sincere zeal did not help Ko Hŭi-man avoid a fate of many of his fellows. For a while it indeed seemed that he was rewarded for his pro-Kim positions. He was "elected" a Supreme People's Assembly member in 1957 and promoted to the position of minister of forestry in 1958. The next year, however, Ko became a victim of the purges and disappeared forever; see *Pukhan inmyŏng sajŏn.*

6. Samsonov, record of conversation with Ko Hŭi-man, August 31, 1956.

7. This phrase hints at an episode in Ch'oe Yong-gŏn's career: his formal chairmanship in the Democratic Party, which is discussed in chapter 2.

8. Memoirs of Kang Sang-ho, manuscript, copy in the author's archive; Kang Sang-ho, interview with the author in Leningrad, October 31, 1989.

9. Hoxha Enver, *The Artful Albanian,* 177–178.

10. This discussion has been studied by Masao Okonogi. See Okonogi, "North Korean Communism."

11. Pak Sang-hong, "Chikŏp tongmaeng saŏp-eso chegitwenŭn myŏch' kaji munje" (Some problems from the trade unions' activity), 40–42.

12. *Chosŏn chŏnsa,* vol. 28, 291.

13. In North Korea the trade unions' activity in the mid-1950s was even more restricted than in other "people's democracies." As Balazs Szalontai noticed, even the Hungarian diplomats were surprised that in the DPRK it was the state (instead of the trade unions) that dealt with all social security, holiday, and other issues. Moreover, already in early 1955 some criticism emerged in the trade unions that targeted the "wartime work style," a common euphemism for dictatorship and hierarchy.

14. Kim Hak-jun, *Pukhan 50 nyŏn sa,* 190.

15. B. K. Pimenov (first secretary of the Soviet Embassy), record of conversation with Kim Yŏng-ju (head of the Organization Department of the KWP Central Committee), April 11, 1959. When asked about the goals of Ch'oe Ch'ang-ik's group, Kim said: "Ch'oe Ch'ang-ik's group was revisionist; [they] wanted, after the establishment of their control [over the DPRK and KWP], to reach an

agreement with Yi Sŭng-man [Syngman Rhee], [which would be] based on de-
claring Korea a 'neutral' state and breaking the DPRK away from the socialist
camp."

16. Lim, *Founding of a Dynasty,* 229.

17. Samsonov, record of conversation with Ko Hŭi-man, August 31, 1956.

18. Kim Chu-bong, interview with the author in Moscow, February 2, 1990.

19. Lazarev, record of conversation with Ko Hŭi-man, September 18, 1956.
In mid-September, just a couple of weeks after the meeting in Moranbong
Theater with Samsonov, Ko Hŭi-man was in Moscow, where he met another
Soviet diplomat, Lazarev, with whom he again spoke of the recent plenum.

20. Ye. L. Titorenko (second secretary of the Soviet Embassy), record of conversation with Ch'oe Sŭng-hun (deputy chairman of the KWP Committee of
Ryanggang Province), October 23, 1956. It is interesting that, according to
Pukhan inmyŏng sajŏn, at this time Ch'oe Sŭng-hun was a section chief *(kwajang)*
at the KWP Central Committee—a contradiction with the archive document.
Perhaps Ch'oe had just been transferred to (or from) Ryanggang Province. This
might be a coincidence; there might be another Ch'oe Sŭng-hun, although it is
rather unusual to meet two Koreans with exactly the same surnames and given
names. If this is the same person, which is highly probable, it is also noteworthy
that in spite of making such a liberal statement in 1956, he was lucky to survive
politically (let alone, physically) until at least 1965, when he was deputy head
of a department *(pubujang)* of the KWP Central Committee.

21. N. M. Shesterikov (counselor of the Soviet Embassy), diary, September
16, 1956; Titorenko, record of conversation with Ch'oe Sŭng-hun, October 23,
1956. According to some sources obtained by the embassy, Pak Ch'ang-ok was
not a deputy director but the director of the mill. See Okulov and Vasiliev,
record of conversation with Sin Ch'ong-t'aek, February 3, 1957; and Shesterikov, diary, September 14, 1956. Still, this hardly makes much difference.

22. The exact date of Kim Sŭng-hwa's departure is not known. What is
known is that it took place no earlier than July 25 and no later than September
12 (on September 12 he was referred to as "Kim Sŭng-hwa, who has left for the
USSR to study"; N. M. Shesterikov, diary). It is likely that he had left Korea just
prior to the August plenum, although one year later, on October 26, 1957, B. K.
Pimenov remarked that Kim Sŭng-hwa had left Korea in September 1956; B. K.
Pimenov (first secretary of the Soviet Embassy), record of conversation with Pak
Kil-yŏng (head of the first Department in the DPRK Ministry of Foreign Affairs),
October 26, 1957. Kim Hak-jun, in his more recent study of North Korean his-
tory, listed Kim Sŭng-hwa among the participants of the plenum; Kim Hak-jun,
Pukhan 50 nyŏn sa, 190. Because the precise time of Kim Sŭng-hwa's departure
for Moscow is still unknown, his participation in the plenum cannot be completely ruled out; however, it seems unlikely. Had he been one of the challengers, he would hardly have been permitted to leave the country afterward.

Nevertheless, by mid-September he definitely had already been overseas. It is more likely that the defectors, whose accounts were used by Kim Hak-jun for his research, confused Kim Sŭng-hwa's participation in the conspiracy, which was quite real, with his direct participation in the plenum.

23. Pimenov, record of conversation with Pak Kil-yŏng, October 26, 1957.

24. Samsonov, record of conversation with Ko Hŭi-man, August 31, 1956.

25. Kang Sang-ho, interview with the author in Leningrad, October 31, 1989.

26. Ibid.

27. Ibid.

28. G. Ye. Samsonov (first secretary of the Soviet Embassy), record of conversation with Yi Song-un (chairman of the Pyongyang City Committee of the KWP), November 23, 1956. Yi Song-un was one of Kim Il Song's trusted henchmen; he was a prosecutor during show trials against Domestic Communists (1953) and Pak Hŏn-yŏng (1955) and played a significant role in a witch hunt of the late 1950s. Later he was to occupy some important positions, including a stint as ambassador to the USSR (1960–1964). Kim Hak-jun, *Pukhan 50 nyŏn sa,* 169, considers him "unusually able for somebody with a Guerrilla faction background."

29. *Nodong sinmun,* September 15, 1956.

30. Shesterikov, diary, September 18, 1956.

7. THE SOVIET-CHINESE DELEGATION AND THE SEPTEMBER PLENUM

1. For a detailed account of the Eighth Congress and reforms approved by the convention, see Sullivan, "Leadership and Authority in the Chinese Communist Party."

2. The delegation dispatched to the congress consisted of Ch'oe Yong-gŏn, Yim Hae, Li Chu-yŏn, and Ha Ang-ch'on (*Nodong sinmun,* September 13, 1956). Ch'oe Yong-gŏn as head of the KWP delegation was mentioned by *Nodong sinmun* in its report about the official reception on September 17, but on September 20 the newspaper stated that the customary congratulatory address to the congress had been delivered by Yim Hae.

3. V. V. Kovyzhenko, interview with the author in Moscow, August 2, 1991.

4. Ibid.

5. Among many jokes about Mikoyan's remarkable versatility, my favorite is this one: Mikoyan is visiting his friends. When it is late and guests are leaving, somebody notices it is raining and suggests that Mikoyan take an umbrella. "Never mind," Mikoyan says. "I'll pass between the drops—I know how to do it."

6. Rothschild, *Return to Diversity,* 156.

7. V. V. Kovyzhenko, interview with the author in Moscow, August 2, 1991.

8. Kim Il Song was quoted by a participant of the December Plenum of

1957 during the latter's meeting with a Soviet diplomat. See Pimenov, record of conversation with Pak Kil-yŏng, December 8, 1957.

9. G. M. Plotnikov, interview with the author in Moscow, February 1, 1990. Colonel Plotnikov worked in North Korea in the 1950s and was a witness to Mikoyan's visit, although he had nothing to do with the plenums or Mikoyan's mission as such.

10. V. D. Tihomirov, interview with the author in Moscow, September 25, 1989.

11. V. V. Kovyzhenko, interview with the author in Moscow, August 2, 1991.

12. I tried to get hold of these papers, which are currently in one of the Russian archives. Their existence was confirmed, but access to this material was unequivocally denied.

13. Kovyzhenko himself thought that the entire plan to overthrow Kim Il Song was a Chinese provocation. In his opinion, Mao Zedong took great pains to encourage the Soviets to interfere actively in the Korean situation. Were it a failure, Mao could always have pointed to this as an example of Soviet interference in the internal affairs of a fraternal country, a good proof of alleged "Soviet hegemonism." Were the removal of Kim Il Song a success, Mao Zedong would also derive advantage from the event, given that the most likely candidate for the succession would be a member of the Yan'an faction (i.e., pro-Chinese). V. V. Kovyzhenko, interview with the author in Moscow, August 2, 1991.

14. Pimenov, record of conversation with Pak Kil-yŏng, December 8, 1957.

15. *Nodong sinmun,* September 29, 1956.

8. THE PURGES

1. V. I. Pelishenko (counselor of the Soviet Embassy), record of conversation with Pak Kŭm-ch'ŏl, November 22, 1956.

2. Samsonov, record of conversation with Yi Song-un, November 23, 1956.

3. *Nodong sinmun,* October 19, 1956.

4. For an analysis of this short period of relaxation, see Kim Sŏng-su, "1950 nyŏndae Pukhan munhak-kwa sahoejuŭi riŏllijŭm" (Socialist realism and North Korean literature of the 1950s), 141–145.

5. Ye. L. Titorenko (second secretary of the Soviet Embassy), record of conversation with Yu Sŏng-hun (rector of Kim Il Song University), September 11, 1957. The assumption of some scholars that Pak Ch'ang-ok managed to escape to the USSR is a mistake.

6. Samsonov, record of conversation with Yi Song-un, November 23, 1956.

7. Pelishenko, record of conversation with Pak Kŭm-ch'ŏl, November 22, 1956.

8. Suh Dae-sook, *Kim Il Sung,* 152; Ye. L. Titorenko (second secretary of the

Soviet Embassy), record of conversation with Ch'oe Chŏng-hyŏn (postgraduate of Kim Il Song University), September 11, 1957.

9. *Nodong sinmun,* January 16, 1957.

10. Filatov, record of conversation with Ch'oe Ch'ang-ik, July 23, 1956.

11. *Nodong sinmun,* October 28–November 25, 1956.

12. Ye. L. Titorenko (second secretary of the Soviet Embassy), record of conversation with Yu Sŏng-hun (rector of Kim Il Song University), February 7, 1957.

13. Ibid.

14. *Nodong sinmun* (January 10, 1957) published a note about their return (another sign of the relative openness at that time) and explained that it was necessary, "taking into consideration the difficult situation in Hungary, . . . in order to ease the burden" of the Hungarian people.

15. Ibid.; Ye. L. Titorenko (second secretary of the Soviet Embassy), record of conversation with Song Kun-ch'an (head of the Department of Marxism-Leninism, Kim Il Song University), January 21, 1957. Transcription of the name "Song Kun-ch'an" is verified by *Nodong sinmun,* August 6, 1957.

16. V. I. Pelishenko (provisional chargé d'affaires), record of conversation with Kim Il Song, February 12, 1957.

17. G. Ye. Samsonov (first secretary of the Soviet Embassy), record of conversation with Chang Ik-hwan (deputy minister of education), May 23, 1957. The figure of three thousand itself sounds very high, so we cannot rule out a possibility of some mistake—say, in translation or typing. In 1948 in the primary and secondary schools nationwide there were 35,176 teachers, of whom in 1946 about 15 percent were working in Pyongyang and South P'yongan Province; *1946, 1947, 1948 nyŏndo Pukhan kyŏngje t'onggye charyojip* (The collection of the statistics on the North Korean economy in 1946, 1947, and 1948). The teachers' numbers greatly increased by 1957, for that decade was a period of intense educational developments, but even in this case the replacement of three thousand teachers would mean that from one quarter to one half of all teachers in the province lost their jobs. The figure sounds a bit excessive, so it has to be approached with some doubt.

18. This was the opinion of Chang Ik-hwan, deputy minister of education. See Samsonov, record of conversation with Chang Ik-hwan, May 23, 1957. Such an attitude toward the university is also confirmed by the frequent mention of alleged subversive activity of the "splittists" there in the official press in late 1957 and 1958.

19. Titorenko, record of conversation with Yu Sŏng-hun, September 11, 1957.

20. Ibid.; *Nodong sinmun,* August 6, 1957. Incidentally, Yi Ch'ŏng-won was one of the first persons to use the term *"chuch'e"* (albeit in slightly different form, *"chuch'esŏng,"* but explicitly citing Kim Il Song's then recent speech). He did so in his speech delivered to the Third KWP Congress, April 27, 1956; *Nodong sinmun,* April 28, 1956.

21. *Nodong sinmun,* August 6, 1957.

22. Ye. L. Titorenko (second secretary of the Soviet Embassy), record of conversation with Ch'oe Chŏng-hyŏn (postgraduate of Kim Il Song University), November 4, 1956, AVPRF, fond 0102, opis 12, delo 6, papka 68.

23. Titorenko, record of conversation with Song Kun-ch'an, January 21, 1957.

24. Samsonov, record of conversation with Chang Ik-hwan, May 23, 1957.

25. On September 11 his arrest was still "recent news." Titorenko, record of conversation with Yu Sŏng-hun, September 11, 1957.

26. V. S. Zahariin (head of the Consular Section, Soviet Embassy), record of conversation with Pak T'ae-sŏp (Soviet citizen), November 12, 1957.

27. Ye. L. Titorenko (second secretary of the Soviet Embassy), record of conversation with Yi Tae-p'il (deputy chairman of the Pyongyang City Committee of the KWP), October 10, 1957.

28. Ye. L. Titorenko (second secretary of the Soviet Embassy), record of conversation with Chang Chu-ik (corresponding member of the DPRK Academy of Science), October 17, 1957.

29. Ibid. The case of "Kim So Ryon" poses a difficult problem that arises from the transcription of Korean personal names in Russian documents. Though the reliable and standard Russian transcription system (the Kholodovich system) has existed since the 1930s, in the 1950s it was used by a handful of academics in Korean studies, while others, diplomats included, transcribed the names as they heard them. Because of the considerable difference between Russian and Korean phonetics, it is usually impossible to reconstruct the original names of not-so-well-known figures, if they are not mentioned in the available Korean materials. Therefore I retranscribe Russian transcriptions and use question marks in brackets to indicate this difficulty and uncertainty of the suggested transcription.

30. Good examples include an article by Mun Sŏk-pol (August 23), an editorial on September 4, and an article on the situation in domestic retail trade on September 17 (in which Yun Kong-hŭm, who had been minister of commerce prior to the August incident, was accused of sabotage). Eventually the accusations of sabotage (but not of spying) were widely used against the opposition in 1957–1959. For example, in August 1959, Yi Song-un accused Kim Sŭng-hwa and Pak Ŭi-wan, both senior officials in the construction industry, of sabotaging the introduction of new construction technologies to the DPRK; Yi Song-un, "P'alwol chŏwonhŭi-wa tang taeryŏl-ŭi t'ongil tangyŏl."

31. *Chŏngch'i chisik,* no. 2 (1958), 26. *Chŏngch'i chisik* was a party periodical that published mostly propaganda material, to be used in political indoctrination sessions by the party propagandists. In regard to the quoted remark, it must be mentioned that the concept of human rights per se was not denied by the Communist legal theory of the 1950s (actual legal practice, as it is well known, was entirely another matter). Only in the late 1970s, when Western propaganda

(and forces of internal dissent) made "human rights protection" a major political issue in the Soviet Union and some other Communist countries, did this term gain clearly negative connotations in the official Communist usage.

32. Ibid., 15.

33. Titorenko, record of conversation with Yi Dae-p'il, October 10, 1957.

34. O. V. Okonishnikov (first secretary of the Soviet Embassy), record of conversation with Kim T'aek-yong (deputy minister of justice), October 14, 1957.

35. B. K. Pimenov (first secretary of the Soviet Embassy), record of conversation with Won Hyŏng-gu (deputy head of the Organization Department, KWP Central Committee), July 22, 1958.

36. Kim Hak-jun, *Pukhan 50 nyŏn sa,* 191–192.

37. Ye. L. Titorenko (second secretary of the Soviet Embassy), record of conversation with Yu Sŏng-hun (rector of Kim Il Song University), April 6, 1957.

38. V. I. Pelishenko (provisional chargé d'affaires), record of conversation with Pak Chŏng-ae (deputy chairperson of the KWP Central Committee), December 17, 1956.

39. V. I. Pelishenko (provisional chargé d'affaires), record of conversation with Nam Il (minister of foreign affairs), January 4, 1957.

40. B. K. Pimenov (first secretary of the Soviet Embassy), record of conversation with An Un-gong[?] (lecturer in the Institute of National Economy, former head of the first Department of the Ministry of Foreign Affairs), September 8, 1957.

41. Kurdiukov, record of conversation with Yi Sang-jo, August 9, 1956.

42. B. N. Vereshchagin (counselor of the Far Eastern Department), record of conversation with Yi Sang-jo (DPRK ambassador to the USSR), October 20, 1956.

43. A special role of Andropov in negotiations, as well as his resolute refusal to give the defectors away, is mentioned in many documents. For an example, see N. M. Shesterikov (counselor of the Soviet Embassy), record of conversation with Pak Kil-yŏng (head of the first Department of the Ministry of Foreign Affairs), February 17, 1958.

44. V. I. Pelishenko (provisional chargé d'affaires), record of conversation with Kim Il Song, January 30, 1957. In general the Yi Sang-jo affair generated a large amount of exchanges, and it is mentioned in dozens of the contemporary Soviet documents.

45. Shesterikov, record of conversation with Pak Kil-yŏng, February 17, 1958.

46. B. K. Pimenov (first secretary of the Soviet Embassy), record of conversation with An Un-gong[?] (former head of the first Department of the Ministry of Foreign Affairs), January 30, 1957. In March 1959. Pak Kil-yŏng told a Soviet diplomat that, with one exception, all former staff members of the North Korean Embassy in Moscow had been fired from the Foreign Ministry after their return to Pyongyang; N. Ye. Torbenkov (counselor of the Soviet Embassy), record of conversation with Pak Kil-yŏng (deputy minister of foreign affairs), March 15, 1959.

47. Lim, *Founding of a Dynasty*, 231.

48. On the Chinese official reaction to the Eastern European crisis of 1956, see Teiwes, *Politics and Purges in China*, 180–182.

49. Now a documentary record is available of the exchanges during the CPSU Presidium (Politburo) meeting on October 30, where, among other matters, the declaration was discussed:

> CDE. SABUROV [first deputy prime minister]: I agree with the need for a Declaration and withdrawal of troops. At the XX [CPSU] Congress we did the correct thing, but then did not keep control of the unleashed initiative of the masses. It's impossible to lead against the will of the people. We failed to stand for genuine Leninist principles of leadership. We might end up lagging behind events. . . . We must reexamine our relations. Relations must be built on an equal basis.
>
> CDE. KHRUSHCHEV: We are unanimous. As a first step we will issue a Declaration.

This exchange was followed by a lengthy discussion of the draft of the October Declaration. See Kramer, "The 'Malin Notes.'"

50. I have quoted here the Korean text published in *Nodong sinmun*, November 1, 1956, because it was the text that influenced the relevant developments.

51. On this campaign, see Teiwes, *Politics and Purges in China*, 216–258.

52. The first such article appeared on July 7.

53. Paek Chun-gi also considers that the 1957 crisis in Moscow was one of the important influences on North Korean politics. Paek, "Chŏngjŏn hu 1950 nyŏndae Pukhan-ui chŏngch'i pyŏndong-gwa kwonlyŏk chaep'an," 54–55.

54. Hobsbawm, *Age of Extremes*, 73.

55. B. K. Pimenov (first secretary of the Soviet Embassy), record of conversation with Pak Kil-yŏng (head of the First Department in the DPRK Ministry of Foreign Affairs), November 28, 1957.

56. Ibid. Among the wrongdoings allegedly recognized by Mao and Peng during the Moscow meeting, Kim Ch'ang-man briefly mentioned "attempts of the Chinese People's Volunteers to print Korean money." It is not clear what was meant by these words. Perhaps they imply that Chinese troops were engaged in producing counterfeited DPRK bills to meet their own demand for local currency.

57. V. I. Pelishenko (counselor of the Soviet Embassy), record of conversation with Nam Il (minister of foreign affairs), October 9, 1957. According to Suh Dae-sook's data, Kim Ch'ang-hŭp lost his ministerial position in September 1957, just before this conversation between Pelishenko and Nam Il; Suh Dae-sook, *Korean Communism, 1945–1980*, 463.

58. Pimenov, record of conversation with Pak Kil-yŏng, December 8, 1957.

59. *Chosŏn chŏnsa*, vol. 28, 294.

60. Ibid.

61. Pimenov, record of conversation with Kim Yŏng-ju, April 11, 1959. At this stage it is not clear what Kim meant by his remark about alleged plans of the "South Korean ruling circle" to stage a rebellion in February–March 1956. This is too early for the August Plenum, so it is probable that Kim hinted at some other allegations against some other groups that the investigators wanted to connect with the August "factionalists." It is also noteworthy that Kim Yŏng-ju recognized that no direct evidence had been found of connections between Ch'oe Chang-ik's group and "the American and Yi Sung-man's agents." Taking into consideration methods routinely and successfully employed by Stalinist states to extract confessions, we must surmise that for some reason such "direct evidence" was not deemed necessary. Indeed, the charges of espionage, which had been applied to all previous oppositions, were dropped this time. Perhaps Kim Il Song considered such charges to be too offensive to the USSR and China, whose connection with the opposition was clear.

62. The report took quite a few pages in *Nodong sinmun*, March 4, 1958.

63. V. I. Pelishenko (counselor of the Soviet Embassy), record of conversation with Nam Il (minister of foreign affairs), February 14, 1959.

64. Kim Hak-jun, *Pukhan 50 nyŏn sa*, 196–198.

65. Ye. L. Titorenko (second secretary of the Soviet Embassy), record of conversation with Ch'oe Sŭng-hun (deputy chairman of the KWP Committee of Ryanggang Province) and Chu Ch'ang-jun (deputy head of the Propaganda Department of the KWP Central Committee), March 5, 1958.

66. N. Ye. Torbenkov (counselor of the Soviet Embassy), record of conversation with Pak Kil-yŏng (deputy minister of foreign affairs), July 6, 1959. The list of the disgraced Central Committee (CC) members included Hyŏn Chŏng-min, Yi Yu-min, Hŏ Sŏng-t'aek, Cho Yŏng, Hŏ Pin, Chin Pan-su, Yi Kwon-mu, Ch'oe Chong-hak, Kim Won-bong, and "Yi Sang-hyŏk." The latter's name is absent from the available CC rosters and other documents, but it is highly probable (indeed, almost certain) that Pak Kil-yŏng or his Soviet interlocutor made a mistake, and by "Yi Sang-hyŏk" they really meant Kim Sang-hyŏk. Of these persons, Hŏ Pin and Ch'oe Chong-hak were Soviet Koreans; Chin Pan-su, Yi Kwon-mu, Yi Yu-min, Cho Yŏng, and Hyŏn Chŏng-min belonged to the former Yan'an exiles; and Kim Won-bong, Hŏ Sŏng-t'aek, and Kim ("Yi") Sang-hyŏk were surviving South Korean Communists. This group was replaced by Chŏng Ch'il-sŏng, Sŏk San, O Chin-u, "Kim Chun-sam" (unidentified, position given as deputy minister of the interior), Kim Pong-yul, Hyŏn P'il-hun, Pak Se-ch'ang, An Yŏng, and Kwon Yŏng-t'ae. Four of these new appointees were former guerrillas (Sŏk San, O Chin-u, An Yŏng, and Kwon Yŏng-t'ae), two represented the Soviet faction (Kim Pong-yul and Pak Se-ch'ang), one was a domestic Communist from the South (Chŏng Ch'il-sŏng, soon to be purged), and one was from the North (Hyŏn P'il-hun).

67. Pelishenko, record of conversation with Pang Hak-se, October 24, 1959.

68. Ibid.

69. In some reference materials Kim Ik-sŏn is mentioned as a former Soviet Korean (see, e.g., *Pukhan inmyŏng sajŏn*, 97). Nevertheless, I have never come across his name in such a context, so the assertions about his Soviet background are dubious.

70. Ibid. Perhaps the list is not complete; the document mentions that the tribunal had five members, but only four are named.

71. It was the chief of North Korean secret police, Pang Hak-se, who briefed a Soviet diplomat about the secret trial and the eventual execution of the opposition leaders; V. I. Pelishenko (counselor of the Soviet Embassy), record of conversation with Pang Hak-se (minister of the interior), February 12, 1960. To the best of my knowledge, the fact of their secret trial and consequent execution has remained unknown to scholars.

72. On the fate of Kim Ung after 1968, see *Pukhan inmyŏng sajŏn*, 89–90. By the way, Kim Ung's political resurrection is not unique; it was also the fate of some other important North Korean politicians, once purged and presumed dead, but surviving the exile or imprisonment and restoring their former fortunes (for example, such prominent personalities as Ch'oe Kwang and Pak Chŏng-ae).

73. G. K. Plotnikov, interview with the author in Moscow, February 1, 1990.

74. *Chosŏn kongsanjuŭi undong-ŭi wanjŏnhan t'ongil-ŭi silhaeng* (The complete realization of the unity of the Korean Communist movement), 32.

75. Ibid., 33.

9. NORTH KOREA CHANGES COURSE

1. On August 3, *Nodong sinmun* published a rather lengthy article about the activities of the Kaesong society of Hanmun (classical Chinese) poetry, as well as some examples of their verses. The verses were about appropriately political topics, like unification, but only a few short years later such a "flunkeyist" society would be unthinkable.

2. See, for example, Hobsbawm, *Nations and Nationalism since 1780*, 91–92.

3. Yi Hyang-gyu, "Pukhan sahoejuŭi pot'ong kyoyuk-ŭi hyŏngsŏng" (The formation of North Korean primary education), 52–53.

4. The *General Sherman*'s raid in the 1860s and the subsequent American landing on the Kanghwado—two rather insignificant episodes—have always been featured prominently in North Korean textbooks as examples of a century-old history of the "U.S. imperialist aggression against Korean people." Now the same episodes enjoy popularity among the increasingly influential anti-American nationalists in the South.

5. A. M. Puzanov (Soviet ambassador), official diary, January 5, 1959.

6. For the official information on the tempo of collectivization, see *Chosŏn chŏnsa,* vol. 28, 235; vol. 29, 69.

7. *Nodong sinmun,* April 30, 1956.

8. Brugger, *Contemporary China,* 125.

9. *Chosŏn chŏnsa,* vol. 29, 79–83.

10. Measures aimed at eliminating private commerce, Archives of the Hungarian Ministry of Foreign Affairs, XIX-J-1-j Korea 1945–1964, box 11, 24/b, 00254/1958. These data were provided to me by Balazs Szalontai.

11. Hungarian Embassy to the DPRK, report, October 22, 1954, KA, 11, doboz, 22/a, 08103/2/1954. Document provided by Balazs Szalontai.

12. Brugger, *Contemporary China,* 126.

13. These trials are even mentioned in later official North Korean texts: *Chosŏn chŏnsa,* vol. 29, 57–58; *Pukhan ch'onglam,* 302.

14. Pak Tong-hwan, "Hyŏkmyŏngjŏk kyŏnggaksŏng-ŭl chegohaja" (Let's increase the revolutionary vigilance!), 65.

15. Ibid., 67.

16. Kim Hak-jun, *Pukhan 50 nyŏn sa,* 198.

17. *Pukhan ch'onglam,* 302–312.

18. As cited in Kim Hak-jun, *Pukhan 50 nyŏn sa,* 201.

19. Pelishenko, record of conversation with Pang Hak-se, February 12, 1960.

20. Kim Il Sung, *Works,* vol. 11, 327–328.

21. Kim Hak-jun, *Pukhan 50 nyŏn sa,* 194.

22. Kim Sŏng-su, "1950 nyŏndae Pukhan munhak-kwa sahoejuŭi riŏllijŭm," 146–154.

23. *Chosŏn chŏnsa,* vol. 29, 225–226.

24. Hamm, *Arming the Two Koreas,* 127.

25. In its issue of November 15, 1958, *Nodong sinmun* reported the production of the first Korean tractor, aptly called Ch'ŏllima. It was presented as a major news item: the newspaper ran a large headline at the top of the front page, and the entire page (as well as a substantial part of other pages) contained articles related to this topic. In the same style, *Nodong sinmun* reported the production of the first North Korean excavator (November 18, 1958) and truck (November 19, 1958).

26. Pelishenko, record of conversation with Nam Il, January 4, 1957.

27. Ye. L. Titorenko (second secretary of the Soviet Embassy), record of conversation with Chang Chu-ik (corresponding member of the DPRK Academy of Science), November 17, 1957. Dr. Kim Mil-ya, a daughter of Kim Chae-uk's, provided me with interesting information about the Sixth High School; Kim Mil-ya, interview with the author in Tashkent, January 27, 1991.

28. V. S. Zahariin (head of the Consular Section, Soviet Embassy), record of conversation with Pak Kil-yŏng (head of the First Department, Ministry of Foreign Affairs), January 28, 1958.

29. Such a passivity had some precedents. As Balazs Szalontai pointed out to me, in the 1920s a considerable part of the ruling elite in Mongolia consisted of the Buryats (essentially, Soviet Mongols), whose role was quite akin to that of the Soviet Koreans in the early DPRK. Nevertheless, in the late 1930s the Mongolian dictator Choibalsan, with obvious Soviet approval, purged all Buryats and replaced them with the local Mongols (Khalkhas), who were generally less educated. These purges opened great career opportunities for the locals and consolidated Choibalsan's control over the country. Perhaps the similarity between these two cases is somewhat superficial, though. In Mongolia the "Soviet Mongols" were ostensibly sacrificed for the sake of greater political stability for a staunchly pro-Soviet regime, whereas in Korea the likely reasons of the Soviet passivity were, first, a hope to avoid further complication of the increasingly difficult relations with Pyongyang and, second, an inability to intervene effectively.

30. Kim Hak-jun, *Pukhan 50 nyŏn sa*, 428.

31. In the Chinese draft of the joint declaration that announced the troop withdrawal was an explicit suggestion that, in the case of war, the Chinese troops would move back. The Korean side insisted that this promise would be taken out of the final text. See Shesterikov, record of conversation with Pak Kil-yŏng, February 17, 1958.

32. Zoia Pak (widow of Kim Ch'il-sŏng), interview with the author in Tashkent, February 1, 1991. According to her information, Kim Ch'il-sŏng was arrested on November 28, 1958.

33. *Mirok Chosŏn minjujuŭi konghwaguk* (Secret records of the Democratic People's Republic of Korea), 371–372.

34. Alexander Song (son of Song Won-sik, a prominent Soviet Korean cadre) was an officer of the North Korean Air Force in the late 1950s. Correctly or not, he believes that his Soviet citizenship saved him from arrest when terror in the armed forces reached an unprecedented height around 1960. Alexander Song, interview with the author in Tashkent, January 31, 1991.

35. V. S. Zahariin (head of the Consular Section, Soviet Embassy), record of conversation with Tyugai M. F., Yun Ye. K., and Yugai N. A., November 16, 1959.

36. Ibid.

37. V. S. Zahariin (head of the Consular Section, Soviet Embassy), record of conversation with Pak Il-mu, October 10, 1959.

38. V. S. Zahariin (head of the Consular Section, Soviet Embassy), record of conversation with Pak Kil-nam, November 5, 1959.

39. G. K. Plotnikov, interview with the author in Moscow, February 1, 1990.

40. In regard to Pak Kil-nam (translated from Korean), AVPRF, fond 0541, opis 10, delo 9, papka 81; in regard to Pak Il-mu (translated from Korean), AVPRF, fond 0541, opis 10, delo 9, papka 81.

41. V. S. Zahariin (head of the Consular Section, Soviet Embassy), record of

conversation with Yi Chong-ch'an[?] (head of the Consular Department, DPRK Ministry of Foreign Affairs), October 31, 1959.

42. Pak Pyŏng-yul, interview with the author in Moscow, January 25, 1990.

43. N. Ye. Torbenkov (counselor of the Soviet Embassy), record of conversation with Pak Tŏk-hwan (counselor, Ministry of Foreign Affairs), June 13, 1960.

44. Sim Su-ch'ŏl, interview with the author in Tashkent, January 17, 1991.

45. Pelishenko, record of conversation with Nam Il, February 14, 1959.

46. Torbenkov, record of conversation with Pak Tŏk-hwan, June 13, 1960.

47. S. P. Iugai (Yu Sŏng-hun's nephew), interview with the author in Moscow, January 26, 1990; Ye. L. Titorenko (second secretary of the Soviet Ministry of Foreign Affairs), record of conversation with Yu Sŏng-hun, February 20, 1960.

48. The date of Hŏ Chin's spectacular escape is not known, but the Soviet Embassy papers mentioned that the North Korean operatives, charged with the task of his kidnapping, left Pyongyang in mid-February. Shesterikov, record of conversation with Pak Kil-yŏng, February 17, 1958.

49. G. Ye. Samsonov (first secretary of the Soviet Ministry of Foreign Affairs), record of conversation with Yi Sang-gu (North Korean citizen), October 16, 1959.

50. V. P. Tkachenko, interview with the author in Moscow, January 23, 1990. V. P. Tkachenko is a Soviet diplomat and party official who, from the early 1960s up to August 1991, had worked in the Korean sector of the CPSU Central Committee. The kidnapping incident and its consequences are described in the official diary of the Soviet ambassador to the DPRK, February 1–15, 1960, entry of February 1, AVPRF, fond 0102, opis 16, delo 6, papka 85; and Ye. L. Titorenko (second secretary of the Soviet Ministry of Foreign Affairs), record of telephone conversations with Kim U-jŏng (first secretary of DPRK Embassy), November 26, 1959 (this latter document contains the date of Yi's forced departure as well as another description of the incident provided by the KGB). "Kim U-jong," of the Russian document, is tentatively identified as the Kim U-jŏng who eventually became a prominent North Korean diplomat (Russian transcription does not make a distinction between "o" and "ŏ" nor between "n" and "ng"). It is interesting that the name of the victim was changed from "Yi Sang-gu" in earlier documents to "Yi Sang-un" in later ones. Taking into account the importance of the documents and the entire affair, as well as a reasonably good command of Korean by some Soviet diplomats (at least by Titorenko himself), we can rule out the possibility of mistake regarding the name. Hence the purpose of this change is currently unknown.

51. G. K. Plotnikov, interview with the author in Moscow, February 1, 1990. G. K. Plotnikov himself dated the incident as having occurred in 1958, but considering the unreliability of human memory, I prefer to place it in the "late 1950s."

52. Hungarian Embassy to the DPRK, report, August 15, 1960, KTS, 8, doboz,

5/f, 0033/RT/1960; Hungarian Embassy to the DPRK, report, December 8, 1960, KTS, 5, doboz, 5/ca, 001/RT/1961; Hungarian Embassy to the DPRK, report, February 18, 1961, KTS, 6, doboz, 5/c, 003629/1961. All documents kindly provided by Balazs Szlantai.

53. N. P. Kurbatskii (attaché), record of conversation with Pak Sin-dŏk (head of the Ch'ŏngwudang Organizational Department), August 21, 1956.

54. Kim To-man (head of the Department of Agitation and Propaganda of the KWP Central Committee), record of conversation with B. K. Pimenov (first secretary of the Soviet Embassy), August 20, 1958.

55. Materials on the reactionary conspiracy exposed in the Ch'ŏngwudang Party, the Democratic Party, and the Committee for the Promotion of Peaceful Unification, AVPRF, fond 102, opis 14, delo 9, papka 75. Note that the materials still qualify the alleged activities of these parties as both anti-Communist and anti-Soviet: in spite of all the attempts to limit the Soviet influence, traditional appearances were still kept.

56. Ibid.

57. A. M. Iulin (first secretary of the Soviet Embassy), record of conversation with Kim To-man (head of the Agitation and Propaganda Department of the KWP Central Committee), February 11, 1959.

58. Ye. L. Titorenko (second secretary of the Soviet Embassy), record of conversation with Ch'oe Hak-ryon (head of the Legal Department of the DPRK Supreme People's Assembly), March 16, 1959.

59. Iulin, record of conversation with Kim To-man, February 11, 1959.

60. A. M. Iulin (first secretary of the Soviet Embassy), record of conversation with Kim Yŏng-ju (head of the Organization Department of the KWP Central Committee), August 7, 1959.

61. Hwang, *Yŏksa paljŏn-esŏ inmin taejung yŏkhal-gwa kaein-ŭo yŏkhal* (The role of the individual and the people's masses in historical development), 35.

62. Kim Sŏk-hyang, "Pukhan-ui myŏngjŏl-gwa ki'nyŏmil" (North Korean holidays), unpublished manuscript. I thank Dr. Kim for providing this interesting material.

63. For example, the first Korean truck, produced in November 1958, left the factory's gate with a huge portrait of Kim Il Song fixed on its front (photo in *Nodong sinmun*, November 19, 1958).

64. *Chosŏn chŏnsa*, vol. 29, 171.

65. *Nodong sinmun*, December 13, 1958. The rooms are mentioned in a lengthy article by Chu Kwan-ok, vice-chairman of Northern P'yongan KWP Committee. This is the earliest mention of the "rooms for study of the Great Leader Marshal Kim Il Song's revolutionary activity" that I came across in the contemporary North Korean press (of course, there could be earlier references that I did not find).

66. Puzanov, official diary, January 5, 1959.

10. THE INCEPTION OF THE "GUERRILLA STATE"

1. Yi Song-un, "P'alwol chŏwonhŭi-wa tang taeryŏl-ŭi t'ongil tangyŏl." This is the same Yi Song-un whose name we have already encountered quite a few times, as a former guerrilla and a leading persecutor of the opposition.

2. Yim, "Panil minjŏk haebang t'ujaeng-e issŏsŏ kyŏnsilhan kongsanjuŭijadŭl-ŭui yŏkhal" (The role of true Communists in the anti-Japanese national liberation struggle)." This article was written (or at least signed) by Yim Ch'unch'u, a top-level party cadre.

3. Kim Si-jung, "Uri tang-i kyesŭnghanŭn pich'nanŭn hyŏkmyŏngjŏk chŏnt'ong" (The shining revolutionary tradition, continued by our party).

4. Hwang and Kim, "Yi Ch'ŏng-won chŏ *Chosŏn-e issŏso p'ŭroret'ariat'ŭ hegemoni-rŭl wihan t'ujaeng-e taehayo*" (In regard to *Struggle for the Proletariat Hegemony in Korea*, by Yi Ch'ŏng-won).

5. This issue was probably the first publication to mention a new invention of North Korean propaganda—slogans allegedly written on the bark of trees by the anti-Japanese guerrillas. This was to become a tradition, upheld even till now. These slogans were "discovered" during many major campaigns, and— what a surprise!—their content always confirmed the current ideological line. However, the first slogans, allegedly found near Poch'ŏnbo and cited in *Nodong sinmun* on July 4, did not contain explicit referrals to Kim Il Song. It is even possible, but unlikely, that they were authentic.

6. The first article (or at least one of the first) with this new expression appeared in *Nodong sinmun* on July 10 and was written by Kim Ŭn-yŏp. In earlier publications the term "revolutionary tradition" had no fixed adjective or was sometimes described as "*yŏnggwangsŭroun*," or "glorious" (for example, in a set of articles published on June 4 and in an article on June 5). From July 1958 onward the North Korean press widely used "shining revolutionary tradition" as a fixed, virtually invariable expression.

7. Kim Il Sung, "Chosŏn inmingun-ŭn hang'il mujang t'ujaeng-ŭi kyesŭngja ida."

8. *Chosŏn chŏnsa*, vol. 29, 171.

9. According to Nicholas Eberstadt, the population of North Korea in 1960 reached 10,568,000. Eberstadt, *Korea Approaches Unification*, 59.

10. *Chosŏn chŏnsa*, vol. 29, 372.

11. Ibid., 171.

12. Notably, the author of one of the earliest publications on this topic stated that "in 1932, Kim Il Song joined the Communist Party"—without specifying that it was the Chinese Communist Party; Yi Na-yŏng, *Chosŏn minjok haebang t'ujaeng sa* (The history of the national liberation struggle of the Korean people), 338. Nevertheless, if compared with later biographies, this one had a degree of

openness, since every reader could easily guess which party Kim Il Song joined—no Korean Communist Party existed then, after all.

13. Kim Il Sung, "Chosŏn inmingun-ŭn hang'il mujang t'ujaeng-ŭi kyesŭngja ida," 71.

14. For example, a long article published in *Kŭnloja* in 1959 dealt with the necessity of redesigning the political indoctrination in order to conform to the new line of promoting Kim's guerrillas as the only exponents of the "true Communism" in Korea; Han, "Hyŏn sigi tang sasang saŏp-esŏ-ŭi myŏch' kkaji munje" (Some question of the party's ideological educational activity at the current stage). In 1958–1960, *Kŭnloja* published materials on the "revolutionary tradition," as personified by Kim Il Song and his guerrillas, in almost every issue. All other early proponents of the Communist movement were either ignored or depicted as factionalists or even traitors.

15. Yi Song-un, "P'alwol chŏwonhŭi-wa tang taeryŏl-ŭi t'ongil tangyŏl."

16. Wada, *Kim Il Sŏng-gwa manju hang'il chŏnjaeng.*

17. The main biographical data are from *Pukhan inmyŏng sajŏn.* The information about Yun Kong-hŭm and Sŏ Hwi is from Kim Hak-jun, *Pukhan 50 nyŏn sa,* 191–192. The date of Yun Kong-hŭm's death is as mentioned in *Mirok Chosŏn minjujuŭi konghwaguk: Ha* (Secret records of the Democratic People's Republic of Korea: Part 2), 76. The information about Kang Sang-ho and Pak Kil-yŏng is my own (I met them both and am especially thankful to General Kang for his help and support). Regarding the purge of Pak Kŭm-ch'ŏl, see, for example, Ch'oe Sŏng, *Pukhan chŏngch'i sa,* 166–167. Regarding Han Sŏl-ya's fate, see Myers, *Han Sŏl-ya.*

CONCLUSION

1. Some modern publications insist that living standards in North Korea in the 1950s were higher than in the South. Perhaps this indeed was the case. However, without intending to start an argument, I must mention that in 1956 Yi Sang-jo, the then DPRK ambassador to the USSR, frankly told a Soviet diplomat: "Economic conditions in the South are slightly better than in the North. If a South Korean worker has a job, his living standards are better than those of a North Korean worker, but the real income of the workers of the South is somewhat lower than it used to be under the Japanese." See Kurdiukov, record of conversation with Yi Sang-jo, June 16, 1956.

2. Pak Myŏng-lim, *Hanguk chŏnjaeng-ŭi palbal-gwa kiwŏn,* vol. 2, 357.

3. *Uri-nŭchinan 100 nyŏn tong'an ŏttŏkhe sarassŭlkka?* (How did we live during the last hundred years?), vol. 2, 44.

4. Grajdanzev, *Modern Korea,* 76.

5. In Korea in the early 1940s there were 246,000 civil servants and government employees of Japanese origin. Cumings, *Korea's Place under the Sun,* 153.

6. V. V. Kovyzhenko, interview with the author in Moscow, August 2, 1991.

7. Pimenov, record of conversation with Won Hyŏng-gu, June 21, 1958.

8. Yi Hyang-gyu, "Pukhan sahoejuŭi pot'ong kyoyuk-ŭi hyŏngsŏng: 1945–1950," 52–53.

9. Filatov, record of conversation with Pak Ch'ang-ok, March 12, 1956.

10. Biakov, record of conversation and Song Chin-p'a, February 15, 1956.

11. Kim Mil-ya, interview with the author in Tashkent, January 27, 1991.

12. Valentina Dmitrieva, interview with the author in Moscow, January 30, 1990.

13. Titorenko, record of conversation with Ch'oe Chŏng-hyŏn, November 4, 1956. The correct spelling of Ch'oe Chŏng-hyŏn's name can be ascertained from an article in *Nodong sinmun* on August 6, 1957. It mentioned him as the student who made accusations against the "factionalists," including his former teacher.

14. Okulov and Vasiliev, record of conversation with Sin Ch'ong-t'aek, February 3, 1957.

15. Ibid.

16. Scalapino and Lee, *Korean Communism,* 752–756, 784–785.

Bibliography

Note: AVPRF = Archive of Russian Federation Foreign Policy, Moscow.

1946, 1947, 1948 nyŏndo Pukhan kyŏngje t'onggye charyojip (The collection of the statistics on the North Korean economy in 1946, 1947, and 1948). Ch'unch'on: Hanlim taehakkyo ch'ulp'anbu, 1994.

Bell, John. *The Bulgarian Communist Party from Blagoev to Zhivkov*. Stanford, Calif.: Hoover Institution Press, 1986.

Biakov, I. S. (first secretary of the Soviet Embassy). Record of conversation with Song Chin-p'a (former editor of *New Korea* magazine), February 15, 1955. AVPRF, fond 0102, opis 12, delo 6, papka 68.

———. Record of conversation with Yi Ho-gu (deputy chairman of the central office of the Korean Society for International Cultural Exchange), February 18, 1956. AVPRF, fond 0102, opis 12, delo 6, papka 68.

Brugger, Bill. *Contemporary China*. London: Croom Helm, 1977.

Chen Jian and Yang Kuisong. "Chinese Politics and the Collapse of the Sino-Soviet Alliance." In Westad, *Brothers in Arms*, 246–295.

Ch'oe Sŏng. *Pukhan chŏngch'i sa* (Political history of North Korea). Seoul: Pulp'ich', 1997.

Chosŏn chŏnsa (The general history of Korea). Pyongyang: Kwahak paekkwa sajon ch'ulp'an sa, 1981.

Chosŏn kongsanjuŭi undong-ŭi wanjŏnhan t'ongil-ŭi silhaeng (The complete realization of the unity of the Korean Communist movement). Pyongyang: Chosŏn nodongdang ch'ulp'ansa, 1962.

Chosŏn mal sajŏn (Dictionary of the Korean language). Pyongyang: Kwahakwon ch'ulp'ansa, 1961–1962.

Cumings, Bruce. *Korea's Place under the Sun: A Modern History*. New York: Norton and Co., 1997.

Eberstadt, Nicholas. *Korea Approaches Unification*. New York: M. E. Sharpe, 1995.

Fairbank, John, and Merle Goldman. *China: A New History*. Cambridge: Harvard University Press, Belknap Press, 1998.

Filatov, S. N. (counselor of the Soviet Embassy). Record of conversation with Ch'oe Ch'ang-ik (vice-premier and member of the KWP Standing Committee), July 23, 1956. AVPRF, fond 0102, opis 12, delo 6, papka 68.

———. Record of conversation with Kim Sŭng-hwa (minister of construction), May 24, 1956. AVPRF, fond 0102, opis 12, delo 6, papka 68.

———. Record of conversation with Kim Sŭng-hwa (minister of construction and member of the KWP Central Committee), July 24, 1956. AVPRF, fond 0102, opis 12, delo 6, papka 68.

———. Record of conversation with Pak Ch'ang-ok (deputy premier of the DPRK cabinet and member of the presidium of the KWP Central Committee), July 21, 1956. AVPRF, fond 0102, opis 12, delo 6, papka 68.

———. Record of conversation with Pak Ch'ang-ok (vice-premier and member of the presidium of the KWP Central Committee), March 12, 1956. AVPRF, fond 0102, opis 12, delo 6, papka 68.

———. Record of conversation with Pak Ŭi-wan (vice-premier), January 24, 1956. AVPRF, fond 0102, opis 12, delo 6, papka 68.

———. Record of conversation with Pak Ŭi-wan (vice-premier), February 21, 1956. AVPRF, fond 0102, opis 12, delo 6, papka 68.

———. Record of conversation with Pak Ŭi-wan (vice-premier), February 29, 1956. AVPRF, fond 0102, opis 12, delo 6, papka 68.

———. Record of conversation with Pak Yŏng-bin, February 25, 1956. AVPRF, fond 0102, opis 12, delo 6, papka 68.

———. Record of conversation with Yun Kong-hŭm (minister of commerce), August 2, 1956. AVPRF, fond 0102, opis 12, delo 6, papka 68.

Gluchowski, L. W. "Khrushchev, Gomulka, and the 'Polish October.'" *CWIHP Bulletin* 5: 44–45.

Grajdanzev, Andrew. *Modern Korea*. New York: Institute of Pacific Relations, 1944.

Hamm, Taik-young. *Arming the Two Koreas: State, Capital, and Military Power*. New York: Routledge, 1999.

Han P'yo-yŏp. "Hyŏn sigi tang sasang saŏp-esŏ-ŭi myŏch' kkaji munje" (Some question of the party's ideological educational activity at the current stage). *Kŭnloja* 1959, no. 3 (1959).

Hobsbawm, Eric. *The Age of Extremes*. New York: Vintage books, 1994.

———. *Nations and Nationalism since 1780: Programs, Myth, Reality*. Cambridge: Cambridge University Press, 2000.

Hoxha, Enver. *The Artful Albanian: Memoirs of Enver Hoxha*. Ed. Jon Halliday. London: Chatto and Windus, 1986.

Hwang, Chang-yŏp. *Yŏksa paljŏn-esŏ inmin taejung yŏkhal-gwa kaein-ŭo yŏkhal* (The role of the individual and the people's masses in historical development). Pyongyang: Chosŏn nodongdang ch'ulp'ansa, 1957.

Hwang Chang-yŏp, and Kim Hu-sŏn. "Yi Ch'ŏng-won chŏ *Chosŏn-e issŏso p'ŭroret'ariat'ŭ hegemoni-rŭl wihan t'ujaeng*-e taehayo" (In regard to *Struggle for the Proletarian Hegemony in Korea,* by Yi Ch'ŏng-won). *Kŭnloja* 1957, no. 12 (1957).

Iulin, A. M. (first secretary of the Soviet Embassy). Record of conversation with Kim To-man (head of the Agitation and Propaganda Department of the KWP Central Committee), February 11, 1959. AVPRF, fond 102, opis 15, delo 8, papka 81.

———. Record of conversation with Kim Yŏng-ju (head of the Organization Department of the KWP Central Committee), August 7, 1959. AVPRF, fond 0541, opis 10, delo 9, papka 81.

Ivanenko, V. I. (first secretary of the Soviet Ministry of Foreign Affairs). Record of conversation with Pak Kil-yŏng (deputy minister of foreign affairs), May 17, 1956. AVPRF, fond 0102, opis 12, delo 4, papka 68.

Ivanov, V. (Soviet ambassador to the DPRK). Memo to N. T. Fedorenko (deputy minister of foreign affairs), September 28, 1956. AVPRF, fond 0102, opis 12, delo 6, papka 68, list 331. (Handwritten original: list 333–340.)

Kim Hak-jun. *Pukhan 50 nyŏn sa* (Fifty years of North Korean history). Seoul: Tong'a Ch'ulp'ansa, 1995.

Kim Il Sung. "Chosŏn inmingun-ŭn hang'il mujang t'ujaeng-ŭi kyesŭngja ida" (The Korean People's Army is heir to the glorious traditions of the anti-Japanese armed struggle). In Kim Il Sung, *Kim Il Sŏng chŏjak sŏnjip* (The selected works of Kim Il Song), vol. 2, 65. Pyongyang: Chosŏn nodongdang ch'ulp'ansa, 1967.

———. *Kim Il Sŏng chŏjak sŏnjip* (The selected works of Kim Il Song). Pyongyang: Chosŏn nodongdang ch'ulp'ansa, 1967–.

———. *Works.* Pyongyang: Foreign Languages Publishing House, 1980–.

Kim Nam-sik. *Namnodang yŏngu* (Study of the South Korean Workers' Party). Seoul: Tolpegai, 1984.

Kim Si-jung. "Uri tang-i kyesŭnghanŭn pich'nanŭn hyŏkmyŏngjŏk chŏnt'ong" (The shining revolutionary tradition, continued by our party). *Kŭnloja* 1958, no. 7 (1958).

Kim Sŏk-hyang. "Pukhan-ui myŏngjŏl-gwa ki'nyŏmil" (North Korean holidays). Unpublished manuscript.

Kim Sŏng-su. "1950 nyŏndae Pukhan munhak-kwa sahoejuŭi riŏllijŭm" (Socialist realism and North Korean literature of the 1950s). *Hyŏndae Pukhan yŏngu* (Studies of modern North Korea) 2, no. 2 (1999): 121–160.

Kim To-man (head of the Department of Agitation and Propaganda of the KWP Central Committee). Record of conversation with B. K. Pimenov (first secretary of the Soviet Embassy), August 20, 1958. AVPRF, fond 102, opis 14, delo 9, papka 75.

Koon Woo Nam. *The North Korean Communist Leadership, 1945–1965: A Study of Factionalism and Political Consolidation.* Tuscaloosa: University of Alabama Press, 1974.

Kramer, Mark, trans. and annotator. "The 'Malin Notes' on the Crises in Hungary and Poland, 1956." *CWIHP Bulletin* 8–9 (1996): 392–393.

Kurbatskii, N. P. (attaché). Record of conversation with Pak Sin-dŏk (head of the Ch'ŏngwudang Organizational Department), August 21, 1956. AVPRF, fond 0102, opis' 12, delo 6, papka 68.

Kurdiukov, I. F. (head of the First Far Eastern Department of the Soviet Foreign Ministry). Record of conversation with Yi Sang-jo (DPRK ambassador to the USSR), June 16, 1956. AVPRF, fond 0102, opis 12, delo 4, papka 68.

——. Record of conversation with Yi Sang-jo (DPRK ambassador to the USSR), August 9, 1956. AVPRF, fond 0102, opis 12, delo 4, papka 68.

——. Record of conversation with Yi Sang-jo (DPRK ambassador to the USSR), August 11, 1956. AVPRF, fond 0102, opis 12, delo 4, papka 68.

Lazarev, S. P. (first secretary of the Soviet Foreign Ministry). Record of conversation with Ko Hŭi-man (head of department in the KWP Central Committee), September 18, 1956. AVPRF, fond 0102, opis 12, delo 4, papka 68.

Lim Ŭn. *The Founding of a Dynasty in North Korea.* Tokyo: Jiyu-sha, 1982.

Lisikov, V. K. (third secretary of the Soviet Embassy). Record of conversation with Kim Sŏng-yul (chairman of the Pyongyang City Committee of the Democratic Party of North Korea), May 8, 1956. AVPRF, fond 0102, opis 12, delo 6, papka 68.

Mirok Chosŏn minjujuŭi konghwaguk (Secret records of the Democratic People's Republic of Korea). Seoul: Chung'ang ilbo sa, 1991.

Mirok Chosŏn minjujuŭi konghwaguk: Ha (Secret records of the Democratic People's Republic of Korea: Part 2). Seoul: Chung'ang ilbo sa, 1993.

Myers, Brian. *Han Sŏl-ya and North Korean Literature.* Ithaca, N.Y.: Cornell University Press, 1994.

Nongŏp hyŏpdonghwa undong-ŭi sŭngli (The success of the agricultural cooperative movement). Pyongyang: Chosŏn nodongdang ch'ulp'ansa, 1958.

Okonishnikov, O. V. (first secretary of the Soviet Embassy). Record of conversation with Kim T'aek-yong (deputy minister of justice), October 14, 1957. AVPRF, fond 0102, opis 13, delo 6, papka 72.

Okonogi, Masao. "North Korean Communism: In Search of Its Prototype." In *New Pacific Currents,* 177–207. Honolulu: University of Hawai`i Press, 1994.

Okulov, R. G. (*Pravda* correspondent), and S. V. Vasiliev (TASS correspondent). Record of conversation with Sin Ch'ong-t'aek (deputy minister of communications), February 3, 1957. AVPRF, fond 0102, opis 12, delo 6, papka 68.

Otnosheniia Sovetskogo Sojuza s Narodnoj Korejej: Dokumenty i Materialy (Relations of the Soviet Union and People's Korea: documents and materials). Moscow: Nauka, 1981.

Paek Chun-gi. "Chŏngjŏn hu 1950 nyŏndae Pukhan-ui chŏngch'i pyŏndong-gwa kwonlyŏk chaep'an" (North Korean political changes and power re-alignment in the 1950s). *Hyŏndae Pukhan yŏngu* (Studies of modern North Korea) 2, no. 2 (spring 1999).

Pak Myŏng-lim. *Hanguk chŏnjaeng-ŭi palbal-gwa kiwŏn* (Sources and origins of the Korean War). Seoul: Nanam, 1998.

Pak Sang-hong. "Chikŏp tongmaeng saŏp-eso chegitwenŭn myŏch' kaji munje" (Some problems from the trade unions' activity). *Kŭnloja* 1957, no. 7 (1957): 40–42.

Pak Tong-hwan. "Hyŏkmyŏngjŏk kyŏnggaksŏng-ŭl chegohaja" (Let's increase the revolutionary vigilance!). *Kŭnloja* 1957, no. 5 (July 1957).

Pelishenko, V. I. (counselor of the Soviet Embassy). Record of conversation with Nam Il (minister of foreign affairs), October 9, 1957. AVPRF, fond 0102, opis 13, delo 6, papka 72.

———. Record of conversation with Nam Il (minister of foreign affairs), February 14, 1959. AVPRF, fond 0541, opis 15, delo 8, papka 81.

———. Record of conversation with Pak Kŭm-ch'ŏl, November 22, 1956. AVPRF, fond 0102, opis 12, delo 6, papka 68.

———. Record of conversation with Pang Hak-se (minister of the interior), October 24, 1959. AVPRF, fond 0541, opis 10, delo 9, papka 81.

———. Record of conversation with Pang Hak-se (minister of the interior), February 12, 1960. AVPRF, fond 0541, opis 15, delo 9, papka 85.

Pelishenko, V. I. (provisional chargé d'affaires). Record of conversation with Kim Il Song, January 30, 1957. AVPRF, fond 0102, opis 13, delo 6, papka 72.

———. Record of conversation with Kim Il Song, February 12, 1957. AVPRF, fond 0102, opis 13, delo 6, papka 72.

———. Record of conversation with Nam Il (minister of foreign affairs), January 4, 1957. AVPRF, fond 0102, opis 13, delo 6, papka 72.

———. Record of conversation with Pak Chŏng-ae (deputy chairperson of the KWP Central Committee), December 17, 1956. AVPRF, fond 0102, opis 13, delo 6, papka 72.

Petrov, A. M. (counselor of the Soviet Embassy). Record of conversation with Song Chin-p'a (former editor of *New Korea* magazine), December 15, 1955. AVPRF, fond 0102, opis 12, delo 6, papka 68.

Petrov, A. M. (provisional chargé d'affaires). Diary. AVPRF, fond 0102, opis 12, delo 6, papka 68.

———. Handwritten memo to Ambassador V. I. Ivanov. AVPRF, fond 0102, opis 12, delo 6, papka 68, list 332.

———. Record of conversation with Nam Il (minister of foreign affairs), July 24, 1956. AVPRF, fond 0102, opis 12, delo 6, papka 68.

———. Record of conversation with Yi P'il-gyu (head of the Department of Construction Materials) on July 14 [July 20], 1956. AVPRF, fond 0102, opis 12, delo 6, papka 68, list 333–340. Handwritten.

———. Record of conversation with Yi P'il-gyu (head of the Department of Construction Materials), July 20, 1956. AVPRF, fond 0102, opis 12, delo 6, papka 68. Typed.

Pimenov, B. K. (first secretary of the Soviet Embassy). Record of conversation with An Un-gong[?] (former head of the First Department of the Ministry of Foreign Affairs), January 30, 1957. AVPRF, fond 0102, opis 13, delo 6, papka 72.

———. Record of conversation with An Un-gong[?] (lecturer in the Institute of National Economy, former head of the First Department of the Ministry of Foreign Affairs), September 8, 1957. AVPRF, fond 0102, opis 13, delo 6, papka 72.

———. Record of conversation with Kim Yŏng-ju (head of the Organization Department of the KWP Central Committee), April 11, 1959. AVPRF, fond 0102, opis 14, delo 8, papka 75.

———. Record of conversation with Pak Kil-yŏng (head of the First Department in the DPRK Ministry of Foreign Affairs), October 26, 1957. AVPRF, fond 0102, opis 13, delo 6, papka 72.

———. Record of conversation with Pak Kil-yŏng (head of the First Department in the DPRK Ministry of Foreign Affairs), November 28, 1957. AVPRF, fond 0102, opis 13, delo 6, papka 72.

———. Record of conversation with Pak Kil-yŏng (head of the First Department in the DPRK Ministry of Foreign Affairs), December 8, 1957. AVPRF, fond 0102, opis 13, delo 6, papka 72.

———. Record of conversation with Won Hyŏng-gu (deputy head of the Organization Department, KWP Central Committee), June 21, 1958. AVPRF, fond 0102, opis 14, delo 8, papka 75.

———. Record of conversation with Won Hyŏng-gu (deputy head of the Organization Department, KWP Central Committee), July 22, 1958. AVPRF, fond 0102, opis 14, delo 8, papka 75.

Pukhan ch'onglam (North Korean review). Seoul: Pukhan yŏnguso, 1985.

Pukhan inmyŏng sajŏn (Biographical dictionary of North Korea). Seoul: Chung'ang ilbo sa, 1990.

Puzanov, A. M. (Soviet ambassador). Official diary. AVPRF, fond 0102, opis 15, delo 7, papka 81.

Rothschild, Joseph. *Return to Diversity: A Political History of East Central Europe since World War II.* New York: Oxford University Press, 1993.

Samsonov, G. Ye. (first secretary). Record of conversation with Ko Hŭi-man (head of department in the KWP Central Committee), August 31, 1956. AVPRF, fond 0102, opis 12, delo 6, papka 68.

Samsonov, G. Ye. (first secretary of the Soviet Embassy). Record of conversation with Chang Ik-hwan (deputy minister of education), May 23, 1957. AVPRF, fond 0102, opis 13, delo 6, papka 72.

———. Record of conversation with Yi Song-un (chairman of the Pyongyang City Committee of the KWP), November 23, 1956. AVPRF, fond 0102, opis 12, delo 6, papka 68.

Samsonov, G. Ye. (first secretary of the Soviet Ministry of Foreign Affairs). Record of conversation with Ki Sŏk-pok (a referent in the Ministry of Culture), May 31, 1956. AVPRF, fond 0102, opis 12, delo 6, papka 68.

———. Record of conversation with Yi Sang-gu (North Korean citizen), October 16, 1959. AVPRF, fond 0541, opis 15, delo 8, papka 81.

Scalapino, Robert, and Lee, Chong-sik. *Korean Communism*. Berkeley and Los Angeles: University of California Press, 1972.

Shesterikov, N. M. (counselor of the Soviet Embassy). Diary. AVPRF, fond 0102, opis 12, delo 6, papka 68.

———. Record of conversation with Pak Kil-yŏng (head of the First Department of the Ministry of Foreign Affairs), February 17, 1958. AVPRF, fond 0102, opis 14, delo 8, papka 75.

Suh Dae-sook. *Kim Il Sung: The North Korean Leader*. New York: Columbia University Press, 1988.

———. *Korean Communism, 1945–1980: A Reference Guide to the Political System*. Honolulu: University of Hawai`i Press, 1980.

Sullivan, Lawrence. "Leadership and Authority in the Chinese Communist Party: Perspectives from the 1950s." *Pacific Affairs* 1986, no. 4 (1986): 605–633.

Taejung chŏngch'i yŏng'ŏ sajŏn (The popular dictionary of political terms). Pyongyang: Chosŏn nodongdang ch'ulp'ansa, 1959.

Teiwes, Frederick. *Politics and Purges in China*. 2nd ed. New York: M. E. Sharpe, 1993.

Titorenko, Ye. L. (second secretary of the Soviet Embassy). Record of conversation with Chang Chu-ik (corresponding member of the DPRK Academy of Science), October 17, 1957. AVPRF, fond 0102, opis 13, delo 6, papka 72.

———. Record of conversation with Chang Chu-ik (corresponding member of the DPRK Academy of Science), November 17, 1957. AVPRF, fond 0102, opis 13, delo 6, papka 72.

———. Record of conversation with Ch'oe Chŏng-hyŏn (postgraduate of Kim Il Song University), November 4, 1956. AVPRF, fond 0102, opis 12, delo 6, papka 68.

———. Record of conversation with Ch'oe Chŏng-hyŏn (postgraduate of Kim Il Song University), September 11, 1957. AVPRF, fond 0102, opis 12, delo 6, papka 68.

———. Record of conversation with Ch'oe Hak-ryon (head of the Legal Department of the DPRK Supreme People's Assembly), March 16, 1959. AVPRF, fond 0541, opis 15, delo 8, papka 81.

———. Record of conversation with Ch'oe Sŭng-hun (deputy chairman of the KWP Committee of Ryanggang Province), October 23, 1956. AVPRF, fond 0102, opis 12, delo 6, papka 68.

———. Record of conversation with Ch'oe Sŭng-hun (deputy chairman of the KWP Committee of Ryanggang Province) and Chu Ch'ang-jun (deputy head of the Propaganda Department of the KWP Central Committee), March 5, 1958. AVPRF, fond 0102, opis 14, delo 8, papka 75.

———. Record of conversation with Song Kun-ch'an (head of the Department of Marxism-Leninism, Kim Il Song University), January 21, 1957. AVPRF, fond 0102, opis 13, delo 6, papka 72.

———. Record of conversation with Yi Tae-p'il (deputy chairman of the Pyongyang City Committee of the KWP), October 10, 1957. AVPRF, fond 0102, opis 13, delo 6, papka 72.

———. Record of conversation with Yu Sŏng-hun (rector of Kim Il Song University), February 7, 1957. AVPRF, fond 0102, opis 13, delo 6, papka 72.

———. Record of conversation with Yu Sŏng-hun (rector of Kim Il Song University), April 6, 1957. AVPRF, fond 0102, opis 13, delo 6, papka 72.

———. Record of conversation with Yu Sŏng-hun (rector of Kim Il Song University), September 11, 1957. AVPRF, fond 0102, opis 13, delo 6, papka 72.

Titorenko, Ye. L. (second secretary of the Soviet Ministry of Foreign Affairs). Record of conversation with Yu Sŏng-hun, February 20, 1960. AVPRF, fond 0541, opis 16, delo 5, papka 85.

———. Record of telephone conversations with Kim U-jŏng (first secretary of DPRK Embassy), November 26, 1959. AVPRF, fond 0541, opis 15, delo 8, papka 81

Torbenkov, N. Ye. (counselor of the Soviet Embassy). Record of conversation with Pak Kil-yŏng (deputy minister of foreign affairs), March 15, 1959. AVPRF, fond 0541, opis 15, delo 8, papka 81.

———. Record of conversation with Pak Kil-yŏng (deputy minister of foreign affairs), July 6, 1959. AVPRF, fond 0541, opis 15, delo 8, papka 81.

———. Record of conversation with Pak Tŏk-hwan (counselor, Ministry of Foreign Affairs), June 13, 1960. AVPRF, fond 0541, opis 15, delo 8, papka 81.

Uri-nŭchinan 100 nyŏn tong'an ŏttŏkhe sarassŭlkka? (How did we live during the last hundred years?). 2 vols. Seoul: Yŏksa pip'yŏng sa, 1998.

Vereshchagin, B. N. (counselor of the Far Eastern Department). Record of conversation with Yi Sang-jo (DPRK ambassador to the USSR), October 20, 1956. AVPRF, fond 0102, opis 12, delo 4, papka 68.

Wada Haruki. *Kim Il Sŏng-gwa manju hang'il chŏnjaeng* (Anti-Japanese War in Manchuria and Kim Il Song). Seoul: Ch'angjak-kwa pip'yŏn sa, 1992.

Westad, Odd Arne, ed. *Brothers in Arms: The Rise and Fall of the Sino-Soviet Alliance, 1945–1963.* Washington, D.C.: Woodrow Wilson Center Press; Stanford, Calif.: Stanford University Press, 1998.

Yi Hyang-gyu. "Pukhan sahoejuŭi pot'ong kyoyuk-ŭi hyŏngsŏng: 1945–1950" (The formation of North Korean primary education: 1945–1950). PhD thesis, Seoul National University, 2000.

Yi Na-yŏng. *Chosŏn minjok haebang t'ujaeng sa* (The history of the national liberation struggle of the Korean people). Pyongyang: Chosŏn nodongdang ch'ulp'ansa, 1958.

Yi Song-un. "P'alwol chŏwonhŭi-wa tang taeryŏl-ŭi t'ongil tangyŏl" (The August Plenum and the unity of the party ranks). *Kŭnloja* 1959 no. 8 (1959).

Yim Ch'un-ch'u. "Panil minjŏk haebang t'ujaeng-e issŏsŏ kyŏnsilhan kongsanjuŭijadŭl-ŭui yŏkhal" (The role of true Communists in the anti-Japanese national liberation struggle). *Kŭnloja* 1957, no. 5 (1957).

Zahariin, V. S. (head of the Consular Section, Soviet Embassy). Record of conversation with Pak Il-mu, October 10, 1959. AVPRF, fond 0541, opis 10, delo 9, papka 81.

———. Record of conversation with Pak Kil-nam, November 5, 1959. AVPRF, fond 0541, opis 10, delo 9, papka 81.

———. Record of conversation with Pak Kil-yŏng (head of the First Department, Ministry of Foreign Affairs), January 28, 1958. AVPRF, fond 0102, opis 14, delo 8, papka 75.

———. Record of conversation with Pak T'ae-sŏp (Soviet citizen), November 12, 1957. AVPRF, fond 0102, opis 13, delo 6, papka 72.

———. Record of conversation with Tyugai M. F., Yun Ye. K., and Yugai N. A., November 16, 1959. AVPRF, fond 0541, opis 10, delo 9, papka 81.

———. Record of conversation with Yi Chong-ch'an[?] (head of the Consular Department, DPRK Ministry of Foreign Affairs), October 31, 1959. AVPRF, fond 0541, opis 10, delo 9, papka 81.

Index

267

About the Author

ANDREI LANKOV GRADUATED from the Leningrad (now Petersburg) State University in 1986 and received his PhD from the same school in 1989. He has worked and studied in North and South Korea, Russia, and Australia. Since 1996, Lankov has been a lecturer with the Faculty of Asian Studies, Australian National University. He has published a number of books and articles on North Korean history, including *From Stalin to Kim Il Sung* (2002).